THE GABRIELS

Election Year in the Life of One Family

Other Books by Richard Nelson
Available from TCG

The Apple Family: Scenes from Life in the Country

INCLUDES:

That Hopey Changey Thing
Sweet and Sad
Sorry
Regular Singing

Frank's Home

Goodnight Children Everywhere and Other Plays

ALSO INCLUDES:

Franny's Way
New England
Some Americans Abroad
Two Shakespearean Actors

Illyria (forthcoming)

Rodney's Wife

IN A TRANSLATION SERIES
WITH RICHARD PEVEAR AND LARISSA VOLOKHONSKY:

The Cherry Orchard

The Inspector

Molière, or the Cabal of Hypocrites and *Don Quixote*

A Month in the Country

The Seagull

Uncle Vanya

THE GABRIELS

Election Year in the Life of One Family

RICHARD NELSON

THEATRE COMMUNICATIONS GROUP
NEW YORK
2018

The Gabriels: Election Year in the Life of One Family is published by
Theatre Communications Group, Inc., 520 Eighth Avenue, 24th Floor,
New York, NY 10018-4156

The publication of *The Gabriels: Election Year in the Life of One Family* by Richard Nelson, through TCG's Book Program, is made possible in part by the New York State Council on the Arts with the support of Governor Andrew Cuomo and the New York State Legislature.

TCG books are exclusively distributed to the book trade by Consortium Book Sales and Distribution.

ISBN 978-1-55936-548-2 (paperback)
ISBN 978-1-55936-870-4 (ebook)

A catalog record for this book is available from the Library of Congress.

Book design and composition by Lisa Govan
Cover design by Mark Melnick
Cover image: Archangel Gabriel Weathervane, c. 1840,
American Folk Art Museum/Art Resource, NY

First Edition, November 2018

CONTENTS

WHAT REMAINS

By Oskar Eustis

On Tuesday, November 8, 2016, we opened Richard Nelson's *Women of a Certain Age* at The Public Theater in New York.

It was the third play of Richard's that we premiered that year. His trilogy, collectively called *The Gabriels*, was written to chart the election year through the life of one family in Rhinebeck, New York. Each of the three plays was written to open on the day it took place; each had new writing added on its opening night to be sure that it felt as current as possible; each discussed the election and its meaning without being about the election. The Gabriels, like all of us, had their own family dramas that were separate and distinct from the nation's drama.

Women of a Certain Age took place on the eve of the presidential election, and it opened on that night. The Public had set up TV screens in the lobby and in our restaurant upstairs, The Library, thus turning the whole theater into an election-watching party. The lucky two hundred of us who got to watch the world premiere of *Women* happily began filling the theater at about 7:45 P.M. The news from the polls, while not definitive, certainly seemed to be bearing up the commonly held assumption that Hillary Clinton would be our next president. (That morning, the *New York Times* had predicted her election as a ninety-eight-percent probability.)

When we left the theater, profoundly moved and affected by Richard's beautiful play, we walked into a different world. We could feel it instantly in the uncomfortable atmosphere of the lobby and Library, and the numbers on television bore out that unease. By ten P.M. Eastern Time, when the show ended, the inexorable movement toward the Republican candidate was clearly visible. Donald Trump was going to be the 45th President of the United States.

Certainly this result would have been as surprising to the Gabriels as it was to all of us: the very title of the final play was gesturing toward the expectation that we were about to elect our first female president. They all talk to each other with the understanding that Hillary was probably going to win. But Richard's plays are so beautifully observed and felt, so exquisitely crafted, that now, rereading them, we can see and feel all the fault lines in the American compact that would lead to the election of Trump.

The Gabriels themselves were not Trump voters; George expresses resentment when a rich employer assumes he might be. But the struggles and dis-ease of this New York family capture the dislocated feeling that so many voiced November 8 with their votes.

The Gabriels struggle with their finances: George and Hannah, his wife, are educated working-class people who are trying to make ends meet, and finding it increasingly difficult to do in a world of dramatic economic inequality. As a carpenter and furniture maker, George finds he has less and less leverage with the wealthy clients he depends on for a living. Patricia, the matriarch of the family, has had to sell her home and piano to afford the nursing home she now lives in, and even so finds herself unable to make the payments to keep a roof over her head. The entire play takes place in the Gabriel family home, which is not even theirs anymore: they are just temporarily residing there, in their own home, until the new owners throw them out.

The Gabriels struggle, most of all, with their sense of belonging. They are resentful of the "weekend people," the rich New Yorkers who increasingly use their town as a getaway, and who demonstrate contempt for the culture and history of their home town. They feel Hillary's connection to the powers that be, on Wall Street and in Washington, and distrust her claims to care about people like them. They increasingly feel that they are slipping backward. Hannah works as a maid in a hotel; George reminds her that his grandparents worked on the same property, as servants to John Jacob Astor.

The mention of Astor is not accidental: the Gilded Age is being re-created in our time, with the economic and cultural riches in the country being increasingly monopolized by a small group of the very wealthy, and with the un-moneyed masses feeling powerless and cast aside. Richard's artistic heroes, Anton Chekhov and Harley Granville Barker, were writing in the last Gilded Age, when the increasing alienation from their leaders led the educated and cultured to feel incapable of controlling their own destinies. Reading *The Gabriels*, like reading Chekhov, leaves us with the unmistakable feeling that something is going very wrong, but that no one knows how to fix it. Nelson's characters, like Chekhov's, are undeniably appealing people, but lack the power, the agency, to become heroes.

They feel, in other words, like us.

But there is also hope in these plays, a deep and powerful hope, which springs not from politics or ideology but from the love and connection of this family that we grow to know so well. Early on, Richard decided that the plays would be set in the kitchen and center on cooking. In each of the plays the characters prepare and cook a meal onstage, in real time, the sounds and smells of the food permeating the whole theater. In this magnificently simple way, Richard affirms the continuity and power of life and family. Cooking is not inherently dramatic; food changes as it is cooked, but cooking has no reversals or dramatic action. Cooking sustains us, physically and communally. Cooking is life-giving, and life is based on hope. It is the simple, small actions we take to sustain our communal life that give us hope that the world, full of loss, can nonetheless be good.

Richard's determination to put real life onstage, to tell the truth by avoiding all grandstanding and theatrical flourishes, has created a masterful trilogy of plays that show us, not only the way we live now, but the way we live. I came back to each successive Gabriel play with the sense of returning home, saddened by what had been lost, but joyous to be back with these people I loved.

Mary ends these plays, as we do, listening to a piano that no one else onstage can hear, a piano that has long been sold off to pay debts, played by a husband who died the year before. It is the only theatrical flourish Richard allows himself to make, and its effect is electric. The thing that matters most is the love we have for each other. Love can survive economic and electoral disasters. It can even survive death.

New York City
July 2018

HUNGRY

For Bobbie and Cindy

PRODUCTION HISTORY

Hungry was commissioned by and first produced at The Public Theater (Oskar Eustis, Artistic Director; Patrick Willingham, Executive Director) in New York City on March 4, 2016. The director was Richard Nelson; the set design was by Susan Hilferty and Jason Ardizzone-West, the costume design was by Susan Hilferty, the lighting design was by Jennifer Tipton, the sound design was by Scott Lehrer and Will Pickens; the production stage manager was Theresa Flanagan, the stage manager was Jared Oberholtzer. The cast was:

MARY GABRIEL	Maryann Plunkett
PATRICIA GABRIEL	Roberta Maxwell
GEORGE GABRIEL	Jay O. Sanders
HANNAH GABRIEL	Lynn Hawley
JOYCE GABRIEL	Amy Warren
KARIN GABRIEL	Meg Gibson

In December 2016, the complete series of *The Gabriels* was presented at The Public Theater with rotating repertory.

CHARACTERS

THOMAS GABRIEL, a playwright and novelist, died four months ago, at the age of sixty-four.

MARY GABRIEL, Thomas's third wife, and widow, a retired doctor, sixty.

PATRICIA GABRIEL, Thomas's mother, eighty-one.

GEORGE GABRIEL, Thomas's brother, a piano teacher and cabinet-maker, sixty-one.

HANNAH GABRIELl, George's wife, and Thomas's sister-in-law, works for a caterer, fifty-two.

JOYCE GABRIEL, Thomas's sister, an assistant costume designer, lives in Brooklyn, fifty-three.

KARIN GABRIEL, Thomas's first wife, an actress and now teacher, fifty-four.

TIME

Friday, March 4, 2016. 6:00 P.M. to approximately 8:00 P.M.

SETTING

The kitchen of the Gabriels' house, South Street, Rhinebeck, New York.

PUNCTUATION

Double quotation marks are used when someone is reading from something or directly quoting. Single quotation marks are used when someone is paraphrasing or generalizing.

Like most other humans, I am hungry . . .

—*M. F. K. Fisher*

An empty room: the kitchen of the Gabriels' house. South Street, Rhinebeck, New York.

Refrigerator, stove/oven (electric), sink; large wooden and rustic table used as a kitchen counter (with a drawer for silverware) is set beside another smaller table making an L-shape; a bench with a back is to one side, facing the tables; a small desk; upstage a small cupboard. Chairs and a bench set upside down of the tables.

Exits: upstage to the unseen dining room; down left to the mudroom, back porch and backyard; down right leads to the rest of the house—living room (where there is a piano), the stairs to the bedrooms on the second floor, and to the front porch.

In the dark, Lucius's "Wildewoman" plays through the main speakers.

Mary, Hannah, Joyce and Karin enter with trays full of kitchen objects. They will create the 'life of the kitchen.' They take the chairs and bench off the table and desk, and set them around the table and at the desk. They place a dish rack, dish towels, dirty dishes, glasses, napkins, bowls, a colander, pasta pots, etc., around and under the sink; notebooks, letters, catalogues, an iPod dock, etc., on the desk;

Mary's purse on the back of the desk chair; a timer, coffeepot, etc. on the top of the stove; a plastic trash can next to the sink; aprons on hooks on the refrigerator; oven mitts on hooks on the stove; fridge magnets on the refrigerator; salt and pepper, sugar bowl, cookbooks within bookends, a knife block, flour, sugar, a glass jar with reading glasses, a small tray of spices, a plate with the leftover crumbs from a sandwich, a mug for tea, etc., on the tables. George too has entered, with a plastic box of old cookbooks; he sets some of the books on the bench and table, and the box on the floor by the bench.

All but Mary leave; the lights and music change:

The Roosevelt Museum

Music ("Wildewoman") now plays on the iPod. The timer ticks on the stove.

Mary sits alone, having finished her late lunch, looking through an old cookbook. After a few moments, she takes her plate and mug to the sink, and washes them. She brings a cutting board from the dish rack and sets it on the table; turns off the music.

The sound of the timer ticking is now heard louder.

Mary goes to the refrigerator, takes out a towel-covered bowl, and brings it to the table. She takes off the towel; she flours the cutting board, and takes bread dough out of the bowl, puts it on the cutting board, and begins to knead the dough.

After a moment, Karin, with a small paperback in hand, enters from the living room, startling Mary.

KARIN: They're back, Mary.

MARY *(Startled)*: What?! *(Seeing Karin)* Sorry, I forgot you were here. What did you say?

KARIN: They just got back . . . You asked me to tell you.

MARY: Karin . . . Did you find something? What did you find?

(Karin hands Mary the book.)

You found this. They just published this. Most are his old plays . . .

KARIN: I remember him writing one or two of those.

MARY: You do?

KARIN: In our apartment on Cranberry . . .

MARY: Karin, we've got a whole box of these. *(The book)* We don't even know what to do with them. Take it. *(Hands it to her)* If you want . . . Thomas would want you to have one. A memento.

HANNAH *(Entering with her coat on)*: You're still here, Karin. I thought you had to go.

KARIN *(As she goes)*: I do. I have to go soon. Thank you, Mary. Thank you . . .

(She is gone.)

MARY: You all were gone a long time. Take off your coat.

HANNAH *(Explaining)*: Now we're going to take a walk. Joyce 'needs to get some air.' She's had it with her mom. You want to come? She wants us to sneak out the back . . . George is coming.

(Mary shakes her head.)

MARY: So how was the 'all-new, remodeled' Roosevelt museum?

HANNAH *(Shrugs)*: It's what it now is . . .

MARY: What does that mean?

HANNAH: What has Karin been doing? I'm surprised she's still here.

MARY: Looking through the bookshelves. Whatever. She's been doing it for hours in the living room. *(Before Hannah can say anything)* It's fine, Hannah.

HANNAH: You're baking bread.

MARY: I felt like making something.

JOYCE *(Entering, having passed Karin)*: Karin's still here?

(Joyce has her coat on too.)

HANNAH: We were just talking about that.
JOYCE *(Over this)*: Is she staying for dinner?
HANNAH *(To Mary)*: She's not?
MARY *(Over this)*: No. She's not staying for dinner. I did not ask her to stay for dinner.
HANNAH: Good.
JOYCE: So you can say 'no.'
MARY: I know how to say 'no,' Joyce.
HANNAH: And I think you've done enough for Karin today. *(To Joyce)* Karin just said she was about to go . . .
JOYCE: I've hardly said five words to her.
HANNAH: She didn't come to see you. Where's my husband?
JOYCE: He's coming. Getting Mom comfortable for her nap . . . He's prying himself loose. *(To Mary)* We're going for a walk— Have you been out?
HANNAH: She doesn't want to go.
MARY *(Over this)*: The Stop&Shop . . . How was the museum? I want to know.
HANNAH: I wasn't as bothered as Joyce and George—
JOYCE: It has really been fucked up, Mary.
HANNAH *(To Mary)*: She's slightly exaggerating.
JOYCE: Only slightly.

(The timer has gone off.)

I'm not even saying I was that *bothered.* Or even surprised. Why should we be surprised anymore? *(To Mary)* Your timer went off . . .
MARY: I know . . .
JOYCE: It's not what it *had been.* That's all I'm trying to say. It's very different. *(To Mary)* And— *(The second thing she wanted to say)* Thomas would have really hated it. He

loved the Roosevelt Museum. He loved the way it was. But this is the world we now live in.

MARY: I'm happy I didn't go then . . . I'd like to remember that museum the way *Thomas* liked it.

(Mary washes the bowl in the sink.)

HANNAH: You need any help?

(Mary shakes her head and will go to the cupboard to get a bread pan.)

MARY: What did they do to it?

JOYCE: The museum? Everything. You feel they are *pushing* things on you now. Like you can't think for yourself anymore. I'm sure it's what the Bush libraries are like. In *Texas.*

HANNAH: I'll bet you the Bush libraries are even worse, Joyce.

(Mary will get butter out of the refrigerator, and will butter the bottom and sides of the pan as:)

JOYCE *(To Mary)*: Mom seemed to enjoy herself though.

MARY: Good.

(George enters from the living room, still in his coat.)

HANNAH: Here comes my husband . . .

JOYCE: Come on, let's go. Let's get some air.

GEORGE: Why is Karin still here?

HANNAH *(Over the end of this)*: She's not staying for dinner.

JOYCE *(To George)*: Let's go.

GEORGE: You go. I'm going to stay.

JOYCE: What? Why? *(Confused)* Mom in bed? She taking her nap?

GEORGE *(Hesitates, then)*: Not yet . . .

JOYCE: What?? Are you kidding me, George?

GEORGE *(Over this)*: Joyce, she decided . . .

JOYCE: What?? What has Mom decided now? What the hell is she deciding now?

HANNAH: Joyce—

GEORGE: She decided she doesn't need a nap.

JOYCE *(It just comes out)*: No.

GEORGE: She says she wants to stay up.

JOYCE: No. Please god, no. I knew this would happen.

GEORGE: Joyce—

JOYCE *(Defensive)*: She's tired, that's all what I mean. I'm thinking of her . . . I am . . .

HANNAH *(To George)*: I'm sure she is.

JOYCE *(To George)*: She looks exhausted . . . She should be in bed. *(To the others)* Or am I wrong? Tell me I'm wrong. *(To Mary, defensive)* I had to help her up the porch steps.

HANNAH: I think she just lets us do that, Joyce.

MARY: She does 'let' you do that . . .

(Mary shapes the bread dough into a loaf and puts it in the bread pan.)

JOYCE: I don't think so.

GEORGE *(To Joyce)*: *You* want to tell her to take a nap? Go ahead and tell her. *I* told her. *(Points)* She's right in there, in her chair . . .

JOYCE: I guess then we're *not* taking a walk . . .

(Joyce starts to take off her coat.)

(To George) If she doesn't take her nap now, she's going to . . .

(Hannah is taking off her coat.)

GEORGE: She's going to what? She'll be fine.

(Mary will take the cutting board, etc., to the sink and wash them.)

HANNAH *(With her coat, to Joyce)*: Give me your coat. I'll hang it up.

JOYCE *(To George)*: Mom looked absolutely exhausted. That's all I was saying.

MARY: I'm sure, today wore her out.

JOYCE *(Over this)*: She had to see everything. I mean every *thing*. She sat down on every goddamn bench. We must have been in there five hours . . .

MARY: She's old.

JOYCE: Thanks for that news . . . *(Trying to explain)* I haven't been here like you, so . . .

HANNAH: I'm sure each time there's a bit of a—surprise . . .

GEORGE: You could have come for Christmas, Joyce.

MARY *(To George)*: She had just been here.

JOYCE: I had just been here.

(George now tries to hand Hannah his coat.)

(To George, incredulous) Hang up your own coat. She's not your servant . . .

(He starts to put his coat on a chair.)

Don't leave it there. That's a chair. There are *hooks* . . . The same hooks that have been out in that hallway forever.

GEORGE: I know where the hooks are.

HANNAH: Give me the coat. I'll hang it up.

JOYCE: Don't spoil him, Hannah. He's spoiled enough.

MARY: Joyce . . .

HANNAH: Joyce, the other night—

GEORGE *(To Hannah)*: What??

HANNAH *(Three coats in her arms)*: The other night we're watching a film. Japanese.

GEORGE: I was joking, Hannah. Come on.

HANNAH *(Over this)*: And this guy comes home, in the film, and slips off his shoes; the wife hurries to get his robe, and as he takes off his jacket he just drops it on the floor. Just drops it.

GEORGE: I was teasing . . . She'll believe you.

HANNAH: The wife's standing right there. So she has to reach down and pick it up. George turns to me and says—'see.'

JOYCE *('Outraged')*: Oh for Christ sake . . . That's embarrassing. She's your wife not your slave.

MARY: He was kidding . . .

HANNAH *(To George, as she heads off)*: I know you were joking . . .

GEORGE: Then why tell the story?

HANNAH: Because it's funny.

(Hannah goes off with the coats.
Mary wipes the table.)

MARY *(To say something)*: Did you have any lunch? I think there are still some cold cuts . . .

GEORGE: We ate at the Eveready. Even got a booth right away.

(Then:)

My brother loved the Roosevelt Museum. Thomas did some research in that library, didn't he? Or am I wrong?

JOYCE: For his Roosevelt play?

GEORGE: The last thing you're faced with, just before you leave? There's a movie—with—guess whose voice is on it, Mary? *Bill Clinton's.*

(Hannah enters having heard this:)

HANNAH: You didn't let her guess.

MARY: That's not *FDR*.

GEORGE *(Emphatic)*: No.

HANNAH *(Shrugs)*: He was a president . . .

MARY: I was going to guess Hillary.

JOYCE: Not Trump?

GEORGE *(Over this)*: You used to be able to walk in there and you felt you were in the presence of *that man*.

HANNAH *(To Mary)*: You should go, see for yourself.

GEORGE *(Continuing, over this)*: It's about what *they* want you to believe. To think. They feel they need to tell you what to think. So that you'll vote for us *Democrats*? It's not history anymore, it's now just politics. What the hell happened to history?

JOYCE *(To George)*: So where did you leave Mom? If she didn't go upstairs to take a nap. You know—she's probably sick of us too.

MARY: I doubt if your mother—

JOYCE *(Hearing herself)*: I mean—

GEORGE *(Be quiet)*: Joyce . . .

JOYCE: Mom can't hear. She can't hear if you're sitting right next to her . . .

GEORGE *(Answering the question)*: She was still in her chair, in the living room.

HANNAH: I peeked in. She's talking to Karin . . .

JOYCE: *At* Karin is more like it. So poor Karin got trapped . . .

HANNAH: It sounded like she was telling Karin about her voting for Roosevelt.

JOYCE: Is that even possible?

GEORGE: Who knows? Why Karin? *(Answers his own question)* Because she's polite and still listens . . . Should we go and rescue Karin?

JOYCE *(To Mary)*: Hannah told us at lunch, you don't remember actually inviting her . . .

MARY: I must have.

JOYCE: I don't think I've seen her in decades.

GEORGE: She was at Thomas's memorial in the city.

JOYCE: I wasn't looking for her then.

HANNAH: She visited in October. Thomas asked Mary to get in touch . . .

JOYCE: Did he? Maybe I knew that . . . Huh. *(To Mary)* You okay with that?

HANNAH: She seemed really 'pleased' to be there. This morning . . . So—we all did a nice thing.

(No one knows what to do, where to go; they watch Mary work.)

MARY: I just felt like *making* something . . .

GEORGE: Makes sense.

HANNAH *(Trying to make a joke)*: I wake up like that sometimes too. Then I don't make anything. *(To George)* Do I?

GEORGE: Yes, you do . . .

(Joyce is looking into the coffeepot on the stove.)

MARY: I should make a fresh pot, Joyce.

JOYCE: It's still—sort of warm. I'm going to buy this house a coffee maker. They cost like ten bucks.

(She will take a cup from the dish rack.)

GEORGE *(To Joyce)*: You going to stay tonight in my room? Your old room's full of crap—

MARY: I made up a bed in George and Thomas's old room . . .

JOYCE: I don't care where I sleep.

(Karin appears in the doorway from the living room.)

Look, she's escaped. Good for you. Good for Karin.

KARIN *(Over the end)*: I wasn't escaping.

GEORGE *(Over this)*: My sister's always joking.

KARIN *(To Mary)*: Patricia wonders if she could get a cup of tea. I could do that. Just tell me where you keep the tea, Mary . . .

JOYCE: Karin—my mother means: go and get *(George and herself)* her 'children,' and make them come back in there.

That's what she means—by 'cup of tea.' It's code. *(To George)* Isn't it?

GEORGE: That is what our mother means . . .

HANNAH *(To Karin)*: Sit down. Join us . . .

JOYCE *(A joke)*: You're safe in here.

(Karin will sit at the table.)

KARIN *(Confused)*: What do you mean?

HANNAH *(To Karin)*: So their mom voted for Roosevelt?

KARIN: At least five times she said.

(As Joyce pours her coffee:)

MARY: I'm going to make a new pot . . . That's not even hot—

(Mary will empty the pot in the sink, take out the grounds, wash the pot; get water from the sink, coffee from the freezer, and start to make coffee as:)

GEORGE *(To Hannah to say something)*: Mary was surprised we got a table right away at the Eveready.

HANNAH: Unlike last night.

JOYCE: What happened last—?

HANNAH *(Over this)*: We wanted to go out for dinner. And how rare is that?

KARIN *(Standing there, interrupts)*: I should probably be going soon . . .

MARY: Do you have to go already?

KARIN: I guess not. I'm not in the way?

MARY: No. Of course not. *(Pointing to the bench)* Karin, all those books were Thomas's too. Research for something. I thought they belonged in here. You'll see why. Take a look.

(Karin will sit on the bench and look through the books.)

HANNAH *(Continues, to Joyce)*: Every place in Rhinebeck Village, packed to the gills. On a *Thursday* night. One place even laughed at me . . . 'Oh we're usually booked out from Wednesday . . .'

JOYCE: In Rhinebeck?? When did that happen?

HANNAH: It happened. When? We don't know. We never go out . . .

GEORGE: Joyce . . . Mom's in there all by herself . . .

JOYCE: I'm almost done.

(Joyce takes a sip of her coffee.)

MARY *(Ready to put in the scoops of coffee)*: How much am I making? Who's going to want coffee? *(No one does)* Then what am I making it for?

HANNAH *(To Mary)*: Leave it. We'll want it later . . .

JOYCE *(Over this)*: Oh, Mary, I almost forgot . . . Here . . . *(Out of her pocket, a small booklet)* This is for you . . . A present.

MARY *(Wiping her hands on her apron)*: What—? What is it? *('Smiles')* A present for me?

GEORGE: It cost like two dollars.

HANNAH: George . . .

GEORGE *(A joke)*: We all chipped in.

(Mary is handed the booklet.)

JOYCE: Read it. Read the title.

MARY *(Reads)*: *Cookies for Eleanor. (Shows it)*

JOYCE: They had a pile of them at the Val-Kill gift shop.

MARY: I didn't know Eleanor made cookies.

JOYCE: I don't think she did. I think those are the cookies she just liked to eat.

GEORGE *(Standing)*: Joyce . . . Mom sees *me* every day.

(Joyce takes one last 'final' sip of coffee.)

JOYCE: Okay. Okay. I'm feeling guilty. I'm ready . . . Oh give me strength . . .

(She stands.)

KARIN: Patricia said she wanted a cup of tea . . .

GEORGE *(For the thousandth time)*: Our mother, Karin, never says what she means . . .

JOYCE: No, she doesn't . . . *(To Hannah)* Come on, you're coming too . . .

HANNAH: Daughters-in-law *(Looks at Mary)* have been excused.

JOYCE: Who the hell excused you?

HANNAH: I think—*we* did. *(To Mary)* Didn't we?

MARY: I think so.

HANNAH *(To Karin)*: Even *ex*-daughters-in-law, Karin. Stay with us . . . Stay in here . . . You won't regret it . . .

JOYCE *(As she goes with George)*: That doesn't seem fair.

HANNAH *(Calls)*: It does to us!

(They are gone.)

(To Karin) You don't want to be in there . . .

MARY: No. And we speak from experience . . .

(Laughter.)

HANNAH *(To Mary)*: What are you making for dinner?

KARIN: I probably shouldn't stay . . . I don't know . . .

(Then:)

MARY *(To Hannah)*: I was thinking—ratatouille . . . That's easy enough. With—pasta . . .

(The lights fade.)

Three Sisters-in-Law

A short time later.

Off, from the living room, someone is playing the piano: Schumann's Album for Youth, *Op. 68, No. 6., Armes Waisenkind.*

Karin sits on the bench with the cookbooks; Hannah and Mary at the table, in the middle of a conversation.

HANNAH: They've rented out all of Wilderstein.

MARY: How much does that cost?

HANNAH *(Explains everything)*: Rich people.

MARY: Hannah works for a caterer in Rhinebeck, Karin.

HANNAH: When there's work. *(Such as)* Weddings . . .

KARIN *(Over this)*: What's Wilderstein?

HANNAH: A big old beautiful mansion. A park now. In Rhinebeck. A lot of people here have worked really hard to restore it. A lot of local history there. Mary, my boss said she heard they first tried to rent out the Roosevelt home. They said they really wanted a party in there. Mary, what can I do?

KARIN: How can I help? I think it'll be fine . . . I think I can do what I was going to do—later. Tomorrow even. I just can't stay too late. When do you think you'll eat?

MARY *(After a look at Hannah)*: An hour and . . . a half? Something like that. Is that too late?

KARIN: No. No, that'd be fine. Perfect even.

MARY: Good. Good.

KARIN: So what can I do? And it's all right? You're sure?

MARY: Of course. You'll need an apron. Hannah, she'll need an apron. *(To Karin)* You don't want to stain that lovely blouse . . .

(Hannah finds an apron in the cupboard.)

And we'll get you things to cut up . . .

KARIN: I think I overdressed. I thought maybe there'd be more of a—ceremony? I guess. But it was perfect. And I'd never been to something like that before. Hannah, thank you for the boots. I left them in the mudroom . . .

(Hannah gives her an apron. As she puts it on, notices the design:)

I like this . . . *(Smiles, continues)* I hadn't realized—what a dope I am—that it'd be a real walk to the water. I don't know what I'd have done without those boots.

HANNAH: Well, we had to get to the water. That was sort of the whole point, *(To Mary)* wasn't it? What he wanted . . . *(To Mary)* Thomas loved that river . . .

KARIN: Thank you, Mary, for letting me tag along. It meant a lot . . .

MARY *(Looking in the refrigerator)*: So what needs to be cut up . . . ?

(She closes the refrigerator.)

Karin, I keep the *("a list")* mushrooms, onions . . . in the mudroom. *(To Hannah)* I just started doing that.

HANNAH: It's cool out there . . . I should do that.

MARY: The refrigerator was getting too crowded.

HANNAH: Mine's a mess . . .

MARY *(To Karin)*: Would you mind? Bring just what you can carry. That should be enough. They're in little baskets . . .

(Karin starts to go off.)

(Calls to Karin) Also tomatoes! Three or four tomatoes!

(Karin is off.)

(To Hannah) God only knows how good they are this time of year. Or where they come from . . .

(Hannah looks at her.)

(Before Hannah can say anything) We have enough food . . . It's fine.

HANNAH *(To Mary)*: Joyce said it was snowing in the city when she left this morning.

MARY: We got nothing up here. What a crazy winter.

HANNAH *(Putting on her apron)*: That's not my husband playing.

MARY: You can tell that? That it's Joyce?

HANNAH: Patricia's making her play.

MARY: Does she really need to be made? She never seemed to need . . .

(George enters.)

HANNAH: See?

GEORGE: See what?

HANNAH: That it's your sister playing the piano.

GEORGE: I'm sure I'm next . . . Has Karin gone?

HANNAH: In the mudroom.

GEORGE: Mom wants her little sherry glass; she says you're always hiding it, Mary.

MARY: I *wash* it. I put it away. In the dining room.

(George heads to the dining room.)

There were two. She took one to the home. Top shelf, corner cabinet.

(George is off.)

(The obvious place) It's with the sherry . . .

HANNAH: Patricia's got her kids waiting on her. That always makes her happy . . .

MARY *(Back with the coffeepot)*: Do I make coffee or not?

HANNAH *(Looking at her watch)*: Who's going to drink it?

(Mary will put the coffee back in the refrigerator, and the water pitcher.)

MARY *(Back to Hannah's story)*: So *all* of Wilderstein? . . . How rich is the guy? And who has their wedding in early March? There are other aprons . . .

HANNAH *(About the apron)*: This is fine. *(Continues)* I saw . . . Two tents. A truck just to heat the tents. All of us were guessing it must be like *his* fifth wedding.

MARY: Worse than Thomas. What are you serving? At this—fancy wedding?

(Hannah will get the plates, cutting boards, knives, etc., in preparation for cutting and slicing the vegetables, as:)

HANNAH: They're New Yorkers, so they have their own caterer. Their own *New York food.* We just serve it. *(Suddenly to Mary)* Oh I saw their chef! He was wearing jeans and cowboy boots. It's fucking Dutchess County not Deadwood. New Yorkers . . .

(George returns with a sherry bottle and the special sherry glass. Off, Joyce has changed to a faster piece from the Schumann: No. 8, Wilder Reiter.)

GEORGE *(About the piano music)*: Joyce is showing off now . . . *(To Hannah)* She said she hadn't touched a piano in six months . . . Right, Joyce. Right.

(Karin has returned with some vegetables. George looks at Hannah.)

HANNAH *(Explaining)*: Karin can stay for dinner.

GEORGE: Good. Good. The more the merrier. *(Smiles at Karin and he goes off)*

KARIN *(About the vegetables)*: How's this? This enough?

MARY: How many of us are we—now? *(To herself)* It keeps growing . . . *(To Hannah)* You think Patricia is going to eat?

(Hannah takes the vegetables and will go to the sink to wash and clean the mushrooms and tomatoes.)

KARIN: Mary, why all the apples out there? . . . You must have like a bushel—

MARY: I was all set to make my apple crisp. Then Joyce phoned up— *(In Joyce's voice)* 'I think we should have a cake. Treat the day like his birthday or something.' It's not Thomas's birthday. It's sort of the opposite . . . *('Smiles,' then to Hannah)* Joyce says, "I'll pay for the cake."

HANNAH: Has she? Paid for the cake?

(Mary looks at her: of course not.)

MARY: Sit down. Sit, Karin . . .

HANNAH *(At the sink washing vegetables)*: You can still make your apple crisp . . . Come on. *(The tomatoes)* These look pretty good. *(Incredulous)* Stop&Shop??

MARY *(No)*: Adams. *(To Karin)* Kingston.

HANNAH: Mary's apple crisp, Karin, was always Thomas's favorite dessert. I can tell her that right?

KARIN: I didn't know that . . . I never made him—

HANNAH: *Mary's* apple crisp. Only hers.

KARIN: Of course.

(Mary takes out vegetables for the ratatouille as:)

MARY: Talk about rich people, Hannah. When Thomas was rehearsing one of his plays in London, there was this party. *(The connection to Hannah again)* Rich people. I just remembered this the other day. I keep remembering his stories.

HANNAH: Of course you do. That's normal.

MARY *(Continues)*: And this party was hosted by the Lord Mayor of London. For the theater company that was going to do Thomas's play.

(Mary moves the trash can toward the table.)

We can put the peelings in here.

KARIN: You don't compost? I thought everyone in the country—

MARY: We don't. *(Continues, and continues to set up)* And so Thomas went to this party; it was a fundraiser, in the theater's lobby after a show. And the Lord Mayor, Thomas said was drunk, and had a funny chain kind of thing across his chest . . . Thomas wrote me about it. I came across the letter last week . . . I've been rereading a lot of his letters . . .

(Then, continues:)

So the people in charge of this party—get this—they had asked the theater company to have some of the younger, by which I'm sure they meant sexier—

HANNAH: Right.

MARY *(Over this)*: —maybe they even came out and said that—members of the acting company—actresses—

HANNAH: Of course.

MARY: —if they could wear the costumes from the show they had been doing that night at this party for potential patrons . . . Ask me what the show was.

KARIN: What was the show?

MARY: *The Beggar's Opera.*

(They laugh.)

(Saying it yet another way) Rich people . . . Another planet. A whole other universe.

*(Off, the same fast Schumann [*No. 8, Wilder Reiter*] is being played much faster, and with more bravado.)*

HANNAH: Now *that's* George.

(They are listening.)

He too has been practicing. He knew they'd both be asked to play . . .

(Hannah will join Karin at the table; Mary continues to set up, clean up, etc.)

KARIN: How thin do you want me to . . . ? *("cut these")*
MARY: Whatever. I usually . . .
KARIN: What? Tell me.
MARY: Anyway—
HANNAH: Tell her. She wants to do it as *you'd* like.
KARIN: I'll do it any way you want, Mary.
MARY: Quarter inch . . . ?
KARIN: Quarter inch it is.

(Hannah cuts.)

HANNAH: Like that, Mary?

(Mary nods.)

(To Karin) Like that. *(To Mary)* Was that so hard?
MARY *(Continues her story)*: Some actors did wear their costumes at this party. He wrote all about this in the letter. I just read it again last week.
HANNAH: You said.
MARY: Did I? *(Continues)* So they came in these nineteenth-century beggar clothes, their faces dirtied . . . And all these drunks from the city just looking down the girls' dresses . . .
HANNAH: Grow up, men . . . My boss introduced me to the client, "the groom."

(Off, a telephone rings. Hannah starts to get up, the piano playing stops, and then the ringing stops.)

George got it. *(Continues)* She told him I'd worked 'Chelsea's wedding.' He was so impressed.

KARIN: Did you really?

HANNAH: I just served—

KARIN: Still . . .

MARY *(Over this)*: Of course, that type would be . . .

HANNAH: He *had* to know what wines *Chelsea* served.

KARIN: What were they?

HANNAH: There's a winery in Clinton Corners. The *Clinton* Winery. Their wine. Chelsea must have thought it was cute . . .

MARY *(To Karin)*: Clinton Corners it's just . . .

HANNAH *(Over this)*: So this client says: do you think it's too late to get our wine from them too? I don't know what that conjured up . . . *(Explains everything) The Clintons!* . . .

MARY: "I want what they want . . ."

HANNAH *(Over the end of this)*: I get him to order *thirty* cases. Called my friend out in Clinton Corners and told her to charge the fools three times what they usually get.

MARY: Good. Good.

KARIN: And that's what they paid?

HANNAH *(Explaining)*: New Yorkers, Karin, don't know what anything is worth anymore . . .

(George enters.)

GEORGE: Your daughter's on the phone, Mary.

(Mary quickly wipes her hands.)

MARY *(With a 'smile')*: She called . . .

(And begins to hurry off.)

HANNAH *(To Mary)*: Give her our love.
MARY: I will.
GEORGE: I did.

(Mary heads off.)

HANNAH *(Calls after her)*: Tell her we missed her today . . . But that we understand . . .

(Mary is gone.)

(To George) She called . . . *(George nods)*
GEORGE *(Looks at the table)*: We just had lunch.
HANNAH *(As a joke)*: So you're not going to get hungry? Ratatouille. I think Mary's going to make Thomas's apple crisp . . .
GEORGE: Good . . .
KARIN: That was one of Thomas's favorites. I just learned that.
GEORGE: I know.
KARIN: From an earlier marriage? Her daughter? I didn't know Mary had a daughter . . .
GEORGE *(Nods)*: Yeah . . . An earlier marriage . . .
HANNAH *(To Karin)*: She lives in Pittsburgh . . .

(Off, piano music has begun again: another from the Schumann, though slower, No. 9, Volksliedchen.)

GEORGE: Joyce told Mom she hadn't touched a piano in about six months . . . *(Laughs to himself)*

(He will sit and pick up the Cookies for Eleanor *booklet.)*

HANNAH: Did Patricia criticize Joyce's playing?

(No response.)

What did she say? I don't think your mother hears herself sometimes.

(Seeing Mary returning:)

That was quick.

MARY: She's busy. She's going to send an e-card . . . *('Smiles')* I told her she didn't have to do that.

HANNAH: There are a lot of great e-cards now. What's her name, Jackie . . . something?

(Mary turns on the water.)

KARIN *(About her cutting)*: How am I doing?

HANNAH *(Looks)*: Good . . . That knife okay?

KARIN: It's fine.

MARY: I'm glad she thought of calling. She's so busy. Nice to hear her voice . . . *(To George)* You're not going to be missed?

GEORGE: In there? *(Meaning the living room)*

(Shrugs. Reads the title of the booklet, he's been looking at) "*Cookies for Eleanor.*"

HANNAH *(Amazed)*: A cookbook about what Eleanor Roosevelt just liked to eat . . . *(Looks up, to Mary)* Mary, they had a neat display—of everything out of Eleanor's purse from, I think, the 1950s? *(To George)* Or maybe it was when she died?

GEORGE: I don't know. It's a clever idea. 'Inside the woman's purse . . .'

HANNAH *(To George)*: Don't say anything you'll regret. *(To Mary)* Nail scissors. Makeup. Eleanor's handgun license. Who knew Eleanor Roosevelt packed heat?

MARY *(Over this)*: She had a gun license??

(Mary will go to the sink to wash things.)

HANNAH *(To Mary)*: Did you tell her about finding the hair? You wanted to tell your daughter about that.

MARY: She was rushing off somewhere.

HANNAH *(To Mary)*: She has a baby . . . I remember when I had Paulie, I couldn't think about anything else. I missed birthdays . . . Young mothers . . .

(George and Karin are confused. Then:)

GEORGE *(To Hannah)*: What hair? I don't think I know about this . . .

HANNAH: Should I tell him?

(Then:)

Mary found one of Thomas's gray hairs inside a book. One of those? On the bench there? She was trying to go through his boxes. *(To George)* What do you do with something like that? A hair . . .

GEORGE: What do you mean?

HANNAH: Mary told me she almost threw it into the wastebasket. Then thought better of that and set the hair aside—on the top of some unopened box?

(After a look at Mary:)

Then . . . ? She got a phone call or something . . . ?

(Mary works.)

Maybe went to the bathroom? Anyway, Mary comes back and opens up a few more boxes and about an hour later she remembers the hair. She looks all around and she can't find it anywhere. She opens the books . . . She tells herself—it's just a hair . . . 'Why am I crying about a hair?'

(George looks to Hannah: 'She was crying?')

But there's a happy ending, right? When she's getting ready for bed, on the shoulder of her sweater—the hair. Now she's scotch-taped it to an index card and she keeps it in her purse. It's in your purse?

(Mary nods. Hannah goes to Mary's purse hanging on a chair by the desk.)

GEORGE *(Trying to be light)*: A woman's purse.

(Piano music has stopped.)

MARY *(Listens, to George)*: Sounds like your sister has stopped entertaining your mother.

HANNAH: I'm not sure that's something she knows how to stop doing. Here it is.

(Hands the index card to George. He looks at it.)

MARY: It doesn't smell.

KARIN: May I see it?

(Karin reaches for the index card.)

Thomas's hair . . .

(Joyce enters, startling them.)

JOYCE *(To George)*: Where did you go?! The phone rings and you run away . . . *Your turn.*

(Confused) What are you doing?

HANNAH: Making ratatouille . . .

(Hannah takes the index card from Karin and will hand it back to Mary.)

GEORGE *(Standing, to Joyce)*: So where is she? Where's Mom now? . . .

JOYCE: Still in her chair. No doubt still criticizing me.

GEORGE: Joyce, she hasn't been criticizing . . .

(He heads off.)

JOYCE *(Over this, as her mother, to George)*: "Is that how you're going to play it? Is that how you're going to play it?"

GEORGE *(Calls, over this)*: Grow up, Joyce . . .

(He is gone.)

JOYCE *(To 'George')*: Fuck you.

MARY: I thought you sounded great, Joyce . . .

JOYCE: I've been practicing. Don't tell my brother.

(Joyce smiles at Karin.)

HANNAH: Karin is staying for dinner . . .

JOYCE *(Taken aback)*: Good . . .

(Mary has taken the index card to her purse.)

What's that?

HANNAH: One of Thomas's hairs. Mary keeps it taped to an index card, in her purse . . .

JOYCE: Why???

MARY *(Changing the subject)*: I know your mother really appreciates your coming up today, Joyce.

JOYCE: Has she said that? Has she actually said that?

MARY: I think so . . .

(Then:
The lights fade.)

Common Sense in the Kitchen

The same. A short time later. Off, Satie's piano solo, Gnossienne No. 3.

Hannah and Karin sit at the table slicing vegetables for the ratatouille. Mary hovers, cleaning up, getting things ready . . . Joyce sits, looking through an old cookbook that she has found lying on the table.

In the middle of conversation:

JOYCE *(Reading from the old book in hand)*: "Tell me, dear reader, do you often say to yourself, in bitterness of spirit, that it is a mistake to educate girls into a love of science and literature, and then condemn them to the routine of a domestic drudge."

KARIN *(To Joyce)*: *When* was this written?

JOYCE: "1884."

KARIN *(To Joyce)*: And it's a woman?

HANNAH: Has to be a woman . . .

JOYCE *(Reads the cover)*: "Marion Harland." A woman.

KARIN: I think I'm cutting these too thick.

HANNAH: That's fine . . . You're doing great . . .

MARY *(About the music)*: This was one of Thomas's favorites . . .

JOYCE: That's what she wants. That's what Mom's asking for. Pieces Thomas used to play for her . . . *(Reads)* "A talk, as woman to woman." *(The point is proved)* Woman to woman . . . There you go. "An informal preface to what I mean shall be an informal book . . ." A woman talking to women, who's listened to other women . . . *(Just remembers a 'story')* Hannah, I heard a joke this week— A girl tells her mother about her new boyfriend . . . Her mom asks what he does. The mom is shocked: "How can you go out with *him*? Someone who works for the NSA!" The daughter just looks at her mother, her eyes wide open, "But Mom—*he* listens."

(They laugh.)

A friend told me that. A married friend . . .

HANNAH: Keep reading . . . *(To Mary)* I don't think we read this part.

JOYCE *(Reads)*: "My dear fellow-housekeeper and reader."

HANNAH: That's us . . .

JOYCE: "I have before me now a picture of a wife and mother, in slatternly morning-gown at four in the afternoon, leaning back in the laziest and most ragged of rocking chairs, dust on the carpet, on the *open* piano—" I love that touch—her 'readers' all alone at home, playing her piano. *(Then)* I've been there. Who hasn't been there?

(Mary now joins them at the table.)

(Continues to read) ". . . dust on the mantel, the mirrors, even on her own hair, she rubs the soft palm of one hand with the grimy fingers of the other, and with a sickly sweet smile whines out: 'I have no talent for housework.'" *(Looks up, to Mary, about the book)* These were all Thomas's?

(Mary nods.)

HANNAH: We were surprised too.

KARIN: Research for something.

MARY: I don't know what. That whole pile there. I thought they belonged in the kitchen.

HANNAH: She found them in a plastic box in his office . . .

JOYCE *(Looking at the pile of books)*: All of them about cooking? Why would my brother—?

KARIN: Did he start cooking? Thomas never cooked when we were married.

MARY: No. He couldn't cook anything.

(Mary cuts onions.)

JOYCE: That's what I— *('thought')*

MARY *(Over this)*: Maybe pasta. Maybe. That's what he always *said* he could cook. If I hadn't made anything, if I was busy— *(In Thomas's voice)* 'I can cook pasta.'

HANNAH: Did he mean it?

MARY: I don't know. I don't know.

KARIN: You should have—

MARY: Tested him? I know. I know.

JOYCE: That would have been fun.

MARY: It would have been.

(Mary wipes her eyes. Hannah looks at her.)

The onions, Hannah.

HANNAH *(To Joyce)*: He's written notes, quotes from things in the backs of some of them.

JOYCE: Thomas?

HANNAH: In the margins. Thumb through. *(Reaching for a book)* One—something about: how it is the one thing everyone lies about . . . I think it's this one.

KARIN: What is?

MARY: What you eat—when you're alone . . .

HANNAH *(With the book)*: Yes. Here . . . That's what he wrote . . . *(Reads)* "Everyone lies about what they eat when they're alone." *(As she shows Karin)* Do you lie about that? What you eat when you're alone?

(No response.)

I lie about that.

(Joyce continues to read to herself.)

And here . . . Mary thinks he just jotted down things he'd find . . . Something he'd heard or read and just remembered: here: "human beings are the only animals that transform their food. That *cook*."

MARY: He underlines: 'cook.'

HANNAH *(Reads)*: "So it is one of the things that makes us human beings . . ."

KARIN *(As she cuts)*: Some birds—don't they regurgitate what they eat—for their babies?

MARY: That's not cooking.

KARIN: I guess not.

JOYCE *(Looking at the book)*: You haven't tried *my* cooking.

HANNAH: The first time George wanted to cook for me . . . He forgot to wash the lettuce. So you could—hear—the crunch of the dirt, as you ate. Like little bits of gravel. I didn't say anything.

JOYCE: You think he even noticed? I know my brother.

HANNAH: The next night *I* offered to wash the lettuce.

KARIN: That was a nice way to handle that . . . Very generous . . .

HANNAH: I thought so.

KARIN *(Cutting)*: I don't think I'm that generous . . .

JOYCE: Listen to this: "When *I* took possession—"

HANNAH: Thomas?

JOYCE: No, 'Marion Harland.' "When *I* took possession of *my* first real home, the prettily furnished cottage to which I came as a bride, so full of hope and courage; after one day's investigation I knew my lately hired servants—" *(Looks up)* She had servants . . . ". . . knew no more about cookery than I did, or perhaps affected stupidity to determine my capabilities."

HANNAH: Sounds like a nightmare . . . *(To Karin)* That's why I don't have servants.

JOYCE: "And I was too proud to let them suspect the truth, I shut myself up with *my* 'Complete Housewives.'" I guess that's some book. *(Looks at the cover)* It's not this book. *(Reads)* "I do not like to remember that time!"

HANNAH: Poor thing.

JOYCE *(Over this, reads)*: "My wrestling begat nothing but pitiable confusion, hopeless distress, and a three-days' sick headache, during which season I am not sure that I did not darkly contemplate suicide . . ." *(Looks up, then continues)* ". . . as the only sure escape from the meshes that strangle me."

MARY: I didn't read that far . . . God.

KARIN: This is Marion?—

JOYCE: The author. *(Showing her)* It's the introduction: "Familiar talk with my reader."

MARY: I mostly just looked at the recipes. And his notes . . .

(As they chop, peel:)

JOYCE *(Reads)*: "At the height or depth of my despondency, a friend, one with a great heart and steady brain, came to my rescue."

KARIN: How—?

HANNAH: Sh-sh.

JOYCE: "Her cheerful laugh over my dilemma rings down to me now, through all these years. 'Bless your innocent little heart!' she cried, 'ninety-nine out of a hundred cookbooks are written by people who never kept house, and the hundredth by a good cook who doesn't know how to express herself.' Rule Number One: Compile a recipe book for yourself. And take your time. Learn one thing at a time, and when you have mastered it, make a note on it, never losing sight of this principle—you only learn, by doing."
(Looks up) Why wasn't *she* my mother?

MARY: There's nothing wrong with your mother.

(Joyce looks at the book, then looks up.)

JOYCE: When I was like thirteen or something . . . *(To Hannah)* Did I ever tell you this?

HANNAH: Joyce, I don't know what you're going to—

JOYCE: It's Christmas morning—and I unwrap—the fucking *Joy of Cooking*. 'That's all you need, dear heart,' Mom says to me, smiling her smile. 'All you need in life.' Thanks,

Mom. Thank you very much. A really big help. I'm ready for life now! Bring it on!

KARIN: Wasn't she just trying to—?

JOYCE: I know. I know.

HANNAH *(To Karin)*: Let her—

JOYCE: 'Let her' what?

KARIN: I like the *Joy of Cooking*.

HANNAH *(To Mary)*: I know what she means.

JOYCE *(To Hannah)*: As if it were the gift of life. And the way she—'hands' it over, Hannah. *(Gestures)* Like passing some torch. Or an heirloom. My dowry.

MARY: Was it *her* copy?

JOYCE: No. No. Brand-fucking-new. Like she was giving me the goddamn *Joy of Sex*.

(The piano music off has stopped by now. They listen for a moment.)

He stopped . . .

HANNAH: Actually my mom gave me—

KARIN: She didn't. No.

HANNAH *(Over the end of this)*: *The Joy of Sex*. She sort of did. Left her and Dad's copy lying around.

JOYCE: On purpose?

HANNAH *(Shrugs)*: That's what I think now.

JOYCE: At least she didn't 'hand' it to you. *(Turns back to Mary)* Like she was giving me something incredibly 'valuable.' A 'mother-daughter event.' I don't think I even opened it up.

MARY: That must have hurt her.

JOYCE *(Shrugs)*: I was thirteen . . . She should have known better.

KARIN: I agree. *(Remembering her thirteenth year) Thirteen* . . . I hated that age. My skin was like . . .

JOYCE: Another time—I was I think almost seventeen. Trying like hell to get out of here.

KARIN *(As she chops)*: *Seventeen* wasn't much better . . .

JOYCE *(Over this)*: I come into here, this very kitchen—

MARY *(To Karin)*: I thought you and Thomas got married when you were like—*nineteen* . . .

KARIN: Those are two completely different universes: seventeen and nineteen. They were for me. Completely and totally different—planets.

(They let that sink in, then:)

JOYCE *(Starts again)*: I come into this very kitchen, and there's Mom, right there *(Points)* where you are, Karin, she holds a bowl *(Mimes stirring)*. Mixing something. She looks like a witch mixing a potion.

MARY: I like your mom. I like her a lot.

JOYCE: I like her too, for Christ sake. I'm telling a story. Let me tell my story.

HANNAH: And so what happened?

JOYCE: She looks up at me from her 'stirring,' gets that 'look.' We all know that look.

KARIN *(To Hannah)*: What's the look?—

JOYCE *(Same time)*: "What's wrong, Mom?" I say. I *think* I sounded concerned. I tried. I remember trying. *(Mother's voice)* "I'm making my birthday cake, dear heart." It was the 'dear heart.'

MARY: That's cute.

JOYCE: She's not your mother.

KARIN *(To Hannah)*: Her *own* cake. You can't win that . . .

JOYCE: It was her birthday. 'Come on, Mom,' I say in my most 'perky' way, 'I really don't think *you* should be making your own birthday cake, on your own birthday.'

HANNAH: You actually said that? *(Incredulous)* You know you walked right into it.

KARIN *(What could she do)*: She's seventeen.

JOYCE: 'Then who's going to make it?' Mom asks. And suddenly she's not crying anymore but all 'bubbly' and smiley and 'perky' too.

MARY *(Critical)*: Joyce—

JOYCE: I'm being fair. I'm not being unfair. So I start to see where this is all headed. "Why can't we just buy a cake, Mom? I'll go to that bakery in Kingston you like so much. Okay?" She stops being bubbly and smiley and perky. I stand right about where you were Hannah. By your chair. My brothers both sit here. Maybe *they* will make it?

(No response.)

MARY *(Matter of fact)*: So you make your mother a cake. Good for you.

KARIN: I have two brothers. I'm with you.

JOYCE: I make her the goddamn birthday cake. And as I get going I start convincing myself that this is really a special what—honor? My chance to shine maybe? To show up my brothers? So I really work on that damn cake. Right at this table. Here. I work really really *really* hard on it. And when I 'present' my cake? When she sees my great effort, when I am finally done? And push the sweaty hair out of my eyes? Wipe the sweat off my goddamn zitty face? Mom says, "dear heart, you worked so hard."

(This sinks in, then:)

KARIN: Oh boy . . .

MARY: I know what she *meant*.

JOYCE: It's not how *she* would have made it.

KARIN: 'Dear heart' *is* cute. It's old-fashioned.

MARY *(Over this)*: That's not what she said, Joyce. She didn't say that.

KARIN *(Over this)*: That's what she heard.

JOYCE: Thank you, Karin.

(Pause as they chop and cut.)

HANNAH *(Hinting, to Joyce)*: The cake *you* asked Mary to buy for today was store-bought . . .

JOYCE: From Deising's? You got it at Deising's? . . .

MARY: It's from Deising's.

JOYCE: Thomas always loved their cakes. Least I thought of that . . . At least I did something right today . . . Should I keep reading?

(The others: "Yes. Yes.")

(Reads) "And these notes were the first of practical wisdom and receipts I now offer for your inspection."

(Joyce holds up the book.)

She calls recipes 'receipts.' "Never forget that you are mistress of yourself. Have faith in your own abilities. I take it for granted that you, dear reader, are too intelligent to share in the vulgar prejudice against labor-saving machines." *She'd* have a microwave . . .

(Then:)

I have a microwave . . .

KARIN: I couldn't live without my—

JOYCE: Mom knows they don't kill you, right?

MARY: Your mother liked what she had . . .

JOYCE: You don't have to keep explaining my mother to me. *(Reads)* "Many excellent—"

(She starts to read, stops.)

When I told Mom I'd actually bought a microwave for *my* tiny Brooklyn apartment kitchen? It was like I'd robbed someone or kicked a dog . . . Or denied global warming. 'Mom, I didn't do anything wrong.' 'It's wrong.' Not in this century. Or the last one . . .

(Continues to read:)

"... Many excellent housewives have a fashion of saying loftily, 'I carry all my receipts'"—recipes—"'in my head. I never wrote out one in my life.' And so, you, if timid and self-distrustful, are smitten with shame—"

HANNAH: I have an aunt who says that. She says it's all in her head. My mom's little sister. My mom told me not to believe anything she said.

JOYCE *(Continues over this, reads)*: "My advice is—just keep your recipe book out of sight." Like a battle. She's preparing us, suiting us up, for some battle . . . So we're not what? Intimidated?

HANNAH: Times have changed. Thank god. Haven't they?

MARY *(As she chops)*: Thomas has—had—these friends—

KARIN: Who—?

MARY: He met them with me, later; so you probably wouldn't know them. You go to their apartment—first it's always incredibly neat.

HANNAH *(Obvious)*: Then they have a cleaner.

KARIN: I'm sure you're right.

MARY *(Over this)*: The kitchen—a kind of stove that just—*(Makes the point)* intimidates.

HANNAH: I hate those. I really hate those.

MARY: She cooks while she talks. She can do that. While she sips wine and cooks, she tells funny and often self-deprecating stories. How does she do that? Doesn't she have to fucking *measure*? She cleans pots *while* she's cooking *and* telling the stories *and* drinking the goddamn wonderful wine, and almost every time she's in her goddamn bare feet. I hated going there for dinner.

HANNAH: It's the bare feet that takes it over the edge.

JOYCE *(Continues to read)*: "Here I lay down a few safe and imperative rules for your kitchen—" *(Dramatic pause, the others look up)* "—never stand when you can do your work as well while sitting."

(They are all sitting.)

HANNAH: We do *that*. We're good at that.

MARY: We are. *(Makes a check mark)* Check.

JOYCE: "It will sometimes happen that when you have heated your pitch—"

KARIN: What does that mean?

JOYCE: —"swabbed your deck, or made your pudding, the result is—failure. No part of your culinary education is more useful; you have learned how not to do it right, which is the next thing to success." I guess I'm closer to success than I thought. "However, should any such mishaps occur, do not vex or amuse your husband and your guests with the narration . . ." In other words, don't tell them . . .

HANNAH: I'm interested in this.

JOYCE *(Reads)*: ". . . with the narration, still less with visible proof of the calamity." So hide it. "Many a partial failure would pass unobserved but for the clouded brow and earnest apologies of the hostess."

HANNAH: This is about a lot more than cooking.

JOYCE: "Do not apologize!" Exclamation mark. *(Shows them, and reads)* "You will be astonished to find, if you keep your wits about you, how often even your husband will remain in blissful ignorance that nothing has gone wrong, *if* you do not tell him."

HANNAH: "Do not tell him . . ." Have any of you ever done that? Ever happen to you?

(Heads down, they chop.)

I've done that. I'll bet we've all done that. And now we know there's nothing wrong in doing that . . . Let me see that book.

(Joyce hands Hannah the book. Hannah wipes her hands.)

JOYCE: It has someone's recipes—

HANNAH: 'Receipts.'

JOYCE: She's pinned them in—with little pins. Like keepsakes.

KARIN: That's sweet.

HANNAH *(Reads the title page)*: "*Common Sense in the Household. A Manual of Practical Housewifery.*" 1884.

(Shows the title page.)

This sat in someone's kitchen for years and years.

MARY: Maybe generations.

KARIN: The family cookbook.

MARY: Like the family Bible. Maybe more revealing. *(Explains)* What goes on in the kitchen . . .

HANNAH: This is Thomas's handwriting . . . *(Reads)* "The discovery of a new dish does more for mankind than the discovery of a new star."

(Mary will get bowls from the cupboard to collect all the vegetables.)

This is written by someone else, Mary. Maybe the person who gave the woman the book . . . It's old-fashioned handwriting. "Improve each shining hour."

MARY: So he was going to write a story about cooking . . . Or a play . . .

HANNAH *(Reads)*: "Never try experiments"—more advice—"when you have invited guests for dinner. Never risk the success of your meal on a new dish. So introduce your experiments cautiously to your husband, as by-play."

JOYCE: "By-play . . ."? It says that? "By-play"?

HANNAH: "And never be too *shy* of innovations . . . Variety can be not only pleasant, but healthy. The pampered palate will soon grow weary of the same bill of fare." This *is* about a lot more than cooking . . . *(Sees George)*

(George enters.)

GEORGE: Is there any wine, Mary? I'd love a glass of wine . . .
MARY: There's a half a bottle. On the door. Smell it first . . .

(He goes to the refrigerator; she will bring him a glass.)

GEORGE: Mom's asleep. She fell asleep in her chair. *(Before Joyce can say anything)* I couldn't get her to go upstairs, Joyce. I tried. *(Smells the wine)* It's fine. *(Takes the glass)* Thanks. Anyone else?

("No," "Maybe later." No one wants wine now.)

She—insisted on looking through a couple of photo albums. There's the one just of Thomas . . .
MARY: I keep that album out . . .
HANNAH *(To Mary)*: Long day for her . . .
GEORGE *(To Hannah)*: She was crying . . .
HANNAH: I thought your mom did great this morning. *(To Mary)* When you asked if she wanted to help you 'scoop' out any of the ashes . . . I thought—she was going to lose it then . . .
GEORGE: It's good Mom's asleep . . . She needs that.

(The lights fade.)

Patricia Gabriel

The same, a short time later.

Mary is at the sink; Karin, Hannah, Joyce still at the table, chopping, cutting, peeling. George sits, drinking his wine.

In the middle of conversation:

HANNAH: These two big guys knock on your mom's door—she's alone.

MARY *(Over the end of this)*: I was out at the store. If I'd been here . . .

HANNAH: It's not your fault.

(Timer goes off.)

She thinks it's her fault.

MARY: I should have been here.

HANNAH: Come on . . . And these guys tell your mother— *(To George)* Right? *(To Joyce)* They're putting down new asphalt on another driveway down the street, and so—

GEORGE: How her driveway looks 'dangerous.' And a lot of other bullshit.

HANNAH: If someone fell, and so forth. 'Lawsuits.'

JOYCE: They say that: 'lawsuits'?

GEORGE: To scare you.

HANNAH: 'Oh and by the way—'

GEORGE *(Over the end of this)*: 'And by the way—' she's so '*lucky*' because they are right now just down South Street, so that will save Mom a whole lot of money. Normally they wouldn't even be doing this in December. But it's been bizarrely warm . . .

KARIN *(To Mary)*: Your timer . . .

HANNAH: They took advantage of an old woman.

JOYCE: Shit. She wrote a check—?

GEORGE: Mom wrote the check. They 'needed it right away.' They probably ran to the bank to cash it.

HANNAH: By the time Mary is back from the store . . .

MARY: I'd been gone maybe forty, forty-five minutes, Joyce.

GEORGE *(Over this)*: They're already pouring the asphalt.

MARY: George thinks it won't last . . .

GEORGE: It won't. You don't do this kind of job in winter. Even if it's warm for a few days . . . It's just going to crumble.

HANNAH: Seven thousand four hundred dollars.

JOYCE: Shit. Oh shit . . .

(Short pause. Mary lowers the oven temperature, and resets the timer.)

Does she have that kind of money to just . . . ?

GEORGE: The check didn't bounce. We were hoping it would bounce . . .

(Mary takes out a frying pan; she will go and get oil from the pantry cupboard.)

JOYCE: I didn't know anything about this . . .

GEORGE: You haven't been here, Joyce.

JOYCE: I have a phone. A whole brand-new driveway for seven thousand dollars? I didn't even notice a difference.

GEORGE: Ever since Thomas died, Mom has seemed scared. Something happened . . .

HANNAH: Even before . . .

GEORGE: I suppose you always think you're not going to live longer than your kids . . .

(Mary turns on the stove; she will pour oil into the frying pan, and soon collect the vegetables into bowls.)

KARIN *(To Mary)*: You need any help there? . . .

MARY: Maybe in a minute.

(The others will help collect the vegetables into bowls. No one knows what to say.)

GEORGE: We should thank Mary.

MARY: Why?

HANNAH: Why?

GEORGE: For this morning. It was really nice this morning. I didn't think that it would be so nice, *(To Hannah)* did I?

HANNAH: No . . .

GEORGE: I was telling Hannah in the car, I now think I want *my* ashes thrown into the Hudson too. *(A joke, to everyone)* No rush. Please! *(Laughs)* Though maybe next time we can pick a season, Joyce, when we don't have to chop away at the goddamn ice . . .

HANNAH: There was no ice, George.

GEORGE: It was cold. Mom got cold.

MARY: We had thought we were waiting for spring . . .

GEORGE *('Serious' and teasing)*: But Joyce is 'very busy' . . . Unlike us 'country folk' who have nothing to do . . .

JOYCE *(Over this)*: It's a business trip.

GEORGE: 'To Europe.' 'Oh twist my arm.'

MARY: Could you watch this for a minute, Karin?

(Karin goes to stir the vegetables.)

Who wants to help peel apples? We can use the same knives . . . I also have peelers . . .

HANNAH: You've decided to make your apple crisp?

(Mary heads off to the mudroom.)

(Calls) I'll get peelers. *(To George)* She's going to make her apple crisp . . . *(To Joyce)* That was Thomas's favorite.

JOYCE: I know.

HANNAH *(Getting peelers, bowls, etc.)*: We can also have the cake. We can have both . . .

GEORGE *(Back to 'Mom')*: Joyce, last month, Mom . . .

HANNAH: Oh god this is embarrassing.

JOYCE: What? Mom what?

GEORGE *(To Hannah)*: You want to tell her? *(To Joyce)* Last month, Hannah drops by here. Just as Mary and Mom are hurrying out to the bank. To send how much—six hundred dollars, right? To our Paulie . . .

JOYCE: Why? Why did Paulie—? Where was he—?

GEORGE: We thought he was on his senior class trip to Washington. You tell her. You were here.

HANNAH *(Wipes her hands, then)*: 'There you are,' your mother says the moment I walk in. 'We've been trying to call you. We're on our way to the bank and then to the post office. Paulie, he's not on his senior class trip, he's in some trouble in Canada.'

JOYCE: Canada? What are you talking about? *(To George)* What?

(Mary returns with a small bushel of apples, and hears:)

HANNAH: Somehow they knew our son—her grandson—was on a—trip.

MARY: Oh god . . . You're telling her that.

HANNAH *(Over this)*: How did they know?

JOYCE: Who?

MARY: When did I become so stupid?

GEORGE *(Over this)*: I still think it was just a lucky guess.

JOYCE: Who?

HANNAH: Your mother got a phone call: 'Your grandson's crossed the border, and bought an expensive computer and now he doesn't have the money to pay the duty.' *(Explains)* So the customs people at the border are going to confiscate the new computer Paulie's bought, unless we send right away—six hundred dollars. Mary's saying—as I walk in, Mary is saying, 'We're sending him the money.'

MARY: What the heck was I thinking?

HANNAH *(Over this)*: You were worried about our son.

JOYCE: Paulie had called Mom??

HANNAH *(Looks at George)*: Sort of.

JOYCE: I don't understand.

HANNAH: And then I think to ask Mary if she had talked to Paulie *herself*. No. No, but your mother has. Patricia says, 'And Paulie sounds so upset.' So the three of us, we hurry to the bank and take out the money, then to the post office so we can wire a money order. By this time I've called

George at the shop, so George tries to call Paulie on *his* cell phone. He leaves a message. Tell her . . .

GEORGE: And then I call the number—

HANNAH: . . . in Canada where we're supposed to call after we've sent the money. To tell him it's on its way.

GEORGE: A woman answers.

(Then:)

I ask for Paulie. And tell her I'm his father. And then Paulie comes on the line. The connection isn't so great, a lot of static, but I hear him say, 'Hi Dad. Hi. I'm okay. I have a cold. Are you sending the money? Please send the money. I need money.' When . . .

(Looks at Hannah.)

JOYCE: What?

GEORGE: When—*my* cell phone rings. And I pick *that* up, I'm still on the other line, on the land line with Paulie—but on my cell, calling me back—is Paulie. He's in Washington, with his classmates. On his senior class trip.

JOYCE *(Confused)*: I don't understand??

GEORGE: The other—in Canada—was someone else.

HANNAH: Someone who happened to sound like Paulie . . .

GEORGE: With a cold. And a lot of static . . . I ask that person, 'who the hell are you?!' He hangs up.

HANNAH: George calls me and we're still in line at the post office. Thank god there was a line. *(Into 'the phone')* 'Don't send the money. It's a scam.'

GEORGE: It's a 'popular' scam, we learned from the State Police. They couldn't do anything. Mom had her picture in the paper—as a volunteer at the library? We figure they saw that. They look for old people. Old people to them are 'just fish in a fucking barrel.' The cop's words . . .

HANNAH: When you're scared, you're just vulnerable . . .

(Mary brings the apples to the table.)

MARY: She is. We are . . . I can do that now, Karin. Thank you.

(Karin returns to the table.)

JOYCE: How's Paulie doing?
GEORGE: He's applied to fourteen colleges. So we're—waiting.
HANNAH: It's like Chinese water torture, isn't it?
GEORGE *(Nods)*: Every day you watch your son ask himself, 'So what am I worth?' Parents shouldn't have to witness that . . .
JOYCE *(About the apples)*: From Adams? These must be from Adams. They look great for this time of year . . .
MARY: The farmers market . . .
GEORGE *(To Hannah)*: We always forget to go there . . .
JOYCE: The farmers market?
MARY: It's in the winter now too. In the town hall . . .

(They take knives, peelers, and sit and peel apples. Mary has gone back to the stove.)

HANNAH: You know that guy on the *News Hour* who does the business?
MARY: Paul-something . . . what? I forget—
KARIN: I watch him.
HANNAH *(Over this)*: The other day he's interviewing some hedge fund guy who's a little defensive, 'Come on, are we really bad guys?' And then the guy tried to explain, 'Look at those hyenas and the vultures out there on the savanna . . . Come on. Are they *bad* guys? Just because there happens to be a sudden boom in carcasses, is that really their fault?' They're just taking advantage of 'opportunities' . . . ? "They're just hungry . . ."

(Then:)

GEORGE: All of a sudden Mom gets on all these lists. Now that she's in her new place, Mary gets all these phone calls . . . We had no idea. 'I'm calling about your credit card accounts . . .' No they're not. 'It's the IRS.' No you're not.

MARY: 'Congratulations, you've won something or other.' No, you haven't. 'We've got very important information about your Medicare coverage.' No they don't.

GEORGE: They want to pick over her fucking bones . . . She won't show us her checkbook. We don't know what she's been doing . . .

HANNAH: Mary throws away most of the 'solicitations' that come in the mail . . .

MARY: She still gets her mail here. I take her a few things, so she doesn't get too suspicious.

JOYCE: You hear about families and their parents—they fight like hell with their kids about moving into . . . One of these places.

KARIN: My father was like that . . .

HANNAH: She's made it so easy for all of us. Bless her. Bless her . . .

GEORGE: She has friends there . . . People she's known forever . . .

KARIN: Good for your mom. You're lucky.

(As they peel:)

HANNAH: It's a nice place.

GEORGE: Very nice.

HANNAH: I know your mother really wants to show you her apartment, Joyce.

GEORGE: You should go.

JOYCE: Of course I'm going to go. You don't have to tell me to go. I'll go after dinner. I'm looking forward to seeing it. Mom's 'new life.'

GEORGE: Good.

JOYCE: You don't have to make me. I know I should go.

HANNAH: It's just a room. So be prepared. It's a nice room. It's not a house . . .

GEORGE: She took things with her. Her desk. Some rugs. The love-seat from her bedroom. Not much more would fit. She's tried to make it a home. It's just up East Market . . .

JOYCE: I admit to being very surprised, when you called and told me . . . I thought you must have somehow made her . . .

(Then:)

She seemed to have an 'accident' at the diner? At lunch? Or am I wrong?

(Hannah looks to George, then:)

MARY: It happens.

HANNAH: We try not to make anything of it. It embarrasses her. It happens . . .

JOYCE: Maybe she should wear—

MARY: She doesn't like the way she looks in them, Joyce. She says they make her look fat.

JOYCE: Maybe we should insist. For her own—

GEORGE: She *sometimes* wears them. She didn't today, Joyce, because she wanted to look her best.

(Mary will cover the simmering vegetables and join the others at the table.)

JOYCE: Is that Mom's car still out in the drive? I thought we were selling that. When I was here in November, I thought you said you were going to sell that.

(Hannah looks to George.)

GEORGE: Not yet . . .

JOYCE: That's just wasting money. You're still paying insurance, the sticker . . . What? Mom's not still driving, is she? We talked about this . . .

GEORGE: She's not *really* driving, Joyce.

HANNAH: She keeps it at the home. She drove here this morning. We'll drive her back tonight. In the dark . . . She doesn't drive in the dark. She can't see. We'll take two cars . . .

JOYCE: George—

GEORGE: Joyce, you're right, *we* agreed. Mom just didn't agree . . .

JOYCE: What?

GEORGE: She said—no. We thought the place wouldn't allow it. Didn't we? We thought that would settle it. *(Shrugs)* But hey, they do. It's 'independent living.' They said, 'That's not our job.'

JOYCE: She can barely turn her head. She can't see out the back window.

GEORGE: She can turn her head. *(To Hannah)* Can't she?

(No response.
Mary goes to check on the vegetables.)

JOYCE: She's going to kill someone. She's going to run over some kid. You told me you were going to do this . . . You promised.

HANNAH: Mary tell her, your mother hardly drives anywhere.

MARY *(Lists)*: To the Stop&Shop. The library. To here . . .

JOYCE: There are trucks on Route 9. And school buses . . .

(Then:
The lights fade.)

Brigadoon

The same, a short time later.

Mary stirs the vegetables. Joyce, Hannah, Karin and George sit at the table, and slowly, methodically peel apples.

JOYCE: Mary, do you have any red wine?
MARY: In the mudroom.

(Joyce gets up.)

I keep the red out there.
JOYCE: Any particular—?
MARY: They're all basically the same, Joyce. Cheap.

(Joyce is off to the mudroom.)

GEORGE *(To say something)*: Karin, you didn't have to teach today?

(George is about to eat an apple slice.)

HANNAH: They're for the apple crisp, George . . .
KARIN *(Answering)*: Not on Fridays. No 'theater class' on Fridays. I don't know why.

(Mary will taste the vegetables, add salt and pepper.)

HANNAH *(Beginning to slice)*: Mary? Quarters, then halves again?
MARY: Sure.
HANNAH *(To George)*: Quarters, and then halves again . . . Do it how she says.
GEORGE *(Continues to Karin)*: So—long weekends. Not bad.

(Joyce returns with a bottle of red wine.)

Do you go back to the city?

KARIN: I sublet my apartment.

JOYCE: I'm subletting mine for the three months I'm away. You have to. *(Getting herself a glass out of the dish rack)* Anyone else?

(No one wants wine.)

KARIN *(Peeling)*: I don't know how I had the nerve to say I could teach 'playwriting.' I can just hear Thomas, 'You're teaching playwriting? . . .'

JOYCE: They're kids. Make it up . . .

MARY *(About the glass)*: That clean?

JOYCE: It was in the dish rack.

KARIN *(Continues as she peels)*: I had no idea what to expect.

GEORGE: I hope you expected rich kids. Hotchkiss.

HANNAH *(Explaining to Joyce)*: Some teacher got ill all of a sudden. *(To Mary)* Right? Isn't that what happened? That's what Mary said happened.

KARIN *(Over the end of this)*: Needed a body right away. I am that body. I was free . . . *(Which means)* I didn't have a job. Probably the tenth actor they tried . . .

MARY: Karin's been teaching at a school in New York . . .

HANNAH: I didn't know that.

JOYCE: So it's not completely—

KARIN: Teaching *acting*. And it's not really a school. I really don't know what I'm doing.

MARY *(Stirring, adding the tomatoes)*: Thomas used to tell *his* students, when he taught . . .

KARIN: When did Thomas teach? I didn't know he ever—

HANNAH: Oh he hated it. How he hated it.

MARY: The school, not the kids . . .

KARIN: He always told me he'd never teach . . .

MARY: He lasted maybe two years . . .

HANNAH *(Finishing her apples, to Mary)*: What about a salad, Mary? Shouldn't we have a salad?

MARY: Look in the fridge. Check the lettuce. It's been there a while . . . *(About Thomas, to Karin)* Let me get this right. I heard him tell this to a bunch of students when they came to our house in New Haven. *(Trying to get it right)* There are two questions a playwright needs to answer. Two. *(Works to get it right)* 'Why did you write it?' And then, 'Why should we watch it?' *(Pleased with herself)* That was it . . . So what does that mean?

JOYCE: Make it personal. And make it matter. I think I understand that.

(George has picked up the booklet Cookies for Eleanor *and begins to thumb through it.)*

MARY *(As Hannah looks at the lettuce)*: How's the lettuce?

HANNAH: I can pull off the brown leaves . . .

MARY: I don't think that's even washed.

HANNAH *(Over this)*: I'll wash it. And I'll pull off the bad leaves . . .

MARY *(Continuing)*: Oh, and Karin, he had a little sign he'd made for himself. I just remembered this.

(Timer goes off.)

I keep remembering things. All day . . . Over his desk. In his office. "Don't write words, Thomas. Just try and write people."

JOYCE *(To Karin)*: So tell them that . . . Whatever that means . . .

KARIN *(About the sign)*: Actors love hearing that kind of stuff. Thomas loved actors.

MARY: He married one . . . *(Smiles at Karin)*

HANNAH: Mary, your bread.

(Hannah begins to wash the lettuce in the sink. Mary will open the oven.)

GEORGE *(Musing on the booklet title)*: "*Cookies for Eleanor . . .*"

JOYCE: I liked going there today. To Eleanor's house. Let me see.

GEORGE *(About the bread)*: That smells good. I'm getting hungry.

HANNAH *(About George)*: It's a reflex.

JOYCE *(To George)*: Are you done?

GEORGE: I was taking a break . . .

(Mary takes the bread out of the oven.)

JOYCE *(About the booklet)*: Just what Eleanor liked to eat . . . Good for her.

HANNAH *(At the sink)*: Eleanor Roosevelt, I think, was the first woman I ever admired.

MARY: I didn't know that.

HANNAH *(Washing the lettuce)*: I was in, maybe, first grade and we had to draw a picture of someone we admired? Everyone drew their father or grandfather, maybe mother. I drew Eleanor Roosevelt. Of course I put her in a wedding dress . . .

(Laughs. She gets the salad spinner from under the sink as:)

MARY: Of course . . .

JOYCE: Women come from all over.

GEORGE: You mean to Val-Kill?

KARIN: I know women, in the theater, who have come up just to Hyde Park just to see Eleanor's house.

JOYCE: I'm not surprised . . .

KARIN: There's the little wooden bridge—

HANNAH: We saw that today.

KARIN: —did the guard tell you anything about this bridge?

JOYCE: No. She didn't, did she? What?

KARIN: I've been two, three times.

MARY *(Over this)*: What bridge?

KARIN: It's just before you get to the house—and it was made of wood—on purpose.

JOYCE: What do you mean?

KARIN: So any automobile crossing it? It would make a lot of noise. Thump-thump-thump . . . A friend of mine told me this, a guard there had told her—thump thump thump—so all the women who lived there with Eleanor—the ones who made furniture?—would be warned that someone was coming, and so could stop doing whatever they were doing . . .

(Hannah spins the spinner, stopping the conversation. As salad spinner is stopping:)

HANNAH *(To Karin, continuing)*: It seemed to be a very different group who go to Val-Kill, than to—

JOYCE: I'm sure that's true.

KARIN: You noticed that today?

JOYCE *(Nods)*: Than to Franklin's . . . We heard one woman tell her woman friend— *(To Hannah)* Didn't we?

HANNAH: What are you talking about? Just one more time. Sorry.

(She spins one more time, then as it winds down:)

JOYCE: This woman was musing that Val-Kill might be the only real 'monument'?

HANNAH: Oh that.

(Hannah will dry the lettuce with paper towels.)

GEORGE *(Looks up from the booklet)*: What??

JOYCE: —if that's the word—

MARY: It's not a 'monument.'

JOYCE: 'Official' something—whatever you want to call it—to a *woman* in all of the United States.

MARY: Betsy Ross?

GEORGE: That's what I was going to say.

MARY *(Over this)*: In Philadelphia, doesn't she have—?

JOYCE *(Over the end of this)*: That's for the flag, Mary. Not for the woman.

KARIN: Maybe it's not true. Still it feels like it's true.

MARY: Some years ago, when we first moved here . . . Thomas and I went together.

KARIN: To the Roosevelt home?

MARY *(Nods)*: He asked the guard if he could take his wheelchair up in the little elevator—the one FDR would pull himself up in . . .

KARIN: Did they let him?

MARY *(Of course not)*: No . . .

(Hannah has gone back to the refrigerator to look for more salad fixings.)

HANNAH *(To Mary)*: Anything you don't want me to use?

(Mary shakes her head.)

JOYCE: You going to keep the ramps? Outside? I was surprised the ramps were still up. *(To Karin)* George built them.

GEORGE: I'm ready to take them down. I agree, they're in the way . . .

JOYCE *(To Karin)*: My brother's a carpenter.

KARIN: I know.

(Hannah takes a red pepper from the refrigerator.)

MARY *(To Hannah)*: That's been washed.

HANNAH: Why don't you let George take those ramps away, Mary. He can do it this weekend . . .

MARY: What if your mom breaks a leg or something . . .

JOYCE: She doesn't live here now.

MARY: When she visits . . . Anyway, there's no rush, is there?

GEORGE *(Standing up)*: Just tell me when . . . I thought I'd check on Mom. Mary just reminded me that she's still here. I almost forgot.

JOYCE: George, you're just going to wake her up. She'll call us if she needs us . . . Why cause problems?

(He will sit back down.)

HANNAH *(As she takes the vegetables to the table to cut, to Mary)*: Those ramps are ugly . . . Let George get them out of your way. That's not how Thomas would want us to remember him, Mary . . .

JOYCE *(To George, to sort of change the subject)*: So how's your work going? How's business? I haven't asked.

MARY *(Happy that the conversation has moved away from her)*: He's been working on a big order. A whole dining room set. Table. *(To Hannah)* Sideboard?

HANNAH: Some old tree had fallen on the client's property.

KARIN: What do you mean?

GEORGE: An ash . . . A hundred-year-old ash, at least. Beautiful wood. And so they wanted everything made out of *their* tree. I've been drying all of it. My whole shop is full of ash . . .

HANNAH: The client told George how much they loved that tree . . .

JOYCE *(To Karin)*: George makes beautiful furniture.

KARIN: I remember.

MARY: You should peek into his shop sometime.

KARIN: I'd love to.

HANNAH *(Over this)*: He's *already* made some of the furniture . . .

GEORGE *(Knows where she is going with this)*: I have . . .

JOYCE: What?

HANNAH: He finally just met the client with the 'ash' last week. Until then they'd done everything over the phone. The client closes his house in the winter. But he happens to be up here for something and meets George at his shop. And George has now worked out what he'll charge—

JOYCE: You didn't already have a deal?

GEORGE: I talked to him . . .

HANNAH *(Ignoring this)*: And right away, the client's 'negotiating.' The price George has given, you see, is exactly what George wants. No more, no less. He's worked all that out. What he thinks is fair. *(To George)* What you can 'live with.' What 'makes sense.' But the client just cuts twenty percent off. Just like that. *(Snaps her fingers)* I tell George, but that's what he's *used* to doing. Today everybody *assumes* everybody is negotiating . . . about every thing. Isn't that true?

JOYCE: I suppose so . . . Yeah.

KARIN: That's true. Even this job at this school—

GEORGE: I told him I'd take five percent off.

HANNAH: He'd already been working for months; and the guy of course sees this. He's in the shop. So the guy tells George—okay, then if you're not going to 'negotiate,' then fuck you, truck the wood back to my house. He'll get someone else to make his fucking furniture.

(Then:)

George had already begun . . . He'd dried the wood. Cut the wood. Designed two tables, the desk . . . He's already built a little coffee table. George had 'proudly' showed that to the client when he arrived . . .

(Then:)

JOYCE: I bet it'll work out. That asshole just enjoys negotiating. He's having fun with you. They just do that instinctively now . . .

HANNAH: The guy's lawyer has called. 'We want the wood.'

(They work, then:)

JOYCE: Have any of you been up to Hudson recently?

HANNAH: Oh god. What is happening to us? Where do we belong?

KARIN: I haven't been to Hudson.

JOYCE: My boss has a weekend place in Hudson. She is always talking about the parties up there. *(To George)* When *we* were growing up that place was—*poor*.

HANNAH: No one can live there anymore. No one. *(Another case in point)* Saugerties? Who'd have believed that? George has started calling us—the people who grew up here—he calls us the people of Brigadoon. *(Smiles at George)*

JOYCE: Sounds about right.

HANNAH: You watch the Channel 4 news and weather, and there on the weather map—most nights? *Rhinebeck*. Little bitty Rhinebeck on the New York City news. I guess so the weekenders know what the hell to pack . . .

MARY *(Over the end of this)*: I'm sure that's why.

KARIN *(Over this)*: I've seen that.

HANNAH *(To Joyce)*: Oh and this you'll enjoy. *(Standing, to Mary)* Did I see a cucumber?

MARY: In the back. *(Of the refrigerator)*

GEORGE *(Same time)*: Enjoy what?

HANNAH *(To George)*: Next door. *(Points)*

(She goes to the refrigerator.)

MARY: That was a long time ago. When I read that, I wasn't that offended—

GEORGE: You didn't grow up here, Mary.

JOYCE: What are you talking about?

(Hannah will clean the cucumber in the sink, and as they talk, dry it, return to the table, peel it, slice it, and add it to the salad.)

HANNAH *(To Joyce)*: One of the little free papers that are around now—

GEORGE: We had a decent local paper once upon a time.

HANNAH *(Over this)*: They just reprinted last week—I think they found it amusing? An article from back in the '70s; printed excerpts . . . It had been in the *Times Magazine*. *(To Mary)* You still have your copy?

MARY: If I do—on that pile to recycle. In the dining room.

HANNAH *(To Joyce)*: Your mom actually remembers the person who wrote it. She lived next door for about a year?

JOYCE: Who? When?

GEORGE *(Over this)*: You're too young.

HANNAH: She was from Manhattan—and she had rented that house *(To Karin)* that is just next door. Up the hill. She saw herself as some sort of writer—and she wrote about her 'year in Rhinebeck.' As a transplanted New Yorker? I have to show you . . .

(Wiping her hands, she goes off to the dining room.)

GEORGE: I think I sort of remember her.

JOYCE: What did she write?

MARY *(Over this)*: A whole lot of crap.

GEORGE *(Same time)*: Condescending shit. How cute we are. How cute this village is. Its cute people. How—unreal. *(Making his point)* Like Brigadoon . . . She's from 'gritty,' 'real' Manhattan . . . And she comes here, and it's quiet, and still, and soooo scary . . .

JOYCE: Why scary?

KARIN *(Same time)*: Rhinebeck?

GEORGE: It's too clean. Too pretty.

(Hannah returns with the newspaper.)

HANNAH *(Reading)*: ". . . like we're living on the cover of a twenty-five-cent Christmas card. The smooth whiteness of it all!" *(To Mary)* It was on top.

GEORGE *(Making a point)*: "Whiteness."
KARIN: Was she African-American?—
HANNAH: No. *(Obviously)* She was a *New Yorker* . . .
GEORGE: And then she thinks— Oh she's figured us out . . . Read that part . . .

(Mary covers the ratatouille and goes and stands over them at the table—every now and then she will check on the ratatouille.)

KARIN *(To Mary)*: Anything I can—?

(Mary shakes her head.)

GEORGE: Read it to Karin.
HANNAH: She doesn't care—
KARIN: I'm interested . . . I am.
GEORGE *(Reads over Hannah's shoulder)*: Here . . . "I'll tell you where they are, the blotches and blemishes. They're stashed away in their 'homes.'" Read . . .
HANNAH *(Handing him the paper)*: Here . . . You want to read it?
JOYCE: What the hell is she talking about?
GEORGE: She puts 'homes' in quotes. I guess they're not *real.* *(Reads)* "Things are *taken care of* in small towns. Out of the 'goodness' of people's hearts—" 'Goodness' also in quotes. So that's fake too? Our goodness? *(Continues)* "—moves are made so that little that's ambiguous remains to taunt the intellect . . ." She's talking about Rhinebeck . . .
KARIN: Why would they republish something from—?
HANNAH: It still strikes a nerve . . . ? Or once again?
GEORGE *(Reads)*: "It's a workingman's town . . ." Or was.
HANNAH: Still is on most weekdays, at least in the winter . . .
GEORGE *(Over this)*: "—good, solid, working-class prosperity. Dinner at five, church on Sunday and bed before nine-thirty. At school the kids sing songs from *Mary Poppins* in voices sweet as pipes, and while discipline's assumed and the walls are graffiti-free, the children are taught in the old-

fashioned way, as if nothing had happened in the field of education in the last twenty years. Yet twenty-five percent who enter Rhinebeck High don't finish. Instead they marry young . . ." *(Skips, then)* "In seven months I haven't seen one cripple, albino, Puerto Rican, nothing to mar the bland homogeneity of it all. There are no visible poor."

(Closes the newspaper.)

HANNAH: Show Karin . . .
KARIN: Let me see . . .

(He hands her the newspaper.)

HANNAH *(Over this)*: Karin, IBM had just closed in Kingston, in Poughkeepsie. Three huge plants. This town was dirt poor. And this lady got to live in that big house on that hill for next to nothing.
MARY: For two hundred a month! She wrote that.
GEORGE: The dripping condescension. Can they even hear themselves?
HANNAH: Are we just going to bitch in front of Karin?
KARIN: It's fine. Really. Go ahead and bitch . . . I bitch all the time.
GEORGE *(To Karin, over the end of this)*: We work their land, or mow it; we keep up their properties, we fix their houses to make life comfortable for them on the weekends or their summer vacations . . . We build their furniture . . .

(George goes to the refrigerator to pour himself another drink. Mary begins to fill the pasta pot with water from the sink.)

JOYCE: An actor friend was telling me—
MARY *(To Joyce)*: I can't hear. Just a second . . .

(As the water fills the pot, George asks if anyone wants wine. They don't, not yet. Then, when she can hear:)

(To Joyce) What were you saying?

JOYCE: An actor friend, he was telling me—Karin, I think he might teach at the Atlantic Theater School too—

HANNAH *(To George)*: Karin teaches there.

JOYCE *(Over this)*: 'Henry' . . . what? What's his last name? I forget.

KARIN: I think I know who you mean. Henry . . . ?

JOYCE: Whatever my good friend's name is, he said—a lot of his friends instead of having the ambition to say, open up a restaurant, with all that overhead, and loans, and banks and stuff. He said, these days, they're going out and getting themselves a food truck. Like that's the height of their ambition now. A food truck.

KARIN: That sort of thing is getting more and more popular.

HANNAH: With kids?

GEORGE: Like peddlers.

KARIN *(Over this)*: No, not just kids.

JOYCE *(Over the end of this)*: Maybe that's what Rhinebeck needs now. Maybe George, you and Hannah should just start up a food truck. Drive it around to the rich people's houses. Ring a bell. Make 'em a nice latte.

GEORGE: We're laughing now . . .

HANNAH: Who's laughing?

JOYCE *(Teasing)*: I could design you little cute costumes . . . Both of you.

MARY *(To George)*: We went to an art show at Bard last fall? Thomas and me . . . *(To Hannah)* I think maybe it was one of the last times he went anywhere . . .

GEORGE: What was the art show?

MARY: Very contemporary. *(To Hannah)* Didn't I tell you about this?

HANNAH: I don't know.

MARY: Stuff on the floor; videos; things that didn't make a lot sense . . . To me. *(Smiles)* We were being "hip." We're in one room when an elderly African-American man comes in. He's wearing sunglasses, and he has a white cane.

KARIN: So, blind.

(Mary puts the pasta pot on the stove, and turns on the burner.)

MARY: Yeah. And leading him along, guiding him, I guess, are these two very attractive young white women, eighteen, nineteen years old. In very short skirts. It was an odd sight. Thomas right away was curious. The three went from art piece to art piece; and the girls would take turns describing to the blind man what they saw. The colors. Shapes, and so forth. You couldn't help but hear what they told him; they spoke in a little louder than normal voice. So everyone there heard them.

(Mary goes to the cupboard to get the box of pasta.)

And you couldn't help but notice that sometimes, or most of the time, the women would not really be describing the art piece.

KARIN: What?

MARY: If, say, something were yellow, they'd say it was red. And they'd also add things that weren't even there.

GEORGE: *They* were part of the show. They were a piece of art.

MARY: Yes. That's right. George is right. That's just what we realized. Who sees and who doesn't. Who deceives and who is deceived. Who's dependent on whom for what? Thomas loved it. His favorite thing in the show . . . *(Explaining why)* He said whenever he met someone—from Wall Street, with a lot of money—it was always like—

HANNAH: Who would Thomas meet?

MARY *(Lists)*: Board members of theaters—that were doing his plays; or just someone—like George's client. Rich people;

really rich people. Up here some days you trip over them. He said it's like talking to someone who speaks a whole other language. But uses the same words . . . I remember, he said, say one of these people tells you: 'the sky is green.' But you look at the sky and it's blue. What you see with your own eyes is that it's blue . . . So you say, 'What are you talking about, it's blue.' And when you finally get their attention—that's not always so easy, he said—it comes out that they've just changed the meaning of 'sky.' And they think it's their right to do that . . . See, Thomas said, that's what you're going to be up against . . .

(Then:)

GEORGE: So *they're* the young sexy girls in the miniskirts, and *we're* the old blind guy being led along, and having everything explained to us? . . . Sounds about right. I think Thomas got that right . . .

(Then:)

And I can hear him saying that too . . .

(Then:)

HANNAH: Mary told me she didn't want to go to the Roosevelt Museum today, Joyce, because that had been one of Thomas's favorite places.

JOYCE: Uh-huh . . .

GEORGE: But isn't that why we went? *(To Hannah)* I thought that's why we went. Am I wrong?

HANNAH *(Continues)*: Because . . . *(To Mary)* Okay? You mind? Can I tell them?

(Then:)

She's angry at Thomas right now. Right? Really angry. As we were walking back up the hill at the Mills Mansion, back to our cars, Mary told me this. How angry she is at him . . .

GEORGE: Because he's not here?

HANNAH: I think so.

MARY: It's not rational.

HANNAH: And what is?

JOYCE: I can understand that. I suppose I'm angry at Thomas too.

KARIN: I understand too.

MARY: Left behind . . . What it feels like. You'd think being a doctor, I'd be a little more rational . . .

(Then:)

Could we talk about something else? I'd really like to talk about something else. And George, I think, I'd like a glass of wine now too.

HANNAH *(As she looks at her watch)*: I'll join Mary. But I want a nice glass, George. A stem glass. A *real* wine glass . . .

GEORGE: I'm just using—

HANNAH *(Obviously)*: I know what you use . . .

MARY: Me too. A nice glass.

HANNAH: Mary too.

MARY *(Over this)*: I want a damn nice wine glass too.

HANNAH *(Explaining to Karin)*: The good glasses are in the dining room . . .

GEORGE: Karin? Wine?

KARIN: No thanks, I'm driving. And I'm sure the last thing you need is to have to put me up for the night.

(George heads off into the dining room.)

MARY: We have room. *(To Hannah)* Don't we?

HANNAH: There's plenty of room.

(Mary opens the pasta box.)

JOYCE: I always make too much pasta . . .
MARY: My mother taught me how to measure. She had a trick. And it works.
JOYCE: What trick?
HANNAH: We'll need a salad dressing, Mary . . .

(Hannah heads to the refrigerator for salad dressing fixings.)

JOYCE: Can't we just have some Paul Newman—?
MARY: Hannah makes a very nice salad dressing. *(Answering Joyce)* My mother had this trick. Say pasta for two people . . . You imagine you have your hand *(Demonstrates)* wrapped around a man's erect penis. Like this. And that's how much pasta. For two. *(Explaining to Hannah)* How much pasta . . .
HANNAH: She's showed me this. It works. I do it all the time now.

(George returns with the fancy glasses.)

GEORGE: Do what all the time?
MARY *(Ignoring him)*: So if it's five or six—then you do it three times.
JOYCE *(Interested)*: Your mother told you that?
HANNAH: It works.
GEORGE: What?
HANNAH: Nothing, George.

(He will pour and hand out the wine as:)

MARY *(More to the story)*: Once I was measuring it out just as my mother'd taught me, you know— And she was there in the kitchen—and she looks over my shoulder and says—very disparagingly, I thought: 'Who have *you* been going out with?'

(The women laugh.)

GEORGE: I don't understand.
JOYCE: Mothers . . .
GEORGE: What???
HANNAH: Girl talk, George. Never mind.

(The lights fade.)

By Bread Alone

The same, a short time later.
As Hannah prepares her salad dressing; the middle of conversation:

GEORGE: We went with Mom to Bread Alone this week . . .
MARY *(To Hannah)*: Oh, you told me this.
GEORGE: And Peter . . . *(To Hannah)* what's-his-name? He's there. Come on, what's his name? You went to school with him. *(To Joyce)* So did you.
JOYCE: Peter—?
KARIN: What's Bread Alone?
JOYCE *(Over the end of this)*: A little coffee shop on East Market . . .
HANNAH *(To Joyce)*: It hasn't changed yet.
GEORGE: He paints houses now. What's-his-name? Why the fuck can't I remember names anymore? Anyway, he starts telling us—anyone who's in earshot—his 'history of our time.' That's what he calls it.
JOYCE: What does that mean?

(Mary is smiling.)

HANNAH *(Agreeing with Mary)*: It is funny . . .

GEORGE: Everything, he says, every *thing* can be traced back to just—one act.

MARY *(To Karin)*: Anyone talking in any kind of non-whisper and everyone hears it in Bread Alone.

JOYCE: What act?

HANNAH *(Over this)*: That's why everyone goes there, Karin. You really have to watch what you say there.

JOYCE: What act?

MARY *(Over this)*: Especially in the front. The tables are close together in the front. *(To Hannah)* Were you in the front?

HANNAH: We were in the front.

GEORGE *(Continues over some of this)*: Peter what's-his-name is telling everyone how so much of what we now are, what we have now become, and what's now happening to us—can be traced back to one act, during one pizza night, in a small kitchen area, right next to the Oval Office.

JOYCE *(Getting it, to Karin)*: Bill and Monica. We know this. Why do we want to hear this? *(To Mary)* You need any help, Mary?

HANNAH: It's funny, Joyce.

GEORGE: We're all listening now. All of recent American 'history,' he says, is traceable—

JOYCE: Are we still 'fascinated' by this??

GEORGE *(Over this)*: —to that one act of—and he lowered his voice so it's even deeper—one act of 'fellatio.'

JOYCE: And Mom is there with you? Jesus.

GEORGE: Peter what's-his-name says it like it's a musical note: 'Fellatio.'

HANNAH: George . . .

GEORGE: "Let us now see just what directly resulted from that late night of pizza, and—and so forth, so many many years ago."

HANNAH: Peter what's-his-name starts listing every terrible thing from the past twenty years.

GEORGE: He lets the 'fellatio' settle, and then begins the list: Impeachment. No argument there. *(Next)* Ending that law that kept the banks from becoming casinos . . . What was that called?

HANNAH *(Over the end of this)*: Glass something.

JOYCE: Steagall.

OTHERS: Glass-Steagall.

(Others: "We remembered that. We can still remember things!" "If we work together.")

KARIN *(Over this)*: What does that have to do with—

HANNAH: That's what we all ask.

GEORGE *(Over this)*: He explains, Bill and Hillary, were so worried about going broke—personally—after all, didn't she say they were 'dead broke,' that's what they thought the Republicans were really after.

JOYCE: And they were. They were. Of course they were.

GEORGE *(Over this)*: To completely bankrupt them. So that's why, according to Peter, Bill felt he sure as hell was going to need some rich friends—so he turns to Wall Street. And at almost the very last second of his very last days in office, with a stroke of his pen—

HANNAH *(Explaining)*: The banks can become casinos. *(To Joyce)* It's one explanation.

GEORGE *(The list)*: Next: That really rich guy. Mark . . . ?

HANNAH: Rich.

GEORGE: 'Rich.' Now I should have remembered that. Mark Rich. Bill helps out this billionaire friend—

KARIN: Didn't Hillary know his wife?

GEORGE *(Over this)*: So maybe later, if Bill needed help . . . Next *(Continues list)* Gore lost. When Gore should have won easily. And look what we got. Iraq. *(Continues the list)* The great recession—or as Peter calls it, 'the casino goes bust,' directly related, we know now, Peter says—to those very same changes Bill made for his new Wall Street buddies. So Peter what's-his-name begins to add it all up: the loss of something like hundreds of thousands of lives; three or four trillion dollars of treasure; millions of homes underwater; foreclosures; bankruptcies, so forth and so on—all directly traced back to one night of pizza and—and you know what? . . .

JOYCE: Did Mom even understand what he was trying to say?

HANNAH: You mean does she know what the word 'fellatio' means?

JOYCE: I guess that's what I'm asking.

HANNAH: I don't know.

JOYCE: Never mind, I don't want to know.

GEORGE: Mom just kept eating her salad, Joyce. I don't know if she understood or not. But Mrs. Howard—my fifth grade teacher. She must be ninety now. She was a mean teacher. At least to me. She was there too. *(Incredulous, to Joyce)* She's still alive.

HANNAH *(To Mary)*: I forgot to tell you this.

GEORGE: Anyway, once Peter has finished . . . "that one night of pizza and—fellatio . . ." For like a minute, Bread Alone is completely silent. You just hear someone behind the counter, grinding coffee. And then, that's when, Mrs. Howard takes a sip of her tea, wipes her lips, and says out loud, to the whole silent room, *(In her voice)* "Well, I just hope those two got some pleasure out of it."

(Laughter.)

MARY *(Laughing)*: That's not really funny. Mrs. Howard is . . . She's not well, George.

GEORGE: I know. I know.

JOYCE: I didn't know. *(To Hannah)* Mrs. Howard knew what it meant.

(As Mary gets up to put the pasta in and as she shows the women how she has measured out the pasta:)

MARY: Karin, Peter what's-his-name puts his own hand-painted lawn signs all over his front yard about three months before every election. Not for candidates, just for 'ideas.' He's really pissed off. I suppose it makes him feel better.

JOYCE: It must not have been a weekend at Bread Alone. *(Getting up)* What can I do, Mary?

KARIN *(To Hannah)*: Why? I don't— *('understand')*

HANNAH *(Explaining)*: We wouldn't talk like that when the weekenders are around, Karin. *(To Joyce)* It was Monday.

(Mary has set the timer.)

MARY *(To Joyce)*: Stir the pasta? *(To the others)* Thomas said to me once—I just remembered this. I keep remembering things . . .

JOYCE: You said.

HANNAH *(Over this)*: What did Thomas say?

MARY: Thomas told me that years ago, that before the Civil War, slaves were known to do 'shows,' sort of 'plays,' behind their cabins. Just for the other slaves. Making 'fun' of the masters . . . Made them feel not alone, he said . . . Made them feel better . . . I just thought of that. This *('us')* —reminded me of that.

(Then:)

KARIN: Yesterday, I was talking to a sweet young math teacher. Twenty-three, twenty-four. She's new too. This semester. No one talks to her either. She said she goes home each night and watches both MSNBC and FOX News. Just switches back and forth.

GEORGE: Oh god don't do that. Tell her not to do that.

KARIN: We're asking each other: who is supporting him? Who are they? Does any of this make sense?

JOYCE: What are you—?

HANNAH: The election.

KARIN: We're just sitting in the teachers' lounge. And we both find ourselves saying the same thing—we are so damn confused right now. *(Referring to Mary)* I want to feel better.

HANNAH: Our son keeps saying, 'Feel the Bern, Mom.'

GEORGE: I want to be young again . . .

HANNAH: Paulie says he can still win.

JOYCE: He won Colorado.

GEORGE *(Repeats)*: I want to be young again . . .

KARIN: This other teacher was saying—what if our side were to fall apart for some reason. Think about that. It's possible. Maybe very possible. Think what we would be left with. It's hard to fathom.

JOYCE: I can't go there. I'm not going there. *(To Hannah)* I just realized what you're saying—Paulie can now vote! My god, I am so fucking old.

KARIN: If our side—falls apart. It could. She could.

JOYCE: No. No.

HANNAH: I know women . . . Women of a certain age . . . They really dislike Hillary. I have at least two friends who say they'd never ever vote for her.

MARY: I want to vote for Larry David.

(Laughter and "Me too," "I would too.")

JOYCE: Why didn't Warren run?

KARIN: Last week I went on a date to this art show. *(To Hannah)* This relates to . . .

HANNAH: Hillary?

KARIN *(Over this)*: I thought it was a date. Then it wasn't a 'date.' I'm always making that mistake . . . It can be so goddamn confusing . . .

HANNAH *(To Joyce)*: Is it for you too?

JOYCE: Can be. Sometimes.

KARIN: We went to a folk art show in some little gallery. He knew the owner. Oh. And this isn't what I was going to tell you. I just remembered: there was a big wooden carved sign, from I think the early 1800s, hanging from the ceiling, a sign for some old inn; of—the Angel Gabriel.

JOYCE: That's neat.

KARIN: With his horn. We're all Gabriels. I kept the name, it certainly is a better stage name than 'Smith.' *(Smiles)*

JOYCE: Is that why you kept it?

KARIN: Sort of. What I wanted to say was—a needlepoint caught my eye—of a 'Lady Liberty.' Over two hundred years old. Made just after the Revolution. And what was so surprising is that in this needlepoint, Lady Liberty wasn't pictured as some 'ideal woman'—you know, on a cloud, holding a flag, with young and firm pointy breasts—

JOYCE: Right.

KARIN: —shapely legs. As she usually is.

JOYCE: As *men* paint her, George.

GEORGE: I'm not a Neanderthal.

KARIN *(Over this)*: As some 'idealized goddess.' No, this Lady Liberty, she was—kind of normal.

JOYCE: What do you mean?

KARIN: Real. Looked sort of like us. Even had a little weight on her.

JOYCE: Really . . .

KARIN: Her dress wasn't 'sexy.' Just practical. And she even—get this—was of a certain age . . .

HANNAH *(Fact, to Joyce)*: A woman made that Lady Liberty.

JOYCE: Obviously.

KARIN: I thought how interesting. Just after the Revolution, all that had just happened, and *liberty*, for this artist—was what? Not some abstract ideal. Instead, perhaps just a self-portrait. Or maybe a sister or friend modeled for it.

(Then:)

I really would like to see a woman president in my lifetime. And see what that feels like. See if it would make any difference whatsoever. Someone who looked like us.

(Then:)

JOYCE: But is *she* that woman?

KARIN: I understand . . . Fair question.

JOYCE: Maybe it's no longer right to ask that. Maybe we have to stop asking that.

HANNAH: Sometimes I look at Hillary and I see just—a fraud.

KARIN: I know. I know.

JOYCE: Me too.

HANNAH: When I'm catering: I hear some of the people, the 'guests' 'talk.' About doing good things, their causes. And I think they really mean it. They want to do good. And—then you hear them talk about, well . . .

JOYCE: What?

HANNAH: You just get the feeling, listening to them talk to each other, that they really believe they deserve all they've got. Somehow *earned* it. So they want to do good, *and* they deserve to be rich. Is she like them?

JOYCE: Chelsea's in a ten-million-dollar apartment.

KARIN: I think it's a house. *(Shrugs)* Why does she laugh so much?

JOYCE: Hillary?

KARIN *(Over this)*: It doesn't sound real, when she laughs.

MARY: Maybe *that* isn't put on. Maybe that's her. *We* laugh . . .

JOYCE: I know someone with a laugh like that. It can be real.

HANNAH *(To George)*: And there's Fucking Zephyr Teachout.

KARIN: What—??

GEORGE *(To Karin)*: She's running here for Congress.

KARIN: I didn't know that.

HANNAH *(Over this)*: I voted for 'Zephyr Teachout'—against Cuomo. I really liked her. She seemed—real. *(To Karin)* Now, Karin, she's 'rented' a house in our district and running to be our congresswoman. She's 'lived' here for like six months. On weekends. I thought she was a good woman.

GEORGE: She still could be.

HANNAH: One more weekender, Joyce. They not only want our land, and get us working for them, but now they think we should make them our voice. Can't we speak for ourselves anymore? Aren't we allowed even that anymore?

KARIN: Still, Hillary is a woman.

JOYCE: Is that enough? To be a symbol?

KARIN: Obama?

GEORGE: He's been more than a symbol. Hasn't he?

MARY: After last night, I'd vote for Megyn Kelly.

HANNAH: If she wasn't a Republican.

MARY *(Over the end of this)*: If she wasn't a Republican . . .

JOYCE: You watched that? How could you watch that?

MARY *(Over the end of this)*: It was Hannah's fault.

GEORGE *(Over the end of this)*: I went to bed.

JOYCE: It sort of feels to me like we're all about to jump off some crazy high cliff. Doesn't it?

KARIN: Yeah. It does.

HANNAH: Jump or be pushed, Joyce?

GEORGE *(Shouting)*: 'What about us?' 'What about us?'

JOYCE: It feels like a movie. We're just all watching this movie.

GEORGE: Are we in it?

JOYCE: Do you want to be?

HANNAH: A dream.

JOYCE: Nightmare.

HANNAH *(Over this)*: Where there are recognizable 'pieces' of things; but put together in ways so they seem—very strange. Don't you feel something really bad is going to happen?

JOYCE: To us?

(Then:)

HANNAH: God, it's going to be a very long eight months.

MARY *(Smiling)*: "Oh, but don't give up!"

JOYCE: What?

HANNAH *(Same time)*: Why are you smiling?

MARY *(Smiles)*: "Please, don't give up." That's what Thomas would say to me. I remember after one especially bad day, when I felt hopeless . . . By now he was pretty hard to understand, but this time, this day, he speaks really clearly. He sits right here. In his chair.

GEORGE *(In the chair, to Karin)*: This was Thomas's chair.

MARY: He says to me, "Don't give up. Don't give up. Things do happen. They do, Mary."

(Then:)

So do we believe him or not?

(The lights fade.)

"Wildewoman"

The same, a short time later. Lucius's "Wildewoman" plays softly on the iPod dock.

Mary in the middle of a story:

MARY: It was hard to watch. And of course frustrating. Sometimes—and I do mostly think of myself as a pretty good person—but believe me sometimes I had thoughts. Not pretty thoughts. Maybe I even said things to Thomas out of my frustration. I won't tell you what they were. But I'm sorry that I did. Then one day, he's making his way from his chair to the desk. From here to there. Right in here. When Thomas has gone about two feet, in like five minutes, I just can't watch anymore. So I put on some music. Something my daughter had sent me.

JOYCE *(To George and Hannah)*: You know about this?

(They do.)

MARY: I'd had music on before but nothing had ever 'happened.' *(Smiles)* No 'miracle.' But this time—Thomas all of a sudden begins to walk across the kitchen—like normal. In normal time. He picks up something on the desk and begins to walk back. I stop the music. And . . .

(She demonstrates: he moved very slowly.)

I then put on another CD, and another and another. Some work and some don't. We have no idea why. No one knows why. I don't know why. There are these theories about Parkinson's . . . Anyway I kept adding to the list of 'Thomas's music.'

(Timer goes off.)

And so that's all what's on that iPod now—just the music we found that Thomas somehow for some reason—could walk to . . . Why?

(No one knows what to say. Mary goes to pick up the pasta pot.)

HANNAH *(To Mary)*: Bowls or plates, Mary? *(To George)* George . . .

(George will help Mary with the pasta pot and take it to the sink.)

MARY: Plates . . .
HANNAH: Karin, you want to help me?

(The song finishes . . .)

KARIN *(To Hannah)*: Where . . . ?

HANNAH *(To Karin)*: I'll show you. The cabinet, next to the high boy in the dining room. *(Calls back)* The white set, right? *(To Karin)* That's what they've been using . . .

(Hannah and Karin head to the dining room. Joyce opens the drawer in the table to take out the silverware.)

MARY: There are some lovely napkins . . . We haven't used them for a while. Not since your mother moved . . . I was thinking we'd use them tonight. It is a special night . . . They're in the cabinet out here. I happened to see them. *(Goes to the mudroom)*

JOYCE *(To George)*: You think Mom is going to eat with us? How many are we going to be?

(George oils the pasta at the sink.)

GEORGE: We'd better wake her up. She'd be really upset, if we didn't try and wake her up . . . When does she get to see you?

JOYCE *(Taking out the silverware)*: So we'll be six, you think? Do we still have that much silverware that matches?

GEORGE: Does it matter?

JOYCE: We used to . . .

(She counts the silverware.)

MARY *(Returning with the napkins)*: These are nice. They're old. Your mother found them in the basement . . . when we were packing her things . . .

JOYCE: I don't even remember those.

MARY: She thinks they're from Austria. From relatives.

(George, cleaning up, has picked up a couple of Thomas's old cookbooks from the table:)

GEORGE: Look, he used postcards for bookmarks.

MARY: What's that one of?

GEORGE *(Shows)*: A woman hanging laundry . . .

JOYCE: Let me see.

(He shows her.)

MARY: Thomas liked pictures of people doing very simple things. I remember: a woman with a broom. Another: someone writing a letter. Hammershoi. You know him? Women with their backs to us. Chardin? Those two were his favorites. Why?

HANNAH *(Returning with Karin)*: Mary, the blue table cloth? That's special, isn't it? . . .

MARY: That's good.

HANNAH: I took it out.

JOYCE: Mary was just saying today is special . . .

KARIN: Then we'll put the blue one on? Want me to do that? I can do that . . . *(Starts to go)* What can I take?—

HANNAH: The salad dressing . . .

KARIN: Mary, I was looking out the dining room window at your backyard, just now.

MARY: In the dark?

KARIN: You can't see much now, you're right. But I remember coming up and visiting here. So many years ago. And seeing that stream . . .

HANNAH: Landsman Kill.

KARIN: And Crystal Lake. Thomas always used to say to me after one of our visits back here—how lucky he was to grow up in Rhinebeck.

(Karin heads off with the salad dressing.)

MARY: She's been fine. Hasn't she? No problem at all, Hannah. She seems a little lonely.

HANNAH: She's thinking of staying the night . . .

JOYCE: I don't think so. No.

MARY: She's got to get back she said.

HANNAH: She just told me she's thinking about it. She's very 'tempted' she said . . . *(To Mary)* She thinks you invited her.

MARY: Did I do that? Did I?

GEORGE: I will go and wake up Mom . . . Unless, Joyce, you'd rather . . .

(He smiles and heads off.)

JOYCE: Fuck you.

GEORGE: Maybe she's not even hungry . . .

(He is gone.)

MARY: By the way, Hannah, I know that you, or maybe George, got my daughter to call me today. 'Reminded' her to call me. What did you do, phone her, text her? Thank you. I appreciate that . . . Don't tell George I know. *(To herself)* I'll put the apple crisp in while we eat.

(She will set the oven, and begin the final preparations of the apple crisp.

As Hannah and Joyce collect things to take to the dining room:)

JOYCE: I would really like to sit down with Mom sometime and ask her things.

HANNAH: What things?

JOYCE: When I get back. Maybe when I'm back from London, I'll spend more time up here with Mom.

HANNAH: I think she'd like that. Don't you, Mary?

MARY: I know she would . . .

JOYCE: Today, at the museum . . . And please don't hate me for saying this . . . Don't tell George this either. She kept touching me. I know she so wanted me to touch her back. But I found that really hard to do. I don't like touching her. I know that's awful.

(Then:)

HANNAH *(To Joyce)*: What would you want to ask her?

JOYCE *(Shrugs)*: So many things. Some of them are just stupid. Once Mom lost her wedding ring? She found it, because she told us she'd dreamed of seeing it by the side of our stream. Next to the weeping willow. And so in the morning, still in her nightgown, she put on boots and went out into the rain, and there it was—just as she had dreamed it. Did she make that up? *(Another one)* She always knows moments before any of us calls, who is calling.

HANNAH: That's what she says . . .

JOYCE: I feel like I'm fourteen years old when I'm in this house . . . *(Sees George and Patricia arriving)* You're awake. She's awake . . .

(George appears with his mother, Patricia, eighty-one years old. She has just been woken up, and so a little confused. Everyone speaks louder when they talk to Patricia.)

GEORGE *(Helping her in)*: Mom was just telling me a story about Thomas as a little kid. I'd never heard this, Mom.

PATRICIA: I just remembered it. I don't know why . . . ?

JOYCE: Because of today, Mom. What we did this morning. Thomas's ashes . . .

PATRICIA: Maybe.

HANNAH: What story, Patricia?

PATRICIA: You're cooking? You should have let me help.

HANNAH: It's all ready, Patricia.

PATRICIA: What plates are you using?—

HANNAH *(Over the end of this, 'of course')*: The *white* ones.

JOYCE: What story, Mom?

GEORGE *(To Patricia)*: You want to sit down? She just woke up.

PATRICIA: I thought we were eating dinner?

JOYCE: We are, Mom.

PATRICIA *(Insisting)*: In the dining room.

JOYCE: Yes . . . Where else?

(Karin has just returned, Patricia is looking at her.)

HANNAH: It's Karin. Thomas's first wife. She came for today. We invited her. Our guest.

GEORGE: She's been here all day.

HANNAH *(To George)*: And she might stay the night . . .

KARIN: You told me about voting for Roosevelt, Patricia.

PATRICIA *(Defending herself)*: I just woke up. *(To Mary)* What can I do?

MARY: I think everything's under control. I think dinner is ready.

PATRICIA *(Back to Karin; to Mary)*: And you two get along?

MARY: I was the third wife, Patricia. There was one in between us. We both hate her . . .

PATRICIA: What can I take in?

JOYCE: What story, Mom? *(To George)* What story?

PATRICIA *(Ignoring Joyce)*: Give me something.

HANNAH: What can she take?

JOYCE *(Over this)*: I think we're fine, Mom.

GEORGE *(Answering Joyce's question)*: Thomas is about two years old and in diapers. And Mom is by herself for some reason—and taking him on an airplane somewhere. You don't remember where, right? This was in the fifties—so a propeller plane.

PATRICIA *(Seeing the silverware in Joyce's hands)*: Where's the good silverware?

JOYCE: What's the good silverware, Mom? This is the only silverware I remember ever using.

MARY: Patricia, that is our good silverware.

PATRICIA: Is it?

GEORGE *(Continues)*: And they're in the air, and Mom smells that Thomas has pooped in his diaper. So she starts to pick him up off his seat, to walk him to the bathroom, to change him, but he pulls his hand away, gets into the aisle, and somehow rips off his shit-filled diaper and starts running down the aisle swinging it.

KARIN *(Laughing)*: Oh my god! . . .

GEORGE: Thomas's shit flying everywhere!

(They laugh.)

PATRICIA: I wanted to kill him. And for one moment, I opened up my magazine and pretended he wasn't mine.

(She and they laugh.)

But that didn't last long. You soon realize you don't have a choice. We don't have another set of silverware?

GEORGE: I think we got rid of that years ago, Mom.

PATRICIA: I thought because of today . . .

GEORGE: I know. But it's gone. It's gone.

MARY: Everyone—take something. I'm just finishing up Thomas's apple crisp.

PATRICIA: What can I do? I want to do something . . .

KARIN *(To anyone)*: Maybe I *could* stay the night. Let me think . . .

HANNAH: Here, Patricia, you can carry in the salad. Let me just clean this off . . .

(As they pick up things, pitcher of water, the salad dressing, etc.:)

GEORGE *(To Joyce)*: What time's your train tomorrow?

JOYCE: Early.

KARIN: I've got the wine and the water pitcher . . . *(Heads off)* I don't think I had any lunch. I forgot to have lunch.

GEORGE: And I haven't even asked—what's the show you're designing in London?

JOYCE: I'm not the designer, I'm the associate . . . My boss is 'busy.' *Die Fledermaus.*

PATRICIA: She's just the assistant, George.

JOYCE: Thanks, Mom.

(George has the large frying pan of ratatouille.)

GEORGE *(To Joyce)*: Costumes for that should be fun. You'll have fun. London's always fun, right?

(He heads off.)

HANNAH *(Handing Patricia the salad bowl)*: Here, Patricia. You can take this in. I have your arm, Patricia.
PATRICIA: I don't need help. I don't need you to hold my arm.
HANNAH: Mary, the salt and pepper.
PATRICIA: I'll get it.
HANNAH: Patricia . . .

(Patricia goes back to the table for the salt and pepper.)

PATRICIA: You know what I like to do when I travel?
HANNAH: You want help? That's a lot to carry.
JOYCE: When do you travel now, Mom?
PATRICIA *(Ignoring her)*: To foreign countries. I like to visit their grocery stores. I find that so interesting. You should do that. *(Explaining)* What do they have that we don't. What's the same? . . .
JOYCE: I'm not sure, Mom, I will have time for grocery stores.
HANNAH *(To Patricia)*: Let me help you . . .
PATRICIA: Joyce can help me. Joyce, hold on to my arm . . .
HANNAH: Mary, I've got the pasta . . .

(Joyce first goes to wash her hands in the sink.)

PATRICIA *(To Joyce)*: How long will you be gone?
JOYCE: Not that long, Mom . . . George and Hannah are here. And Mary . . .

(Hannah heads off.)

PATRICIA: Mary's going to move to Pittsburgh . . . Her daughter is there.

JOYCE: I know.

PATRICIA: She's got no one left to take care of here.

JOYCE: I know. *(Holding her as they go)* I'll bet you'll hardly know that I was even gone.

PATRICIA: I doubt that . . .

JOYCE *(Heading off)*: I got you, Mom. I got you . . . Hold on to me . . . I'll be back. I am coming back. Are you hungry, Mom?

(They are gone. Mary is alone.)

MARY *(To "Thomas")*: Your apple crisp . . .

(Music: Lucius's "Wildewoman" from the theater speakers.

Mary puts the apple crisp in the oven. She looks over the kitchen: at Thomas's chair, at the journey he made from chair to desk.

Then she picks up the bread, and goes to join the others in the dining room.)

END OF PLAY

WHAT DID YOU EXPECT?

For Maryann and Jay

PRODUCTION HISTORY

What Did You Expect? was commissioned by and first produced at The Public Theater (Oskar Eustis, Artistic Director; Patrick Willingham, Executive Director) in New York City on September 10, 2016. The director was Richard Nelson; the set design was by Susan Hilferty and Jason Ardizzone-West, the costume design was by Susan Hilferty, the lighting design was by Jennifer Tipton, the sound design was by Scott Lehrer and Will Pickens; the production stage manager was Theresa Flanagan, the stage manager was Jared Oberholtzer. The cast was:

MARY GABRIEL	Maryann Plunkett
PATRICIA GABRIEL	Roberta Maxwell
GEORGE GABRIEL	Jay O. Sanders
HANNAH GABRIEL	Lynn Hawley
JOYCE GABRIEL	Amy Warren
KARIN GABRIEL	Meg Gibson

In December 2016, the complete series of *The Gabriels* was presented at The Public Theater with rotating repertory.

CHARACTERS

THOMAS GABRIEL, a playwright and novelist, died in November 2015, at the age of sixty-four.

MARY GABRIEL, Thomas's third wife, and widow, a retired doctor, sixty-one.

PATRICIA GABRIEL, Thomas's mother, eighty-two.

GEORGE GABRIEL, Thomas's brother, a piano teacher and cabinet-maker, sixty-one.

HANNAH GABRIEL, George's wife, and Thomas's sister-in-law, works for a caterer, fifties.

JOYCE GABRIEL, Thomas's sister, an associate costume designer, fifties.

KARIN GABRIEL, Thomas's first wife, an actress and now teacher, fifties.

TIME

Friday, September 16, 2016. 6:30 P.M.

SETTING

The kitchen of the Gabriels' house, South Street, Rhinebeck, New York.

PUNCTUATION

Double quotation marks are used when someone is reading from something or directly quoting. Single quotation marks are used when someone is paraphrasing or generalizing.

You cease to suffer, you cease to hope.

—*Harley Granville Barker,*
The Secret Life

An empty room: the kitchen of the Gabriels' house. South Street, Rhinebeck, New York.

Refrigerator, stove/oven (electric), sink; large wooden and rustic table used as a kitchen counter (with a drawer for silverware) is set beside another smaller table making an L-shape; a bench with a back is to one side, facing the tables; a small desk; upstage a small cupboard. Chairs and a bench are set upside down on the tables.

Exits: upstage to the unseen dining room; down left to the mudroom, back porch and backyard; down right leads to the rest of the house—living room (where there is a piano), the stairs to the bedrooms on the second floor, and to the front porch.

In the dark, Lucius's "Don't Just Sit There" plays through the theater's main speakers.

Mary, Hannah, Joyce and Karin enter with trays full of kitchen objects. They will create the 'life of the kitchen.' George enters, with plastic boxes of Thomas's papers; he sets some notebooks from the boxes on the bench and one of the tables, and the boxes themselves on the floor or on a chair.

As Joyce and George leave, the lights come up and the music fades.

Boxes

Off, from the living room, someone plays the piano—with starts and stops—Fauré's Nocturne No. 1 (Op. 33. No.1). *This is a music lesson.*

The timer ticks on the stove.

Hannah sits, finishing cutting out cookies, using a drinking glass to cut out the round shapes of the cookie dough; she lays out the shaped dough on a cookie sheet.

Mary sits, peeling a potato over a cutting board. Karin, notebook in hand, is in the midst of describing to Hannah something she has read in this notebook:

KARIN: And the windows are lit up; so you can clearly see through.

HANNAH: It's night?

KARIN: It's night. You can't hear the people inside, of course; you can only see them. The family's inside. A child asleep against a woman—the mother. Thomas doesn't tell you that, but—It's obvious, the mother. And a man: the father. And an old man. The whole family. And they seem—at peace.

MARY *(To Hannah)*: Inside the house.

KARIN: Two men have come into the back garden. That's what the stage represents. The garden. They look back—at what we, the audience, see—through the lit-up windows: the family in their house. Someone's drumming his fingers on a table. The mother looks out—one of the men in the garden says to the other, "She's looking at us." But no, no, she can't see. She's looking out into the dark . . . I'm just summarizing.

HANNAH: Sure . . .

KARIN: "What are we going to do?" asks one of the men. "Should I try and get the father's attention? Get him to come outside and tell him that his young daughter's just drowned?" Then watching the family, he adds: *(Reads)* "I have never seen a happier household." The other says, "No, no. Don't go to the window. It's best to tell them of it as simply as we can, as if a commonplace occurrence; and let's not appear too sad, or they'll feel that their sorrow must exceed ours, and they'll not know what to do . . . Let's knock on the side door, and go in as if nothing has happened. Come with me . . ."

(Piano music continues off.)

The other man resists: *(Reads)* "Why do you want me to go too? I'm a stranger here. I was just passing by." "Because a misfortune announced by a single voice seems more definite and crushing. Alone, I'll have to say something right away; the moment I come in. Together, I can take my time, say something, how they found her . . . 'She was floating in the river; her hands clasped . . .' We can blur the pain in details." I don't know why but that moves me. "Blur the pain in details . . ."

MARY: I've done that. As a doctor . . . With . . . details . . .

KARIN *(Continues)*: And the two men continue to talk like this: what to do, what can they do, while all the time—we, the audience, watch, through the window, the family go about their lives. It's an amazing play.

(Timer soon goes off.)

Thomas has made a note to himself in the margins here: "Perhaps they make a meal? Have a dinner? Must feel normal . . . Make it normal . . ."

(Hannah will get up and take a cookie sheet of cookies out of the oven.)

MARY *(To Karin, wiping her hands)*: Where's that page where Thomas has circled everything in magic marker . . . ? *(Takes the notebook from Karin)*

(Hannah will get a pot for the potatoes.)

HANNAH *(To Mary)*: Had you read this play?

MARY *(Shaking her head, looking through the notebook)*: There were so many, Hannah . . . Here . . . One of the men says: *(Reads)* "They are awaiting the night, separated from us by only a few poor panes of glass. They think they are secure in their life, and do not dream that so many others know more of it than they . . ." And *this* is underlined: "And that I, a poor old man—" Thomas wrote in the margin, "that's me, that's me . . ." *(Looks at Hannah, continues)* ". . . a poor old man am two steps from their door, and hold all their little happiness, like a wounded bird, in the hollow of my old hands, and dare not open them . . ."

KARIN: We stayed up most of last night reading this.

(Hannah looks at Mary.)

MARY *(To Hannah, handing the notebook back to Karen)*: We did . . .

KARIN *(As she looks for the page)*: And one of the old men, who's watching the family, says to the other—that he'd seen their daughter—

MARY: The dead daughter.

KARIN: —just this morning. She'd told him she was going to see a friend on the other side of the river.

(Listing:)

How beautiful she was. Her lovely hair . . .

(Turns the page.)

Here: "The daughter was just living this morning!"

(The list:)

What she might have become. All the friends she had. While inside the house now, they're smiling. Someone's playing the piano.

(She notices the coincidence—someone is playing the piano here. And gestures.)

MARY *(To Hannah)*: Playing the piano . . .

(Hannah nods.)

KARIN: Someone inside has said something funny . . .
HANNAH: So then what happens?
MARY: Before the old men get up the courage to tell the family, some people from the town bring the body to the house; and so—the family learns. While still outside, the two men and—
KARIN: —and of course, we, the audience—
MARY: —just *see* this, through the lit window, without *hearing* anything. We just watch—everything going on inside.
KARIN: Finally one of the old men watching all this, says: *(Turns a few pages)* —and this is the last line of the play . . . *(Reads)* "Look." He says, "Look. Their baby is still asleep." The title is "Interior."
HANNAH: I didn't know Thomas even did translations . . .
MARY: He did . . .
HANNAH: He didn't know any languages, did he?
MARY: He worked with friends. *(About the potatoes, over the noise of the water, to Hannah)* These enough?
HANNAH: I don't need more than five . . .

(Hannah goes to the sink to fill a pot with water for the potatoes.)

MARY: I peeled too many then. I got carried away. We can have them tonight then with the sausages . . . Cook them together. I just kept peeling . . . *(Smiles)*

HANNAH *(Wiping her hands)*: May I see?

KARIN *(Handing her the notebook)*: From the French . . .

HANNAH: I was never any good at languages . . .

MARY: Something he got really interested in doing, right before getting sick. I think he and his friends had plans to do a lot more . . .

(She will go and throw out the peelings.)

HANNAH: Translations?

MARY *(Pointing to a page with names; to Hannah)*: Those are his friends. Those two. They're the real translators, he always said. They'd done novels. *(About the potatoes)* You wanted them cut small, right? It's potato salad . . .

HANNAH *(Handing back the notebook to Karin; to Mary)*: Whatever. Doesn't matter . . .

KARIN *(About the notebook)*: He puts a different picture on each notebook—

MARY: Cut-up postcards—

KARIN: Postcards.

HANNAH: What's that one of?

KARIN: A house. Just a house . . .

MARY *(As she cuts the potatoes)*: One day the three of them—

(As Hannah fills the pot with water from the sink:)

The three of them—Thomas and his translator friends—are sitting in the friends' kitchen, working on their first translation together. They worked in the kitchen. *(To Karin)* I told you this . . . *(To Hannah)* And they'd been at it for a couple of days, when one of his friends says. "Thomas, we've been translating for much of our lives—"

(Hannah will take the pot and set it on the stove.)

"And" the friend says, "You just keep asking us one question that we never ever ask ourselves, when translating novels."

HANNAH: What's the question?

KARIN: 'Why?'

MARY: 'Why?'

HANNAH: 'Why' what?

MARY *(About Karin)*: She asked that too. Thomas said he had to explain to his friends that with a play unlike a novel, where you're just trying to get the right words, with a play, what you are really trying to translate are the author's people.

HANNAH: I'm not sure I understand.

KARIN: The characters.

HANNAH: I understood that.

MARY: And so that's why, he said, he was always asking his friends: 'Why does he say what he says or she says, and why now, and why him and not her, and so forth.' To translate the people.

(Hannah will take a bowl of the cut potatoes and pour them into the water on the stove, and turn on the burner.)

Interesting . . . I should probably start our dinner . . .

HANNAH *(To Karin)*: Is that what you tell your Hotchkiss kids?

KARIN: God only knows what they hear . . . *(As a joke)* God only knows what I tell them. Whatever the hell comes out.

MARY: Hannah, I remembered something else last night with Karin . . .

(Mary gathers ingredients for the casserole dish.)

KARIN: What?

MARY: That actor—what he said by . . . *('mistake')*?

KARIN *(To Hannah)*: Oh this is funny.

HANNAH: What?

MARY: The first play of his that Thomas ever took me to see . . . We'd just met. I think it might even have been the first performance. Hannah, there was a scene where an uncle had to kill his nephew, what was the name, the nephew had a funny name?

KARIN: Doesn't matter.

MARY: It doesn't matter. To kill his nephew in order, he said, to save—face? *(Shrugs)* I don't remember why. To save face. Anyway, the actor playing the uncle— *(To Karin)* Thomas used to play squash with him, I just remembered that. *(Continues)* The actor, the uncle, was supposed to say; I have to get this right. Supposed to say: "Come, Nephew, sit and let me save your face."

KARIN *(To Hannah)*: That's what he's supposed to say.

HANNAH: Okay.

MARY: "Come, Nephew, sit and let me save your face." But instead of this, the actor, the uncle, said, and said it really really loud, said, "Come, Nephew, and let me sit on your face . . ."

(Laughter.)

(To Hannah) All the other actors on the stage, they turned their backs to the audience, and you just saw their shoulders going up and down . . . I didn't notice. Thomas told me later . . .

KARIN *(Closing a box)*: I've looked through everything in this one, Mary. Want me to get another?

MARY: A couple more if you can carry them . . .

(Karin gets up and starts to go off to the office with the box.)

HANNAH: How late were you two up last night?

KARIN *(As she goes)*: It was her birthday . . .

MARY: Not everyone goes to bed at ten, Hannah.

HANNAH: I don't always go to bed at—

MARY: It was my birthday.

(Karin is gone.)

(Back to the story) The theater, Hannah! . . . I don't know how the actors learn their lines. And it must get really hard as they get older . . .

HANNAH: You're all right with her . . . ?

MARY: Here? She's paying rent.

HANNAH *(Beginning a list)*: Going through all of Thomas's stuff . . .

MARY: It's not 'stuff.' And there's plenty of room. And I asked her. She wasn't looking to stay. She was going to rent the place she had last time. And she knows theater. That's a big help.

(Off, the phone is ringing.)

(Standing) She's paying rent . . .

HANNAH: Let George—

MARY: He's giving a lesson.

(Piano stops.)

HANNAH: He's getting it.

MARY *(Sitting)*: I remembered something else last night, talking with Karin. *(Phone stops ringing)* Once Thomas was so pleased . . . He'd come across a listing of titles of 'lost plays'—just the titles, the plays didn't exist anymore, by some old Irish writer from the nineteenth century. Somehow they knew the titles—

HANNAH *(Explaining)*: Probably some academic compiled—

MARY: I suppose. And he reads me one title, and says, *(Imitates Thomas)* 'Oh I could make a play from this.'

(Hannah smiles at the imitation. She has been gathering ingredients for her potato salad.)

You know how he loved obscure stuff. That no one else knew about. He was so competitive.

HANNAH: He was a Gabriel.

MARY: He even starts to write it. You want to know what that title was? "*Shakespeare in Love.*"

HANNAH: And then the movie comes out. I never heard this.

MARY *(Over this)*: And he's really pissed off. *(As Thomas)* 'That's my fucking play.' Actually, I tell him, it was this dead Irish guy's play. He says he's going to write it anyway. Who the hell is going to see this stupid movie? We go to Upstate to see it . . .

HANNAH: That's where George and I saw it.

MARY *(Over this)*: It's been playing like four weeks, and we can still hardly get in . . .

HANNAH *(Same time)*: We loved it.

MARY: We can't even sit together. *(Remembering)* You said you wanted to see my Moosewood potato salad recipe.

HANNAH: Never mind. I really do not care whether they like it or not . . .

(Hannah at the refrigerator takes out mustard.)

MARY: I doubt if that's true. You still have your pride . . . I'm going to need the mustard too . . .

HANNAH: Do I still have my pride? Are we so sure?

(She sets herself up to make potato salad.)

MARY *(Another story)*: Once we were at the Book Barn in Hillsdale.

HANNAH: You and Thomas?

MARY: And Thomas has— I didn't tell Karin this. I just remembered this this morning. *(Continues)* Thomas has a book open and he shows me an inscription written inside. 'To Helen' or someone, I forget, 'You deserve to have a whole chapter devoted just to you.'

HANNAH: Sweet . . .
MARY: Guess what the title was? *Bitch.* Some novel . . .
HANNAH: Did he buy the book? Thomas?
MARY: I don't remember. He didn't buy it for me.
HANNAH: This all the balsamic you have?
MARY: You need more?
HANNAH *(Looks at it)*: It should be fine. Onion? *(Mary hands her an onion)*

So Karin is comfortable in the office?

MARY: Upstairs. No complaints.
HANNAH: She's only been there a couple of days, Mary.
MARY: Hannah—
HANNAH: I'm not sure I'd want my husband's ex-wife—
MARY: I didn't know George had an ex-wife.
HANNAH: You know what I mean. Digging through his old things—
MARY: I don't think she's 'digging.'
HANNAH: *Dragging* up then—
MARY: I asked for her help . . . And it doesn't need to be 'dragged up.' It's already there. *(Then, again)* She knows theater. She's an actress. I'm fine.

(Mary has begun to organize a sausage casserole.)

HANNAH: It was probably Joyce on the phone.
MARY: Probably. *(Another memory)* Once Thomas and I were visiting Patricia. This is about almost—twenty years ago—when we first got married? And we drive out to that little shopping plaza on Route 9.
HANNAH: Across from the fairgrounds?—
MARY *(Over the end of this)*: To that wine store. I don't know why he wanted to go to that wine store . . . But there's a mostly comics bookshop there too. It's gone now. But they also had a few used books along with the comics. Thomas *has* to go. I wait outside . . . *(Dramatic pause)*
HANNAH: What???

MARY: He comes out with that huge stupid grin on his face.

HANNAH: I remember that grin.

MARY *(Over this)*: He's got a book under his arm. 'Let's get in the car. Let's go. Let's go.' Then we stop in front of the fairgrounds; and he shows me the book . . . Beautiful jacket. Perfect condition. Thomas explains, 'It was only the first printing that he allowed his photo on the jacket.'

HANNAH: Who?

MARY: The author. That's why it's worth so much. You don't know this?

HANNAH: No.

MARY: This was way before we moved here . . . He paid like four dollars and seventy-five cents for this book. He said he even felt bad cheating the guy in the store. He kept it in a baggie in a bookcase for about five years, then sold it to a dealer in New York. Paid for a trip to Europe . . . *The Catcher in the Rye* . . . We could use that money now.

(George enters.)

We should have kept it.

GEORGE: What should we have kept? What the hell have we thrown away now?

MARY: Nothing, George.

HANNAH: Was that your sister on the phone?

GEORGE: She's picked up Mom. They'll be here in a minute.

HANNAH: How long has Joyce been there?

GEORGE: I don't know. I didn't ask . . . We're almost done.

(George starts to head off.)

HANNAH: Did Danny bring a check?

GEORGE: He forgot . . .

(He goes.)

HANNAH *(Calls)*: Remind him to ask his mother . . . Do you want me to call her? And it's been more than an hour! . . . He always goes over—

MARY: Not always—

HANNAH: And he leaves time between. Because he never wants to keep anyone *waiting*. I tell him *no one* does that. No one. Only George does that. His lessons are supposed to be for one hour . . .

(Karin enters with two boxes. She will set them down near the bench.)

MARY: Joyce called. They'll be here in a minute.

KARIN: There's a full moon . . .

MARY: Is there?

KARIN: Looks huge. *(About the boxes)* There must be twenty, thirty notebooks in this one . . . And files . . .

HANNAH *(To Mary)*: How many boxes are left?

MARY *(Shrugs)*: I don't know . . .

HANNAH: Mary was just telling me, Karin, what a help you are. Because you know the names. You know theater . . .

(The lights fade.)

Arrivals

A short time later. The same.

The piano lesson continues in the living room.

When the water in the pot of potatoes boils, Hannah will turn down the burner, and occasionally poke the potatoes. In the meantime, she continues to prepare the other ingredients in a bowl.

Mary, with a notebook from the new box, is in the middle of explaining an entry:

MARY: He didn't want to be there. Thomas could always make that clear.

KARIN: Oh, yes, he could. He could.

MARY: This time I stick to my guns. I'd taken a course in Greek art in college, so I thought it'd be interesting. And after all I had sat through a *four-and-a-half-hour* fucking play—in *German*. So . . . I figured he owed me this.

(She looks back at the notebook.)

KARIN: I agree.

MARY: 'Go ahead and mope, Thomas . . . Go ahead . . . But you're coming with me to this goddamn museum.'

HANNAH: Fair is fair.

KARIN: *When* were you in Berlin?

MARY *(To Hannah)*: Maybe—twelve, thirteen years ago?

HANNAH: Don't ask me.

KARIN *(As a "joke")*: Thomas never took me anywhere . . .

MARY *(Over the end of this, taking out another notebook; to Hannah)*: I'm looking into a glass cabinet—at papyrus fragments. You push a button and a tray moves . . . *(Demonstrates)* Some of my college education is coming back. Then—I see a label: '*theater*.' I push this button labeled—'*theater*.' 'Thomas,' I say, 'Thomas!' *(Gestures for 'Thomas' to come to her)* He grudgingly comes over to the cabinet, just as this papyrus slowly, very slowly comes into view. They had a description in German and in English.

(Looks at the notebook:)

"The only existing fragment of this play which is by—Euripides." *(Thomas's voice)* "Mary, 'by Euripides!'" My god, I'd found something that interested him! You don't know how hard that was to do . . . *(To Karin)* It was probably easier for you, being an actress . . .

KARIN *(A 'joke')*: Obviously it wasn't.

MARY *(She 'laughs'; hands the notebook to Hannah)*: Here . . . There, read that.

HANNAH *(Wipes hands, takes the notebook)*: That's funny. *(Reads)* "I am a woman, but I have—intelligence . . ."

(The front doorbell is heard from off.)

(To Mary) They're here. *(Reads)* "I am a woman, but I have—intelligence . . ." It's the "but" . . .

MARY: I know.

(Two or three impatient doorbell rings.)

HANNAH *(Obviously, to Mary)*: Joyce.

(The piano music stops.)

MARY: There was just this one papyrus fragment . . . That's all that's left of this play. I remember Thomas writing all this down. He was excited; 'Euripides, Mary!' He said he could use it for something. I don't know what . . .

(Karin has picked up another notebook and looks through it as Mary continues to read:)

(Reads) "In vain, it seems to me, do men mock women; denigrate and speak badly of us. But the truth is, women are better than men." *(Repeats)* "Women are better than men." *(Reads)* "*And*—I shall prove it . . ." *That's* where the papyrus is ripped off . . . The rest is lost . . . "Women are better than men . . ."

(George enters with a bottle of wine.)

GEORGE: Joyce is in the bathroom.

MARY: Did you hear that, George?

GEORGE: Hear what?

MARY: "Women are better than—"?

HANNAH *(Over this)*: Never mind. What's that?

GEORGE *(Holds up bottle)*: Joyce . . . Probably stole it from her boss's party. *(Looking at the label)* It's nice wine . . .

HANNAH: How is Joyce?

GEORGE *(Over this)*: Screw top. That used to mean . . .

KARIN: It used to.

(He puts the wine in the refridgerator.)

GEORGE *(Over this)*: It'll be nice to have a change. Something decent.

HANNAH *(Again)*: Joyce okay?

GEORGE: She had to use the bathroom. I don't know . . .

HANNAH: And your mother?

(He is gone. The timer goes off.)

MARY *(To Hannah)*: You need help?

HANNAH: No.

MARY: It's good Joyce is here. She should be. *(To Hannah, about the timer)* Your cookies . . .

HANNAH: I know.

(Hannah will go to take her cookies out of the oven, and will slowly, with a spatula, separate the cookies from the sheet as:)

KARIN *(With the other notebook, to say something)*: *This* is interesting. The phrase or whatever it is—'Okay'? The phrase—'Okay'?

HANNAH *(Obviously)*: We know the phrase 'Okay.'

KARIN *(Referring to the notebook)*: It comes from 'Old Kinderhook,' the Van Buren campaign for President . . . Thomas wrote that down for some reason . . . Everyone uses 'Okay,' all around the world.

MARY *(To Hannah)*: Kinderhook's just up the road.

HANNAH: Not that close.

KARIN *(Another entry)*: Here's something else. "George Frederic Jones."

MARY *(To Hannah)*: Joyce is going to want coffee . . . I'll heat it up. Who's that, Karin?

HANNAH *(About the coffee)*: How long has that been sitting there?

MARY *(Looking into the coffeepot)*: I don't know.

KARIN *(Skimming the notebook)*: This Jones seems to have had a house in Rhinebeck, near Wilderstein . . . And, I think what Thomas is saying is, this is where the phrase 'keeping up with the Joneses' comes from. Huh. *(Amazed) Rhinebeck!* This whole notebook seems to be about Rhinebeck.

MARY *(Seeing Joyce coming; to Hannah)*: Joyce . . .

KARIN *(Reading in the notebook)*: "Rufus Wainwright was born in Rhinebeck . . ."

MARY *(Greeting)*: Joyce . . . *(Wiping her hands)* My hands are wet . . . Let me . . . *(Keeps wiping them)*

JOYCE *(Over this)*: Hannah . . .

HANNAH *(Working on her cookies, over this)*: I'll give you a hug in a minute, Joyce.

MARY *(Going to give Joyce a hug)*: Karin's here . . .

JOYCE: I know. Nice to see you again, Karin.

KARIN: Back like a bad penny . . .

HANNAH: Don't say that.

MARY: Hannah, she's joking.

JOYCE: Here are Mom's car keys . . . Why haven't we sold that car?

(She sets keys on the table.)

MARY: When the sticker runs out.

HANNAH *(Same time)*: It's worth like nothing. *(Going to give Joyce a hug)* Nice top.

JOYCE: Thrift store. I got lucky.

HANNAH *(Getting up)*: Where's Patricia?

JOYCE: Oh she's coming . . . I behaved.

HANNAH *(Hugging Joyce)*: Really good to see you . . .

JOYCE: You too.

MARY *(Putting the keys in the desk; to say something)*: Karin's rented the guest room above the office.

JOYCE: George told me. I always found up there spooky at night, Karin.

HANNAH: Me too.

MARY: Don't tell her that.

KARIN *(To Hannah)*: Why is it spooky?

MARY: Nothing, Karin. *(To Joyce)* I'll heat up the coffee.

JOYCE: Thanks. Any tea? I'm drinking mostly tea now. Any chai?

MARY: No. *(Looks to Hannah)* No 'chai.' When have we ever had 'chai' in this house, Joyce? How's Lipton? I think we have some Lipton . . . You'll settle for Lipton? *(Looks in the cabinet)*

JOYCE: Anything's fine. I brought wine. George grabbed it from me.

HANNAH *(Over this, about the wine)*: In the refrigerator. It's 'waiting' . . .

JOYCE *(As she checks)*: My boss bought cases and cases. But rich Democrats now don't drink that much anymore. They seem to be mostly young guys watching their weight.

HANNAH *(Seeing George enter)*: Where's your mother?

GEORGE: Taking off her jacket. Very slowly. Just one more practice piece, Hannah, okay?

HANNAH: George . . .

GEORGE *(Over this)*: Danny's been working hard. He's earned it. Listen . . .

(Off, Danny has been playing musical scales.)

(Incredulous) On his own . . .

(He goes.)

HANNAH *(Calls)*: Tell him to ask his mother about the check . . . *(To Joyce)* Danny's mom owes us a check. Your brother keeps forgetting to ask . . .

JOYCE: Sounds like my brother.

MARY: I'll heat your water.

JOYCE: I can do that, Mary. Let me do that. *(To Hannah)* What are you doing? What is all this?

MARY *(Explaining)*: Hannah's making stuff for a picnic tomorrow. If it doesn't rain.

HANNAH *(Quoting George)*: "Even if it rains . . ."

MARY *(A list)*: The cookies . . .

JOYCE *(Over this)*: A picnic. I can't remember the last time I went on a picnic. Watch out for ticks. *(To Mary)* Any mug?

MARY: Doesn't matter.

(Joyce takes a mug from the dish rack, and begins to prepare her tea.)

JOYCE *(To Hannah)*: It's supposed to be nice tomorrow. Not crazy hot like last weekend. The city was unbearable. *(To Mary)* Is there honey?

MARY: On the stove. We keep it there now; so it doesn't get hard. I read that.

(Patricia enters from the dining room.)

PATRICIA: George is almost finished . . . Where do you want me to sit?

JOYCE: It's your kitchen, Mom.

HANNAH: Why don't you sit in your chair, Patricia. *(To Joyce)* This has now become your mother's favorite chair.

JOYCE: Has it, Mom?

HANNAH: It's become that.

(Mary goes to the cabinet, she will take out a couple cans of beans, find a can opener in the drawer in the table, and open the two cans, as:)

JOYCE *(As Patricia sits)*: George's student seems to be a very hard worker.

PATRICIA: Your brother is a wonderful teacher, Joyce.

JOYCE: I know he is. He taught me.

HANNAH: Mary's making your famous sausage casserole . . . How often do we have Joyce to dinner?

PATRICIA: Not very often.

JOYCE: I come when I can, Mom. *(To Hannah)* I left my boss's car at Mom's 'inn.' It's safe there?

HANNAH: Why wouldn't it be safe? *(To Patricia)* I'm glad you're feeling better.

JOYCE: You weren't feeling well, Mom? You didn't say . . .

HANNAH: This morning your mother said she had a headache.

PATRICIA: I did have a headache . . .

(Patricia smiles at Karin.)

JOYCE: That's Karin, Mom, she's—

PATRICIA: I know Karin. I know who she is. Hello, Karin.

KARIN: Hi—Pat.

JOYCE: 'Pat'??

HANNAH: Your mother 'remembered' yesterday—she says, Karin used to call her 'Pat.'

PATRICIA: I just remembered.

JOYCE: Dad called you that.

MARY *(To Patricia)*: You want tea? Now we're making tea. We're branching out.

PATRICIA: No, thank you, Mary.

JOYCE *(Smelling the Lipton)*: I don't need tea. Coffee's fine . . .

(She will pour herself some coffee.)

KARIN: Mary . . . ?

MARY: Wait for George. Then you can work in the living room. It's comfortable in there.

HANNAH *(To Joyce, to say something)*: We all went out last night to that new Indian for Mary's birthday. Your mother too.

JOYCE: I'm sorry I missed your birthday.
MARY: It was a birthday . . .
JOYCE: So there's a new Indian in the village?
HANNAH: It's not cheap.
JOYCE: It's Rhinebeck. What did you expect? Why did you go to the Indian?
MARY: It's new. We hadn't been.
HANNAH: Mary wanted to go somewhere she hadn't been with Thomas. It just opened in January. You want another pillow, Patricia? Let me get you a pillow . . .

(As they watch Mary pour the beans into the casserole:)

PATRICIA: I always made this meal on *Sunday* nights, Mary.
MARY: So did I, Patricia. For Thomas.

(Hannah puts a pillow behind Patricia.)

HANNAH: Is that better? . . .
PATRICIA *(To Hannah)*: You're a dear.
JOYCE *(With her coffee, the notebooks)*: So what's all this stuff, Mary?
HANNAH: Joyce, it's not 'stuff.'
MARY *(Explains)*: We're going through Thomas's old notebooks . . . Seeing what, if anything, we can sell . . .

(The lights fade.)

Mom's 'Inn'

The same. A little while later.

Off, piano music. The lesson continues; still the Fauré.

Hannah and Mary continue their preparations (for the potato salad and casserole, respectively; with Mary cutting up onions and the sausages). Karin listens to Joyce, and continues to look through the notebooks and boxes.

Patricia sits and listens.
Joyce is in the middle of conversation, as she sips her coffee.

KARIN: Did you get to shake Bill Clinton's hand?
JOYCE: He was there for like five minutes. I never even got near him.
MARY: He's had a very busy week—
HANNAH: —filling in. Mary, why won't she drink water?
MARY: I don't know. I'm not her doctor.
HANNAH: Any coffee, Patricia?
JOYCE: You want some, Mom?

(Patricia shakes her head no.)

They say she's all better now.
HANNAH: In one week? From pneumonia? Mary?
MARY: I'm not her doctor.
KARIN: I have a friend, a reporter. He was at a reception with the Clintons? In DC I think. And he took his wife. And she told me that when he talked to her? Bill. You know it's famous how—'you're-the-only-person-in-the-room' when he talks to you? She found that really creepy.
JOYCE: We're not blaming her for that.
HANNAH: What do you need, Patricia?
JOYCE: She doesn't need to be waited on.
PATRICIA: No, Joyce, I don't. Thank you, Hannah. I don't need anything.
KARIN: If I met him, I don't know what I'd say to him.
JOYCE: Met who, Karin??
KARIN *(Obviously)*: Bill Clinton.
MARY: He's done a lot of good too, hasn't he? I remember him doing good.
KARIN: He always sounds so damn convincing. And I always end up so damn 'convinced' . . .
JOYCE: How can I help? Let me do something.
MARY: Hannah?

HANNAH: Chop up the parsley? . . .
JOYCE: Sure. I'll do that. I can do that.
MARY *(Over this)*: Joyce, why do you have to go back tonight?—
PATRICIA: You're going back tonight?
JOYCE: You know that, Mom. I told you.

(Hannah will get the parsley and a cutting board for Joyce.)

Tomorrow's the *millionaires*—for brunch. Last night it was the *billionaires*—and their friends. We think my boss wants to be ambassador to—something. Somewhere where people dress really really well. And change their clothes a lot. Gillibrand's coming tomorrow. That's the rumor.
HANNAH: I'll bet she's a lot of fun. *(To Joyce)* That needs to be washed. I'll need about a cup. *("of parsley")*

(Off, the piano has stopped.)

I think he's done. *(Looks at her watch)*

(Joyce will go to wash the parsley in the sink.)

Patricia, did George tell you we already got a nibble on the piano?

(Patricia nods.)

JOYCE: Did we?
HANNAH *(To Joyce)*: Someone from Bard. A singer. So we had it tuned this morning.
JOYCE: If you had to.

(Then back to the party:)

My boss loaned all us assistants these amazing dresses.
KARIN: What do you mean? What dresses?
HANNAH: She wanted you to look rich. To fit in.

PATRICIA: What was yours, Joyce? Was it very nice? I'd like to see you in a nice dress.

JOYCE: I wear dresses, Mom. *(To Hannah)* Sort of fifties. Big pattern of flowers. Summery.

MARY: Probably something like you once wore, Patricia.

HANNAH *(To Patricia)*: And I'll bet you looked great in it too.

PATRICIA: I think I did.

KARIN: I'm sure you did, Pat.

JOYCE: Perfect neck for me. Squared. Thick straps. She knows . . . Perfect weight. It moved, you know, when you walked, I felt great . . .

HANNAH: You want something to do, Patricia?

(Patricia shakes her head no.)

KARIN: Was there any dancing?

JOYCE *(Of course not)*: No. *(Back at the table to chop the parsley)*

PATRICIA: Joyce doesn't dance, Karin.

JOYCE: I dance, Mom. I dance. Why do you say that?

PATRICIA: I thought you hated dancing.

JOYCE: I hated ballet class, Mom. When I was like eight years old.

PATRICIA *(Her point proved)*: That's what I remember.

JOYCE: Jesus . . . I dance.

PATRICIA: I didn't know that.

JOYCE: My boss had sandals for us too. Waiting in our closets. I looked mine up online. Guess how much, Mom?

PATRICIA: I have no idea, Joyce.

JOYCE: Over a thousand dollars, Mom. *(To the others)* For a couple of thin pieces of leather strips sewn together . . .

HANNAH: For shoes? Who are these people?

JOYCE: They weren't even comfortable.

(Seeing George enter) There you are. Here he is.

HANNAH: Finished?

GEORGE: Danny will ask his mother for a check . . . He's been working so hard . . .

MARY: Good for Danny . . .

HANNAH *(To George)*: Joyce has been telling us about her boss's fundraiser for Hillary in Hudson.

MARY: For very very rich people.

GEORGE *(Getting out the water pitcher from the refrigerator)*: I'm sorry I couldn't make it. I hope they understood. Anyone else want water?

(They don't.)

MARY *(To George)*: Joyce has to go back after dinner. She can't stay the night.

GEORGE: I figured.

PATRICIA *(To Joyce)*: You sure you can't stay?—

JOYCE: No, Mom.

MARY: She has another fundraiser tomorrow. Gillibrand might be there.

GEORGE: What does she need money for?

JOYCE *(Starting a list)*: For Teachout . . .

GEORGE: No. God, please no . . .

(As Karin looks at Mary and starts to get up:)

KARIN: Mary . . .

MARY: Thank you, Karin. We won't be too long.

KARIN *(Over the end of this)*: Of course. *(As she picks up a box)* Maybe I'll find a treasure . . .

MARY: Thank you.

JOYCE AND HANNAH: Thanks.

PATRICIA: Thank you, Karin.

(Karin is gone.)

JOYCE *(To Patricia)*: She lives here now . . .

PATRICIA: I know, Joyce.

MARY: Dinner's not for an hour.

JOYCE: You look good, Mom.

GEORGE: Doesn't she.

HANNAH *(To Joyce)*: What did you think of your mother's new room?

JOYCE *(Turns to Patricia)*: I really liked it, Mom. It's not as crowded as I thought it would feel with a roommate. It's cozy.

HANNAH *(To Patricia)*: Was the roommate there?

(Patricia nods.)

JOYCE: You didn't even know her before, did you, Mom?

PATRICIA: No.

JOYCE: I hadn't known that . . .

(Then:)

So—Mom, what do you pay now? How much a month? I think I need to start there . . .

(Patricia looks to George.)

GEORGE: It's now forty-five hundred a month, Mom.

PATRICIA: It had been more for a single.

GEORGE: It was. And that was a big help. *(To Joyce)* Her moving herself into the double room cut about a thousand-plus off a month.

HANNAH *(To Patricia)*: You did that yourself. *(To Joyce)* You lied and told us you 'wanted company . . .'

JOYCE *(To Patricia)*: So what exactly do you owe them, Mom?

HANNAH *(Trying to be light)*: Joyce, this young guy stopped Mary the other day, when she was visiting your mother. He said, "Mrs. Gabriel, your mother-in-law has no more than a month left." Mary thought—

MARY: Of course I thought . . .

JOYCE: He was from the business office.

HANNAH: You'd think he'd find a different way of putting it.

JOYCE: He said the exact same thing to me. Just now. The moment I walked into Mom's room, he came in. And he knew who I was.

MARY: You signed in. They call back to the office when any of us signs in now . . .

GEORGE: Mom, you owe two months, and now this month. That's about thirteen thousand and change. To get you through the rest of September.

JOYCE: The next two weeks . . .

GEORGE: Yeah.

(Awkward pause.)

JOYCE: Do they kick people out? It's a 'home.' Do they really do that?

GEORGE: It's a business, Joyce . . .

(Then:)

JOYCE: This guy, Mom, from the office showed me some of your bills. *(To the others)* Have you seen them?

HANNAH *(Looking at George)*: I think we have.

JOYCE *(To Patricia)*: 'Guest meals.' What is that, Mom?

MARY *(Before Patricia can answer)*: It's mostly us. *(To Patricia)* You like us to come to dinner now and then, don't you? *(To Joyce)* We can stop doing that. That's our fault.

JOYCE *(The list)*: 'Breakfast in the room'? He said, that's not part of independent living—

HANNAH: You pay extra for that.

MARY: Your mother got a terrible cold, Joyce. Remember?

GEORGE *(Over this)*: We called you.

MARY: She didn't want to get dressed. It wasn't some 'luxurious' indulgence. Your mom's not like that. *(To Patricia)* You're not like that. *(To Joyce)* You know that.

HANNAH: Your mother knows what she's done. And she's facing it. *(To Patricia)* Aren't you?

PATRICIA: I think so. I'm trying. *(To Joyce)* What do you want to say?

(Then:)

JOYCE: Remember telling me, Mom: 'we women, we have to be so damn tough'?

(Then:)

Ever since George called, I've been hearing you say that to me. I remember you sitting me down in this very kitchen, here, and telling me to 'be careful, Joyce. Watch out for yourself.' You never talked like that to Thomas or George.

PATRICIA: No. I didn't.

JOYCE: 'Joyce, we women must be responsible for ourselves. We can't expect others to go around cleaning up our messes.' That used to get me so angry.

PATRICIA: I know. I'm sorry, Joyce.

(Then:)

JOYCE: What are you going to do, Mom?

HANNAH: We told your mother we're ready to dip into Paulie's college fund.

JOYCE *(Shocked)*: What? Are you serious? You can't do that. *(To Patricia)* You'd let them do that?

GEORGE *(Over the end of this)*: Some of it.

MARY: She's against it.

GEORGE *(Over this)*: To get through this.

JOYCE: Are you crazy?

HANNAH *(Over this)*: He'll take out loans. Kids take out loans.

JOYCE: Not that. Not that.

HANNAH *(Over the end of this)*: And some of that was even from your mother. She 'gave' it to Paulie for his college.

GEORGE: She said she could afford it.

JOYCE: You're not doing that.

GEORGE: It's the only savings we have, Joyce.

(Then:)

JOYCE: Mom, Dad's Social Security?

GEORGE: She gets half. She never really worked.

JOYCE: You *worked.*

GEORGE: Hannah checked, her home doesn't take Medicaid; there are other places.

HANNAH: You should see them, Joyce.

GEORGE: But even that . . . Hannah asked a friend who knows about this stuff—

HANNAH: She'd have to own nothing. So you plan for it. There are ways of planning for it. Too late now. We're trying to sell what we can.

GEORGE: Our first thought was to mortgage this house.

JOYCE: Your house, Mom? You'd agree to that?

PATRICIA: I would.

HANNAH *(Over this)*: But we can't, Joyce. It's already mortgaged.

JOYCE: What are you talking about?

PATRICIA: I don't know.

HANNAH: Patricia, you mortgaged it.

JOYCE: Dad paid off this house more than twenty years ago.

HANNAH: Your mother mortgaged it again.

GEORGE *(Over this)*: She just hadn't told us.

JOYCE: When?

PATRICIA: I don't know.

GEORGE *(Over this)*: We don't know yet. We don't know.

HANNAH *(To Patricia)*: It's a different kind. It has been paying you in installments. *(To George)* Isn't that how it works?

GEORGE: We thought that money, her checks, were from investments.

HANNAH: They've let her—maybe urged her, suckered her, to borrow even more. So there's interest now too to pay back on that. Whatever 'that' is . . . We don't know yet.

GEORGE: We don't really know how much of this house Mom owns anymore.

HANNAH: They make it so damn complicated.

GEORGE: I learned about this yesterday.

JOYCE *(All sinking in)*: Oh god, Mom . . . What were you thinking?

GEORGE: Joyce—

PATRICIA: I don't know, Joyce.

HANNAH *(Over this)*: George and your mother have a meeting with these mortgage people; the ones who do these kinds of mortgages. Next Wednesday in Poughkeepsie.

GEORGE: We'll learn then how much we'll need to buy it back. Pay back—of what she's been given. Borrowed. The interest on that.

HANNAH: Fees. The agent told George on the phone to: expect fees.

PATRICIA *(To Hannah)*: What does he mean?

HANNAH *(To Patricia)*: We don't know.

JOYCE: We need to talk to a lawyer.

GEORGE: Hannah and Mom have. She signed a contract.

PATRICIA: George went to high school with him, Joyce.

HANNAH: He did. So he didn't charge us anything.

JOYCE: How could this happen?

PATRICIA: I don't know . . .

GEORGE: It's good to have Joyce here, isn't it, Mom?

PATRICIA *(Getting up)*: It is. It always is.

HANNAH: Let me help you.

JOYCE: She doesn't need help, Hannah.

GEORGE: You going to have a lie-down? Watch some TV on the couch?

PATRICIA: Joyce is right. I don't need help . . .

(She heads to the living room.)

HANNAH: George, if she's going to watch TV, she needs to remember to use both channel changers . . .

(George starts to stand, stops.)

GEORGE: Karin can help her.
MARY: This is hard on her.

(As Patricia leaves:)

GEORGE: Joyce, what if—Hannah and I rent out *our* house . . . ?
JOYCE: What do you mean?
GEORGE: There's still a mortgage, but it's not that big. We could even take out another—
HANNAH: I told you I wouldn't be comfortable with that.
GEORGE: Start to pay off her debts with the rent money from our house. And any money from the things we're trying to sell. *(Beginning of a list)* Her car.
HANNAH: It's worth almost nothing.
GEORGE: We'll save by stopping the insurance. *(Next)* The piano . . . *(Then)* Some furniture . . . Mom has some jewelry . . .
MARY: Whatever Karin and I find that is worth anything . . .
GEORGE: So Mom moves back here to her house. Where she's comfortable.
HANNAH: She can do steps. She's still pretty healthy.
GEORGE: Hannah and I would then live here with Mom. And look after her.
JOYCE *(Looks to Mary)*: And Mary . . . ?
MARY: I'll be moving to Pittsburgh. Not right away, of course. When it starts to feel too crowded. And Karin's just month-to-month. She knows all about this.
JOYCE *(As it sinks in)*: So she doesn't even own her house? How could this happen?
GEORGE: At least part of it. We don't know. She doesn't know. We'll know more on Wednesday.
JOYCE: Fuck.
GEORGE: Don't just say that. Don't just say, 'fuck.' We'll make it work. But we hear you. The last thing we touch—is Paulie's college . . . Okay?

JOYCE: Fuck! How could this happen?

(Then:)

(To George) You know, I remember when Paulie was like ten hours old. And you're holding up a little booklet: 'Look, I'm opening up Paulie's college fund!' You were so damn proud.

GEORGE: With like five dollars . . . Oh that was a real smart investment . . . Put the money in the bank. Let the interest just grow and grow . . . What the hell ever happened to interest from a bank—?

JOYCE: You all know I don't have any money.

GEORGE *(A joke)*: Oh, now that's a surprise . . . *(Teasing)* 'You need to be more responsible, Joyce . . . Grow up, Joyce.'

JOYCE *(Smiling)*: Fuck you.

GEORGE *(Smiling)*: Everyone knows that, Joyce . . . Everyone.

JOYCE: And the two girls I went around Europe with? I didn't tell you this. I was embarrassed. And please, don't tell Mom. They have goddamn trust funds. Who knew? I'm in debt now to both of them . . . I thought we were going to be traveling on the cheap . . .

(Patricia reenters on her way to the dining room.)

HANNAH *(Standing up)*: You need something, Patricia?

JOYCE: We don't have to wait on her. She's not that old.

(Karin has entered right behind Patricia.)

KARIN: Pat would like her sherry, she said.

JOYCE *(To Mary)*: Is there still sherry?

(Patricia heads off.)

MARY: Maybe a little. I haven't been buying it.

GEORGE *(Looks at his watch)*: I think it's that time, Mom . . . It is that time.

MARY: You can come back in here, Karin. I think we're finished. Are we finished?

GEORGE: Find anything we can sell? Any 'treasures'?

KARIN: Not yet . . .

(She goes.)

GEORGE *(To Joyce)*: We finished? For now?

JOYCE: Why didn't you tell me about the house?

HANNAH: He just learned this yesterday, Joyce.

GEORGE: We'll know more on Wednesday . . .

MARY *(Changing the subject)*: Joyce, have you been following Paulie on Facebook?

JOYCE: Of course.

MARY: So have we. Every day.

JOYCE: Does he know that?

GEORGE *(Of course not)*: No.

JOYCE: I can't believe my nephew's already in college . . .

HANNAH: You saw him graduate—

JOYCE: I know . . .

MARY: Here's something that will make you laugh, Joyce. *(To George)* Tell your sister about you and Hannah taking Paulie to Purchase.

KARIN *(Returning with the box, to Joyce):* I've heard this. It's very funny.

HANNAH: You have? She has?

JOYCE: So you used to call Mom 'Pat'?

KARIN: No. No, I never did . . .

(Karin will look through the boxes.)

MARY *(To George)*: Tell Joyce, she could use a laugh.

HANNAH *(To Joyce)*: Did you know it was almost California? . . .

JOYCE: I know. You've told me ten times.

GEORGE: A state school—thank you god . . . Thank you!

JOYCE: What happened?

MARY: They bring Paulie to his dorm . . . *(To Hannah)* Tell Joyce.

HANNAH: He didn't want us even to help. He wanted to say—goodbye Mom and Dad— *(Looks to George)* —in the parking lot. Fortunately, we had a little refrigerator, so he needed 'Dad' to help carry it.

GEORGE *(Laughs)*: Three flights!

JOYCE *(Laughs)*: Oh god.

HANNAH *(Continues)*: We meet his roommate and his roommate's parents—*they're* sitting on the bed, they weren't rushed away by their son.

GEORGE: I think they were just oblivious. They seemed that sort of—

HANNAH: They were from some fancy place in Connecticut. They'd 'heard' of Rhinebeck. 'Friends' have weekend places in 'Rhinebeck.'

GEORGE: We were the *thoughtful* parents.

JOYCE: I'm sure you were.

(Patricia returns with her sherry.)

HANNAH *(Over this)*: 'The new Hamptons' they called Rhinebeck, didn't they? I didn't just dream that?

JOYCE: I've heard that.

PATRICIA: I've heard that too. My god.

GEORGE: I wasn't as bothered as—

HANNAH *(Over this)*: I wasn't *bothered*. How people think of us. Rhinebeck . . .

JOYCE: I hear the same thing. Makes me cringe.

GEORGE: You going to sit there?

JOYCE: Mom, don't you want your chair?

MARY: Patricia, they're telling Joyce about taking Paulie to his college . . .

PATRICIA: Oh, this is a good story, Joyce . . .

HANNAH: You're going to spill that, Patricia.

GEORGE *(Continuing)*: We quickly said our goodbyes—*we* were the good parents who took the hint. We leave his dorm and before we head home, Hannah wants to—

HANNAH *(Over this)*: Not just me.

GEORGE: —take a little stroll around the campus, and—'feel' what it's like? What it's going to be like for *(Making fun, imitating Hannah)* 'our little Paulie'?

JOYCE *(To Patricia)*: You all right?

HANNAH *(Over this)*: Come on, that's not fair. You too!

GEORGE *(Over this)*: We find a bench on a little path; Hannah and I sit down and . . . what? We just start—to cry. *(Laughter)* Tears gushing out. Gushing. Both of us on this bench. How 'we miss our boy.' I don't know all the crazy things we're saying and saying them out loud, when—around the corner, comes a whole gang of college kids, and who should be right in the middle of the gang?

(Laughter.)

JOYCE: No!

MARY *(Explaining)*: Paulie . . .

JOYCE *(Over this)*: It was his first day on his own. What were you two thinking?

PATRICIA: You'd understand better if you had children, Joyce.

GEORGE: Mom . . .

HANNAH: Patricia . . .

JOYCE: God, Mom . . .

MARY: Joyce, I think what your mother is trying to say is: she felt like that when you went to college. She told us this just the other day, that after you'd gone, she slept in your bed for about a week . . .

GEORGE *(To Joyce)*: Did you know that?

(Then:)

JOYCE: So—what did Paulie do?

HANNAH: Walked right past us, Joyce. And pretended he didn't know who the hell we were . . .

(The lights fade.)

George Has a Plan

The same, a short time later.

Patricia sits, sips her sherry, watching all the activity around her: Mary continues to work on her casserole; Karin continues to sort through the box of notebooks; Hannah continues to prepare the potato salad; later she will prepare the dressing for a coleslaw.

All listen to George who is in the middle of telling a story, mostly to Joyce (as the others, except Patricia, have heard most of it.

GEORGE: Joyce, he writes to his publisher saying—he'll be done with his new book within a month. The book—is *Moby Dick*.

HANNAH: But he wasn't calling it that then—

GEORGE: I think he was, Hannah. *Moby Dick*.

HANNAH *(To Joyce)*: It was an entirely different book.

GEORGE *(Over this)*: Now Melville is taking a quick vacation up in the Berkshires. He's got relatives there, with a farm in Pittsfield. It's still there.

JOYCE: Is it?

HANNAH *(Over this)*: Part of a golf course. The clubhouse. *(Looks to George)*

GEORGE: When one day, while a few of his literary friends from New York are visiting—some writer, an editor—Melville and his pals get invited to a picnic. And it's the route of *this* picnic that we're going to be following tomorrow.

HANNAH: If it doesn't rain.

GEORGE: Even if it rains. It rained *then*.

HANNAH: I don't want to go if it's raining.
JOYCE: It's not going to rain.
GEORGE *(Over this)*: We're following the same route—of the most famous literary picnic in the history of American literature.
JOYCE: I don't know anything about this.

(Mary stands to get some Paul Newman lemonade out of the refrigerator.)

MARY *(To Joyce)*: He's told us— *('her, Karin and Patricia')*
JOYCE *(To Hannah, over this)*: Why are you making a face?
GEORGE: The picnic where Herman Melville first met—Nathaniel Hawthorne.
JOYCE: Why don't I know this?
MARY *(Holding up the Paul Newman)*: Anyone?

(No one wants any; Mary will pour herself a glass.)

GEORGE: *After* this day, this picnic, Joyce, Herman Melville will throw away his nearly finished book, and start all over again. And for the next so many months, he will be consumed rewriting, rethinking, what we now know as—*Moby Dick.*

(Then:)

Something happened that day. What happened?
HANNAH: What about Joyce's wine? Can we open that?
JOYCE: I stole it. Open it. Mom got to have her sherry.
HANNAH: George?
JOYCE *(Confused)*: And this guy knows what actually happened?
GEORGE: No. No. *(He gets up)* Of course not.
JOYCE *(To Hannah)*: I thought that's where this was headed. Stop making that face.

(As he gets the wine out of the refrigerator and opens it:)

GEORGE: Ignore her. Who knows what happened, Joyce. No one does. But something did happen. Tomorrow we're going to celebrate that.

JOYCE *(To the women)*: What's—'*that*'??? What are you celebrating?

GEORGE *(Over this)*: Before this picnic, Herman was just a self-taught writer of exotic sea tales. *After* . . . ? Well he'll be different. Something will have set him free, and American literature will be changed forever.

(He goes to the sink for glasses.)

JOYCE *(To the women)*: I've never read *Moby Dick.*

MARY: Me neither.

KARIN: I have.

JOYCE: Like all of the characters are men.

KARIN *(Same time)*: It's really long.

GEORGE: It takes place at sea, of course there are men. *(Picking glasses out of the dish rack)* These all right? *(Continues)* We have no description of the moment these two actually met.

(He holds up a glass.)

MARY: They should be clean.

GEORGE: They're fine.

(Patricia is interested in one of the notebooks.)

JOYCE: Find something, Mom?

PATRICIA: This one is all about Rhinebeck . . .

GEORGE: Mom, should I keep—? Joyce was asking me about the picnic. *(Continues)* Melville, very much wants to meet Hawthorne who is living now near Lennox—

PATRICIA: Where Tanglewood—

GEORGE: His house is still there. On the grounds.

HANNAH: It's been rebuilt two, three times.
PATRICIA: We used to go to Tanglewood . . .

(Patricia stands up, picking up the notebooks.)

HANNAH *(To George)*: Why don't we go anymore?—
GEORGE: Mom? What are you doing?
PATRICIA: I heard all about your picnic last night . . .

(She starts to head to the living room.)

May I borrow these, Mary?
MARY: Of course—
JOYCE *(Same time)*: Where are you going?
HANNAH *(To Patricia)*: You okay?
JOYCE: To lie down, Hannah. She's tired.
PATRICIA *(The notebooks)*: They're all Thomas's?
MARY: They are. All his.
HANNAH *(To George)*: She going to lie on the couch?

(George shrugs. Patricia is gone.)

JOYCE: Restless . . . Like a ghost . . . 'Haunting us.'
HANNAH: Joyce . . .
JOYCE: I can say that, she's my mother.
HANNAH: No, you can't.
JOYCE: It's a joke.
MARY: Joyce, last night, at the restaurant—Patricia said to me: how really sorry she was. How she'd fucked up.
JOYCE: Mom actually said 'fucked up'? Those words?
HANNAH: It's what she meant.
MARY *(Working on her casserole)*: How scared she was about seeing you today, Joyce.
JOYCE: Scared of me?
GEORGE: Didn't you know that?

(Then:)

JOYCE: George, you were telling me about this picnic . . .

(Mary sets the timer for preheating.)

So what happened?

HANNAH: They don't know.

JOYCE: I know nothing about this.

GEORGE *(Over this)*: Hawthorne and his family are living full-time near Lennox where he's trying to avoid a woman in town named Sedgwick. Also a writer. Best-seller after best-seller. His sales pale in comparison. He can't stand her.

HANNAH: He *("George")* likes the *gossip*.

GEORGE: It's not gossip. It's history. Sedgwick's brother, Hawthorne's Boston publisher, Fields, and *the* Doctor Oliver Holmes. They're the other picnickers.

HANNAH: And two women. That's why I have to go.

GEORGE: The wife of the publisher.

HANNAH *(To Joyce, as she shreds the carrots)*: That's me. She wore a blue silk dress. I don't own a blue silk dress.

JOYCE: What are you going to wear?

HANNAH: It's cotton. It's blue . . .

JOYCE: I think this sounds like fun.

HANNAH *(Smiles)*: Fuck you.

JOYCE *(To Hannah)*: Any kind of hat?

HANNAH: I don't wear hats.

GEORGE: They drive together in one carriage the few miles south to the base of Monument Mountain.

HANNAH *(Teasing George, to Joyce)*: It's still there.

GEORGE: Unload hampers of food and champagne.

HANNAH: They're bringing antique straw hampers. I'm bringing Tupperware.

GEORGE *(Over this, continuing)*: And then begin the climb. It's not that difficult a walk—

(He looks to Hannah.)

The women are fine. They follow a ridge. Nathaniel, we know, was a very reserved man. He walks a little ahead of the group, as the others, in party mood, make up rhymes, puns fly in every direction—

HANNAH *(To Joyce)*: Sounds like so much fun, doesn't it?

GEORGE: And that gets the party going. 'So tell me about life in Concord,' Herman asks his idol. 'Well,' Hawthorne says, 'with Thoreau, you just feel embarrassed talking money . . . Emerson on the other hand, he sued to get his share of his first wife's inheritance—'

(Timer goes off.)

'—he's got bank and railroad stock now.' Longfellow—'he's making a hundred bucks a week from *Evangeline*.'

JOYCE: So they just talked money?

HANNAH: According to George's new best friend. The guy worked on Wall Street.

(Mary will put the casserole into the oven to bake, set the timer.)

GEORGE: Somehow Melville's arm got around the older man's shoulders. This surprises everyone; Nathaniel Hawthorne did not like to be touched. The picnickers reach the summit and our two men sit apart and talk.

HANNAH *(To Joyce)*: We don't know what about.

GEORGE: We know from letters that Hawthorne tells Melville that he has stopped reading newspapers.

JOYCE: Was it an election year?

GEORGE: They talk about life insurance, how neither can afford such a thing. And how America 'tames' its artists. When Melville suddenly stands and runs out onto a jutting rock and pretends to be on the bowsprit of a ship, hauling in imaginary ropes. All the time shouting orders to the wind, making his new friend laugh.

HANNAH *(Explains)*: He's drunk.

GEORGE: No one can believe it, when Nathaniel follows his friend onto the jutting rock and shouts to the whole world—that he has found the 'great carbuncle.'

JOYCE *(To Hannah)*: What is that?

HANNAH: Who knows?

GEORGE *(Over this)*: A thunderstorm sweeps across the mountain top; the group finds sanctuary under some protruding cliff; our two friends stand together, soaked, lightning flashes, rolls of thunder, rain whips, as the two men shout into the dark sky . . .

(Then:)

JOYCE: What did they shout?

HANNAH: We don't know . . . So that's what we're doing tomorrow. George and me and George's new rich friend, and the rich friend's rich friends . . . *(To Joyce)* Taste it, tell me what you think. *(Of the coleslaw)* Doesn't it sound like a good time?

GEORGE: It could be fun.

HANNAH: I think it needs more mustard.

JOYCE: So you really don't know what happened?

HANNAH: No. No one does.

GEORGE: We know that from that day on American literature—

HANNAH: I think she's heard enough.

JOYCE: How did you meet this guy?

HANNAH: George met him in the Millerton diner.

GEORGE: He and his wife were in the next booth.

HANNAH *(This explains everything)*: They have a weekend place up here.

KARIN: That diner? It's near Hotchkiss . . . I go there for lunch sometimes.

HANNAH *(Over this)*: That diner's— *(Makes quotation marks with her fingers)* 'authentic *country*.' *(As if this explains everything)* If you're from the city.

(Mary will head off to the mudroom, to collect vegetables for a vegetable marinade.)

KARIN *(To Mary)*: It gets crowded.

GEORGE *(Continues)*: And we got to talking, Joyce; I said I'd spent my whole life here. And he said how rare that was these days to find someone like me.

(Smiles. Then:)

That was nice to hear. We got started talking about the area, its history, and he said he really wanted one day to walk in the steps of the most famous literary picnic—which of course 'as you know' happened only a few miles away. I didn't know. *(To Joyce)* Did you know?

(Mary returns with mushrooms, cauliflower, tomatoes, green beans, and an avocado.)

JOYCE: So then your new friend invited you on his picnic.

HANNAH: He's 'retired.' He's like forty years old.

GEORGE: He's done all this research.

HANNAH: He has an assistant who seems to do most of it.

GEORGE *(Lists)*: What they ate. The poems they read that day . . .

HANNAH: They'll eat whatever tomorrow.

KARIN *(To Mary)*: Let me do *something*. I've just been sitting here . . .

HANNAH: You're finding treasure . . . That's important.

MARY: Karin, if you want, you can help me cut up vegetables . . .

(Karin starts to stand.)

Let me just wash some of this first . . .

HANNAH *(To Joyce)*: Your mother has a hummus mix . . . God knows how old it is. What the hell . . .

(Hannah heads to the cupboard.)

I don't care how old it is . . . As long as it's easy. *(Incredible, about George)* He promised them hummus.

JOYCE: Did they eat hummus? Hawthorne and Melville?

HANNAH: Did they, George?

GEORGE *(Ignoring them)*: We're going to read the poems tomorrow. He has the original books. He has a book dealer who finds him these things.

(Hannah gets the box of hummus mix. Mary is washing the vegetables.)

HANNAH *(To Joyce)*: Here . . . There are directions. You can make it right in the Tupperware. I'll get the . . . *(She will get a Tupperware container for Joyce)*

GEORGE: Last night he also told me something he just learned. Listen to this: when Herman goes to visit Nathaniel a few weeks later at Tanglewood?

MARY *(A joke)*: It must have been out of season, because the traffic gets—

GEORGE: Herman regales— *('him')*

MARY: 'Regales.'

(As Joyce reads the directions on the box of hummus mix:)

GEORGE: —regales him *and* Mrs. Hawthorne with stories of South Sea adventures—Mrs. Hawthorne wrote a letter about this—and describes the *sex* customs of the natives.

(They pay attention to this.)

Maybe his own experiences of sex with the natives? . . . *Then* exactly nine months later, Mrs. Hawthorne gives birth. *(The point)* Nine months later.

KARIN *(To Mary)*: Tell me how you want . . . ?

MARY: It's a marinade. Just cut them up . . .

(Karin works with Mary on the vegetables for the marinade.)

JOYCE *(Over this)*: Are you saying that Melville was the father of Hawthorne's—? *('children')*
GEORGE: That's not what I'm saying, Joyce.

(Mary wipes the mushrooms clean.)

MARY: That's what I thought he was saying too.
GEORGE *(Over the end of this)*: It was the 'excitement' of his stories that night . . .
KARIN: Now *that* would be interesting, if—
JOYCE *(Agreeing)*: If he had sex with Hawthorne's—
GEORGE: Melville didn't have sex with Hawthorne's wife! Forget it.
KARIN: How do we know?
GEORGE: We just do. Come on. *(To Hannah)* And please don't say things like that tomorrow.

(They work. Joyce on the hummus mix; she will need to get a measuring cup, water from the sink and oil. Mary and Karin work on the vegetable marinade.)

HANNAH: Tell your sister about his weekend house.
JOYCE: What about . . . ?
GEORGE: I know, Hannah, but—
HANNAH: George's new rich friend bought this old house in Stockbridge. Very 'historic.' And he's been fixing it up. He has people fixing it up. We're hoping that George can be one of those people fixing it up.
JOYCE: So—you're 'networking.' Good for you.
GEORGE: That's not the only reason—
JOYCE: I didn't think you had that in you.

(George is pouring himself another glass of wine.)

HANNAH: It's why we're going. *(About the wine)* George . . . *(Continues)* He buys his 'historic' house—last winter? He's hardly lived in it. He has some other houses too. The first thing he does is hire scene painters, theater people, to paint each room in a sort of 'scene.' *(Begins to list the scenes)* A forest . . . *(To Karin)* You knew one of them.

KARIN: I did.

HANNAH: So you sit in the living room and you're in a forest . . .

GEORGE: You haven't been—

HANNAH: You told me. *(Continues the list)* Another room: a castle. What else? *(No response)* It's funny. They worked for months. And he and his wife arrive in July, from their house in Italy? And they love it. Love everything about it. They sit there in the forest; they have drinks in the 'castle.' He puts on monks chanting music. He 'loves' the 'feel' of history.

GEORGE: Hannah—

HANNAH *(Over this)*: And two days later, the wife says—'these rooms make me dizzy, like I want to throw up . . .'

JOYCE: Were the painters still—? *('there')*

KARIN: My friend was still there. Living above someone's garage. That's where he got put.

HANNAH *(Over this)*: So they then paint over everything. The same painters. Over all their work. This time—'light blue.' 'Eggshell white . . .' So now they want—bookcases. Floor to ceiling. And built-in cabinets. All looking 'old.' *(In the guy's voice)* 'Really old.' 'That literary cabin-look.' Right? What the hell does that mean? But it'll be a big job. Probably take all winter for a good high-end carpenter . . . *(To Joyce)* That's why we're going on this picnic . . .

(Looks to George.)

Tell her . . . That's George's plan. Like *that*, he thinks he'll get enough work for the year.

GEORGE: And pay for Mom . . . What she owes. Maybe she could even stay in the 'inn' a couple more months . . . Start to pay off the mortgage . . .

JOYCE: You're a good carpenter.

GEORGE: A job like this can—

HANNAH: He doesn't know for sure what it's going to pay. Rich people often don't pay well.

GEORGE: They don't just come along every day. Jobs like this.

HANNAH *(Continuing)*: We know that from experience.

GEORGE: It'd be steady work and for at least the entire winter. Probably longer. Everything custom.

HANNAH: If it works out.

MARY: Tell her what you're really worried about, Hannah.

JOYCE: What?

MARY: That his new friend really only wants George along—because George is a big guy—so he can carry a lot of the stuff for them up the mountain. At this picnic.

GEORGE *(To Hannah)*: I told you I don't think that's true. I don't think that's fair.

HANNAH *(Over this)*: He sees a strong guy. A 'local.'

GEORGE: Hannah—

HANNAH: You know, so like on a safari . . .

JOYCE: A porter? George, as their porter??

HANNAH *(Demonstrating)*: Carrying their baskets on his head? All the other picnickers are coming from New York City. Manhattan. Does he know you have a pacemaker, George?

JOYCE *(To George)*: Does he? Does he, George?

HANNAH: No.

GEORGE: We're just their guests.

HANNAH: Are we?

MARY: And after George mentions to his new rich friend that his wife does catering, Hannah too suddenly gets invited on this picnic . . .

HANNAH: And I get an email with a list of all the stuff they want me to cook . . .

(Then:)

JOYCE *(To Hannah)*: Are they paying you to . . . ?
HANNAH: No. No. Of course not, Joyce.

(The lights fade.)

Joyce's Trip Abroad

The same; a short time later.

Mary and Karin prepare the vegetable marinade; Joyce has paused from making the hummus mix; Hannah continues to clean up; George is finishing his wine.

Joyce, in the middle of conversation with Karin:

JOYCE: Karin, I'd never worked with opera singers before . . .
GEORGE *(Standing; about the dinner)*: What can I do? What do you want me to do? I can help . . .
MARY: George, I think we have everything under— *('control')*
HANNAH: Let him do something. He wants to.
GEORGE: I'm not helpless in the kitchen.
JOYCE: Help your wife. With your 'picnic.'
GEORGE: I don't want to get in her way.
JOYCE *(Joking)*: That's always a good excuse . . .
HANNAH: Ignore your sister. *(Producing a large index card with a recipe)* Here . . . Help with this. Okay?
KARIN *(To Mary)*: 'Okay.' 'Old Kinderhook . . .' 'Rhinebeck.'
GEORGE *(Taking the card)*: Her guacamole.
JOYCE *(Grabbing the index card from George)*: Guacamole. You're really going to trust him with that?
MARY *(Defending him)*: He cooks.
JOYCE *(Giving him back the index card)*: Follow this, George. Ask if you have questions. It's not a crime to ask questions . . .

MARY *(Again)*: He cooks, Joyce.

(George reads the recipe.)

KARIN *(To Joyce)*: What were you saying? About opera singers . . .

(George looks over the table, seeing what ingredients for his guacamole are already out.)

HANNAH: He's fine, Joyce.
KARIN: About your opera in London . . .
JOYCE *(Continuing)*: The singers' corsets, Karin . . . I really thought we were going to get big resistance to them.
KARIN: Because of the . . . *('chest')*
JOYCE *(Over this)*: But they took to the corsets like . . . No problem.
KARIN: Did they think it helped their singing?
MARY *(Giving Karin the word)*: The diaphragm?
JOYCE *(To Karin)*: I thought maybe that. But the costume-shop head, she's been at the ENO like forever . . . I happened to say how I'd been worried about the corsets. After all, they must be terribly uncomfortable. 'So?' she said. 'How comfortable are your high heels, Joyce? And the hours spent putting on your makeup? It's sexy. It's fun. Makes you feel—different. Like you're ready for something . . .'
KARIN: It can feel like that. She's right. *(To the others)* Can't it?
GEORGE: Mary, you keep the vegetables . . . *('out in the mud-room')*
MARY: In the mudroom.

(He heads for the mudroom.)

JOYCE: You want help? Ask . . .

(He is gone.)

MARY *(To Hannah)*: He'll find what he needs.

KARIN *(To Joyce)*: It does sometimes make me feel like that. Mary?

MARY: What? Sure.

JOYCE: She said: 'I'll tell you something that will surprise you. Did you know that *tight-lacing* of corsets—' *(Explains)* That's where you really pull—

KARIN: I guessed that. I know that.

HANNAH *(To Mary)*: You want to show him what you want him to use?

MARY: He's fine . . .

(Hannah will join the women, and work on the vegetable marinade.)

JOYCE *(Continues)*: 'Women who did that, they were seen by men as *fast* girls . . .' *(Explains)* As women 'asserting' themselves. Wanting to be 'educated.' 'Meddlers' they were called.

HANNAH: Really? 'Who do they think they are?'

JOYCE: They were women wanting to 'show off.' Their power.

KARIN: Heels do that. I know that. *(To Mary and Hannah)* Am I the only one . . . ?

MARY: No, no.

HANNAH *(Same time)*: No.

JOYCE: So a lot of the people—the men—who were against corsets, they tried to say their 'movement' was about 'freeing' women from these 'terrible bonds.' That was bullshit, she said. They were just a bunch of conservative men afraid of women.

(George returns with a few avocados, a couple of tomatoes, etc. He will find a knife, a bowl, etc.)

They encouraged women to wear nice loose dresses that wouldn't call attention to what's underneath . . .

KARIN: The simple loose dress.

MARY: Hear that, Hannah?

JOYCE: What?

HANNAH: Shut up.

MARY: She's always looking for that simple loose dress; that she can wear to a fancy party, and can also garden in. I keep telling her *(To Hannah)* there—is—no—such—dress.

(Hannah holds out a knife to George.)

GEORGE: I like this one . . . *(The knife he has)*

JOYCE *(Continues)*: These men spread rumors about women in their corsets—how in order to wear them so tight they'd had their ribs removed. There are newspaper articles that say that. See—these men tried to turn them into freaks. *(To Hannah, what to have with the hummus)* With crudités?

HANNAH: I've got chips.

KARIN: This is interesting . . . *(To Mary and Hannah)* You've heard all this?

HANNAH: She's told us about her trip, moment by moment by moment . . . *(Looks to Mary)*

JOYCE: Karin asked. If I'm boring you—

KARIN *(Over this)*: I'm interested. I'm an actress.

HANNAH *(Over this)*: One woman, Karin . . . *(To Joyce)* You told us this . . . She got into the Guinness book of records—

JOYCE: She had a thirteen-inch waist. That's like this. *(Demonstrates)* This was in the fifties.

KARIN: That's anorexia. That's not power.

JOYCE *(Still demonstrating)*: Like this!

MARY: I had patients with anorexia. My daughter went through that.

(George will get ingredients in the refrigerator, the cabinet.)

HANNAH: You never talk about your daughter. I didn't know that.

MARY: Thank god she got over that . . . It was awful. My ex had no idea how to deal with her. One of the few times he actually called me for advice. Someone very wise had told me years before, the anorexic, she—

KARIN: Is it only girls?

MARY: It can be boys. But way more girls. The anorexic, she is just trying to move some psychological '*stress*'—into a physical stress, because *that* she thinks she can bear. Because it's physical.

(They work. Then:)

JOYCE *(Continues)*: This woman in the costume shop, she gave me this complicated 'explanation' about how clothes and sexual desire are inseparable.

HANNAH: I think she was trying to pick you up.

KARIN *(Smiling)*: Oh I agree, Joyce.

JOYCE: Maybe.

HANNAH *(To Mary)*: She was trying to pick her up.

JOYCE *(Over this)*: That sexual desire with a man, she said, there's obviously a pursuit toward a single-minded goal, a happy 'release' . . .

GEORGE *(Without looking up)*: Sounds about right.

JOYCE: And collapse, and then . . . from zero again.

KARIN: Boy is that true.

JOYCE: But with a woman—I can see her telling me this smoking her third cigarette in a row—

MARY: You can smoke in—?

JOYCE: We were in an alley alongside the ENO. But with a woman, it's all entwined with what she is 'thinking.' It's blended together, so *potentially* there's this desire that is always 'on tap.'

HANNAH *(To Mary)*: 'On tap.'

JOYCE: And that desire is what we clothe.

HANNAH *(To George, peeling avocados)*: You're doing great.

GEORGE: I know.

JOYCE *(To the others, an endearment, about George)*: 'Our cookerer . . .' Helping out 'the women . . .'

HANNAH: Ignore your sister.

GEORGE *(Chops, as if he didn't hear)*: What?

JOYCE *(Continuing)*: She said women instinctively know this.

KARIN: That the desire is always on tap.

JOYCE: We see the world through this lens. And that's why women make such damn good costume designers.

HANNAH: She was flattering you. Did she know you were only the associate designer?

JOYCE: She knew.

KARIN *(Over this)*: I see what she's saying. The best costume designers are women, I think. That's been my experience.

JOYCE: Every piece of clothing can *mean* something. As designers, we try to control or determine this meaning. What's trying to be said. Or better, what we're trying to hide.

KARIN: What the character is trying to hide? Is that what you mean?

JOYCE: I think so.

MARY: I don't think I understand.

JOYCE: Mary, let's say you're cast in a play.

HANNAH: Oh I'd like to see that.

MARY: Be quiet.

JOYCE *(Over this)*: And I'm costuming you. So I study the character you're to play. First, what does she want to hide? That's always a good place to begin. And, then I look to you, Mary the person, and ask the same thing. What are you hiding?

MARY: You mean what I don't like about myself?

KARIN: That's part of it, of course.

HANNAH: You're a fucking costume associate, not a psychiatrist.

JOYCE *(To Karin)*: Is there much difference?

KARIN: Sometimes there really isn't.

JOYCE: Follow me around for a day, Hannah. Go with my boss to a fitting. When she gets going: it's transfixing.

KARIN: The really good ones are like that, Hannah.

JOYCE *(Over this; lists)*: The actor is trying to get her to notice what the actor wants her to notice. *And* also not notice.

What the actor wants to hide, about herself. What's underneath. My boss said the other day, it's like pulling up a mat or rug that's been outside, and suddenly there's all this life underneath. So much that we never see. Instead, we seem to live our lives painting everything in these broad, obvious brushstrokes. Everyone is either this, or that. The 'lawyer,' she wears a suit. The 'jock,' she is in shorts. But people are much more than that, she said. And so of course—much more interesting . . . *(Shrugs)* She can drive me crazy at times—

KARIN: I should show Joyce what I was reading to you this morning . . . People are more than what they want us to see.

HANNAH: What?

KARIN: Edith . . .

HANNAH: Oh you should get that—

MARY: Get it. Get it.

GEORGE: What?

(Karin, standing up, wiping her hands on her apron, to Joyce:)

KARIN: You're sure?

JOYCE: What are you talking about?

HANNAH: This is really hidden.

KARIN: I've been working on a one-woman show, Joyce . . .

MARY *(Over this)*: Just get it.

KARIN: I left it in the living room . . .

MARY: I saw it next to the TV . . .

(As Karin heads off.)

And check on Patricia.

JOYCE *(Over this)*: Edith?

MARY: You'll see . . . It's a surprise.

HANNAH *(To Joyce)*: I agree, people are more than what they want us to see.

JOYCE: I saw a show about fans in Paris. How there were codes and hidden meanings. An entire language of fans. The eighteenth century.

MARY: A language . . . ?

JOYCE: There were fans that on one side had, say, an idyllic rural scene, fauna; and on the other—a naked couple copulating. Completely pornographic.

HANNAH: And . . . ?

JOYCE: So the woman fanning herself, if she were interested, would simply flip the fan, for an instant, showing the man the other side . . . And then he'd know . . .

(Karin returns with the book.)

KARIN: George, your mother can't get the television to work . . .

(He starts to get up.)

GEORGE: I'm coming, Mom. I'll help you . . .

HANNAH: You need to use both channel changers. First the big one then the little. It took me forever to learn that.

GEORGE *(Goes to the sink to wash his hands)*: The order doesn't matter, Hannah.

(They see Patricia entering from living room.)

HANNAH: I thought it did.

PATRICIA: I don't want to watch TV. *(With the notebooks)* Here . . . Mary, his handwriting gets hard to read.

MARY: That happened, Patricia. I know. I know. I got used to it. I can read some things to you.

PATRICIA: What can I do?

MARY: The casserole's already in the oven, Patricia. I think we have everything under control. Hannah, do you need more help with the picnic?

HANNAH: I think I'm fine, Patricia.

MARY: You found the book?

KARIN *(Holding up the book; about Patricia)*: Is this all right for Pat to . . . ?

GEORGE: Sit down with me, Mom. You can watch me make guacamole . . .

PATRICIA: It that an interesting thing to watch?

HANNAH: Join us, Patricia. Let me clear some space . . . Joyce has been telling us more about her trip to Europe.

PATRICIA: I'd like to hear more about that, Joyce . . .

(She has sat at the table.)

JOYCE: What's to tell? And Karin was just about to read us something . . .

KARIN: We don't have to do that.

JOYCE: What are you going to read?

KARIN: Mary?

GEORGE: You okay, Mom?

KARIN *(To Mary)*: You sure this is all right?

JOYCE: What? Something from some 'Edith.' Who's Edith?

KARIN *(Showing the cover)*: Edith—Wharton . . .

JOYCE: Mom, you've read her.

PATRICIA: I have.

GEORGE *(Working)*: She lived in Rhinebeck for a while. *(To Patricia, as a joke)* Did you know her, Mom?

(She likes the joke.)

MARY: Hannah?

HANNAH: Karin's going to do this play, Patricia— She's an actress.

PATRICIA: I know.

HANNAH *(Over this)*: It's a little risqué.

JOYCE: I'm interested.

KARIN: Mary? *(Mary shrugs)* Well, you see photos of Wharton—fur collar, prim, big hat. The picture of a proper lady. With all emotions—pretty much kept at their proper distance. So that's the woman I was planning on portraying. But then, I was telling Mary and Hannah that I came across this—

MARY: Something she wrote.

HANNAH: We found it funny.

KARIN: —in the back of a biography. Never before published. Probably, they think, left unfinished . . .

(She opens the book.)

I'll just read a little of it . . .

(Hesitates, looks at Mary and Hannah.)

GEORGE *(Confused; to Hannah)*: What?

KARIN: Where should I start . . . ? *(Reads)* "The room was warm and softly lit . . . 'Now my darling,' Mr. Palmato said. She let herself sink backward among the pillows . . . her lips were parted by his tongue. Her nipples as hard as coral, but sensitive as lips to his approaching touch . . . His hand softly separated her legs, and began to slip up the old path it had so often traveled in darkness."

(She looks up, then continues to read:)

"But now it was light, she was uncovered, and looking downward, she could see her own parted knees and outstretched ankles and feet . . . And his hand . . . *(Corrects herself) As* his hand stole higher she felt the bud swelling and burst into bloom. His forefinger pressing it, forcing its petals apart, and laying on their sensitive edges a circular touch . . ."

HANNAH *(To Patricia)*: Are you okay with this?

PATRICIA: Are you?

KARIN: ". . . letting herself downward along the divan," I jumped a little, *(Continues)* "until her head was in line with his middle, she began to caress it, with her tongue. She wound her caresses deeper and deeper into the thick firm folds, until, in a thrice—" That's the only thing that makes it seem old: 'thrice,' "—in a thrice it was withdrawn, her knees pressed apart, and she felt it descend on her and plunge into the depths of her thirsting body . . ." That's probably a good place to stop.

(She closes the book.)

JOYCE: Hannah . . . ?
HANNAH *(To Joyce)*: It was funnier this morning . . .
JOYCE: Mom, you okay?

(Patricia finds reading glasses, reaches for the book from Karin.)

What? *(As a joke)* You think you missed something, Mom? *(Smiles)* Why are you so interested? I'm really surprised.
PATRICIA: Joyce, why wouldn't I be? *(Opens the book)*
KARIN: There's a photo of her, the year she wrote that. It's in the middle of the book. She was nearly fifty. She looks completely different than in any of her other photos. All the stiff stuff around her neck is gone. She shows some cleavage . . . What she'd been hiding inside . . .
JOYCE: Oh Edith.
MARY: When I'd just left med school, and doing my first residency. I still thought I'd end up doing research.
JOYCE: What are you—?
MARY: This relates to that.
HANNAH: You never talk about yourself. She never talks about herself.
PATRICIA *(Looks up from the book)*: I know.
MARY: That's not true. I talk about myself all the time. *(Then)* *To* myself. *(Continuing)* I was good at research. I liked the order of things. You start with x, you do the experiment over and over. It's hard to get lost. I think I was scared of that. Feeling lost.

JOYCE: I understand that.

KARIN: Me too.

HANNAH: Who doesn't understand that?

MARY: There was a senior doctor. A wise man. He said—and no one ever told me this in med school—he said: above all else, Mary, besides paying close attention to your patient. Listen to what is beyond or *behind* what he says. Try and enter into his or her stories, his or her predicaments; and *then* try and be *them*. Get *inside* them. *(Looks up)* We were talking about how you can never know what's inside people . . .

(Then:)

When I first met Thomas—this is now years later—one day I tell him about what this doctor had told me. And how what he had said changed my life and made me understand the *complexity* of being a doctor. *And* the joy. The whole art of observing . . . And I told Thomas about a paper I had even helped write—how doctors can learn so much about their patients, from just watching: the way they walk, stand, sit . . . Thomas said to me, 'Mary, just like theater.'

(The others: "Of course." "Theater!" "What else?')
Then:)

JOYCE: What about *your* license, Mary?

HANNAH: I don't think she has done anything yet.

JOYCE: You're renewing your doctor's license.

HANNAH: After five years, she thinks they'll make her take all the tests again.

JOYCE: You doing that?

HANNAH: Will you do that?

JOYCE: Are you?

MARY: Maybe, Hannah. Maybe. I could be helping. I should never have let it expire. That was stupid of me.

HANNAH: You were taking care of Thomas.
MARY: I know . . . But now?

(Then:)

Talking about watching people, and listening to them . . . Thomas and I once had the great good fortune to meet a very special man, a doctor. I don't think I ever told you this, Hannah.

HANNAH: I didn't know.

MARY: Neurologist. He died last year. God bless him. He'd seen two of Thomas's plays, and he too loved the theater; so he agreed to see us. I thought maybe Thomas's condition about being able to walk to music was fairly unique—it's not. There are plenty of other examples with Parkinson's. But we went to his office in the West Village on Horatio, and spent an hour or so together. *(Incredible)* How *that man watched*. That was art.

(Then:)

When he died, someone wrote about him—that as with all the very greatest doctors, his most essential clinical instrument—was his heart.

(She smiles.)

That day with Thomas, this great man took me aside and told me: when you look at those who suffer, he said, who have taken life's hardest hits . . . Try not to see them as in any way diminished, but rather as our warriors, Mary, our tragic heroes, struggling across the abyss . . .

(The lights fade.)

Thomas

The same; a short time later.

Mary, Joyce and Hannah work on the vegetable marinade and hummus.

George works on his guacamole. Patricia listens.

Karin, having gone back into the box of notebooks and books, now holds another book:

KARIN: *This* book has your name, George, in it . . .

JOYCE: That means nothing in this house. As a kid George wrote his name in everything . . . A really nasty habit, wasn't it, Mom?

GEORGE: I was like six years old, Joyce.

JOYCE *(Working)*: Thomas got so fed up with that—

MARY: I don't think I know this.

HANNAH: I do.

JOYCE: —so Thomas convinced George to write his name in one of Dad's *Penthouse* magazines.

GEORGE: It wasn't funny. It really wasn't.

JOYCE: Not to you.

HANNAH: And that's why Patricia, you started calling . . .

PATRICIA: What?

JOYCE: You still do.

HANNAH *(Over this)*: "Put your 'George' right there . . ." *(To Patricia)* You always say it when you want someone to sign something.

PATRICIA: I do?

MARY *(Over this)*: That's why. I never knew that.

HANNAH: You did it just yesterday, with Mary's birthday card. 'Put your George . . .'

KARIN: That's what that was.

MARY: In my family—there was an uncle who always said things without thinking.

HANNAH: You had just one of those?

MARY *(Over this)*: I'm maybe twelve, and he's visiting my parents, and he comes out of the bathroom and holds up to me—for some reason to me—an empty toilet roll and says, 'Mary? Mary?' And I guess I'm supposed to get for him a new roll of toilet paper. But what everyone else only sees is my uncle holding up this empty, and shouting, 'Mary!' For some reason that was funny. And from that day on an empty toilet roll, in my family, will forever be called 'a Mary.' Thomas loved that story. He even used it in one of his plays. He didn't call her 'Mary.'

KARIN *(With an airmail one-sheet letter in hand)*: Maybe here's something . . . This is interesting. An airmail letter. It's from a painter. Kitaj . . . ?

JOYCE: Who?

KARIN: Isn't he famous?

GEORGE: Kitaj. I know who that is.

MARY *(Over this)*: To Thomas?

KARIN: No, no. Wait. 'Sandra'—she's obviously the wife. And this painter blames her death on his critics, on other artists . . . *(Reads)* "I will always believe that her stroke and death (in one weekend thank god) . . ." *(Skims)* ". . . The personal hatreds towards me . . ." "Savages . . ." "I still break down after six months. And to think she never saw the Met show—"

GEORGE *(To Hannah)*: He had a show at the Met.

KARIN: "—and the Kitaj flag flying there . . ." Do you say it 'Kit-I' or 'Kit-agg?' I've heard both.

GEORGE: I don't know. I know his paintings . . .

JOYCE: I know them too . . .

KARIN *(Reads)*: "The Met! Who could have thought such a thing when we were kids at Cooper?" He's writing to old friends. *(Looks at postmark)* Sent from London. "May 1995."

HANNAH *(To Karin)*: *Where* was this?

KARIN: It was just inside this notebook. In this baggie . . .

MARY *(Taking the baggie)*: He kept his valuable things in these . . .

GEORGE: So Thomas knew it was valuable.

KARIN *(Reads)*: "We sure have our share of tsouris . . ." that's a Yiddish word. *(Skims)* "The whole thing is monstrous . . ." "My life has been hellish . . . Sandra lit up everyone's life with her beauty, both inside and out." "My ten year old Max . . ." So they had a son.

JOYCE *(To George)*: 'Ten years,' Sandra couldn't have been that old.

KARIN *(Reads)*: "When the clouds part, let's have a good cry together, meanwhile, I'd like to be with Sandra . . . wherever she is, but Max needs me, so I've become her as well as me. Love and hugs and kisses, dear, dear friends, ever Kitaj . . ." Or—Kitag.

MARY *(With a newspaper clipping from the bag)*: A clipping about him . . . Looks like from the *Times* . . .

JOYCE: That's the *Times*. Is he still alive? Do we know?

GEORGE: I think he died just a couple of years ago. A very good painter. Maybe a great one . . . May I see?

(Karin hands George the letter.)

MARY: Thomas's handwriting . . . *(Reads, from a note found in the baggie)* "Kitaj letter to good friends. Found inside the Tate catalog of Kitaj/Kitag's show; in a used bookshop slash coffee shop in New Haven."

HANNAH: What do you think it's worth? Karin?

KARIN *(Shrugs)*: I know theater . . .

HANNAH *(To George)*: It must be worth something. Handwritten. He's very well known . . . Like a peek into his broken heart . . . People collect that . . .

MARY: Wait. *(Reads)* "Try to return to the son."

HANNAH: What??

MARY: Thomas wrote that: *(Shows them)* "Try to return to the son . . . Too private and too personal to sell." In caps: "PLEASE DO NOT SELL." *(Shows them)*

(No one knows what to say.)

PATRICIA: We're not going to sell that?
GEORGE: I don't think so, Mom . . .

(Phone is ringing off.)

HANNAH: Phone . . .
MARY: I'll research and see if I can find the son.

(Mary takes the letter and folds it and puts it back in the baggie.)

PATRICIA *(Standing)*: I'll get it . . .
GEORGE: Mom.
HANNAH: George . . .
PATRICIA: I will get it; it's my house . . .

(Patricia moves slowly.)

GEORGE *(Wiping his hands)*: Let me come with you, Mom . . .
PATRICIA: I don't need help.
HANNAH: George . . .
GEORGE: Let me just get past you, Mom, and get the phone . . .

(He hurries past her to get the phone; Patricia follows.)

KARIN: I told Thomas he should put this in a play. One year I was watching the Tony Awards with Thomas.
MARY: Where—?
KARIN: In Brooklyn. This is sort of the same thing. Like 'Mary' the toilet roll. We had a mouse problem. So Thomas set a few traps under the sink. We're watching the Tonys,

and—what's the name of that show?—where he's singing, 'I am what I am'? Anyway, right at the climax of the song; the guy's singing full out: 'I am what I am!'

(Piano music off; Bach aria, played haltingly.)

We hear, under the sink: snap. Then—flap. Flap . . . Then . . . flap . . . Whenever I hear that song—that's what I hear—flap.

(George returns.)

GEORGE: It's the opera singer from Bard. She wants to come—
MARY *(Suddenly)*: Who's playing the piano?!
GEORGE: What??
HANNAH *(Concerned)*: Mary—
MARY: Who's playing the goddamn piano, George? If you're not.

(No one knows what to say, then hearing herself:)

(To herself) Shit. Fuck . . .
HANNAH: Mary . . . ?
GEORGE *(Confused)*: Mom. Mom's playing. *(To Hannah)* What . . . ?
HANNAH *(Explaining)*: She thought it was Thomas. She's been doing that.
MARY *(To Hannah)*: He used to play this piece to me . . . *(Then to herself)* Shit . . . Shit . . .

(No one knows what to say.)

GEORGE: The opera singer wants to come over and take a look at the piano. She's on her way into Rhinebeck anyway. What do I tell her? I'll tell her she can come. *(Going out)* She asked if it's really a Bechstein . . .

(Piano music continues off.)

HANNAH: Upright . . . Bechstein *upright.* There's a big price difference we learned. But it'll help. *(To Mary)* The singer's eager. *(To Joyce)* Our sign's been up at Bard for like two days . . .

MARY *(Trying to explain)*: It's going through the boxes, Hannah . . .

HANNAH: I know. I know . . .

MARY: Each one you open and it's like . . .

HANNAH: I know. I see that.

(Then:)

JOYCE *(Trying to make a joke)*: I should go and say, 'Mom is that how you're going to play it?' 'Is that how you're going to play it.'

KARIN *(With some of Thomas's notebooks)*: Mary, when I'd go and see one of Thomas's plays, I'd always think: 'Is that me up there on the stage? Is that character me?' Did you do that too?

MARY: I don't know.

HANNAH: You told me you did.

KARIN: 'That character so sounds like me. Like something I'd say . . .' Of course it was in a completely different context—in a play. Spoken by a character . . .

(She puts a notebook back, and will take out another. George enters.)

GEORGE: She'll be here in a little while. She 'wants to see what we got.' 'It's a Bechstein . . .'

HANNAH: Your mother coming back?

(Off, Patricia plays the Bach.)

GEORGE *(Shrugs)*: Let's leave her alone . . .

JOYCE *(Listening)*: We all played this. We all learned to play this . . .

(They listen.)

GEORGE: Yeah . . .

(Then:)

KARIN *(Another book)*: Thomas gave me a copy of this . . . When I visited last fall . . . When Mary so generously invited me up here . . .

MARY: He asked me to ask you . . .

KARIN: Thomas hardly could speak . . . He had a pile of these on his desk in his bedroom. He gave me one. Why did he have so many copies, Mary?

MARY: He was always talking about adapting it into a play.

(The others: "A play." "Theater.")

He was always trying to get someone to pay him to do that.

HANNAH: What's the book?

KARIN: I love the title: *Wandering Star*. Sholem Aleichem.

GEORGE: I don't know it.

KARIN: I've read it now twice . . .

GEORGE: He wanted to make it into a play? What's it about? Let me see . . . *(Takes the book)*

KARIN: Two young people, a boy and a girl. They live in a 'shtetl'; over a hundred years ago. They're Jewish. Their families have plans for them. But the kids are in love. One day a theater company—

JOYCE *(To Mary)*: I knew there had to be a theater somewhere—

(Off, the music stops.)

KARIN *(Over this)*: —of Yiddish actors, singers, comes to town. The kids run away with these actors, but it just so happens that this theater group is fighting amongst itself and so it splits, one half goes off in one direction, the other in another . . . The boy goes off with one, the girl with the other. They are separated. Right at the point when they thought—they'd be together forever . . . Years pass. One is in Germany, the other in Paris, then London; they write letters that never get delivered, their paths never cross. He becomes a star actor; she a great singer. More years go by, until at the peak of their fame, they each learn the other is in New York City. They plan to meet. They meet—at the zoo. Nice touch . . .

(They notice the piano music start up.)

Each now has married, each has children, they have and have had lovers. They both know, without saying anything, that it's too late for them now. The end.

(Then:)

As I was reading the story, you can tell me if you think I'm imaging this, I can imagine things—

HANNAH *(To George)*: May I see?

KARIN: —this book's a celebration of searching for each other; *and* their forgetting each other; a celebration of both their faithfulness *and* their faithlessness. Of their just being human . . .

MARY: Was he able to write anything in your copy, Karin?

KARIN: No. Nothing . . .

(Then:)

JOYCE: Remember when Thomas all of a sudden decided he was Jewish?

GEORGE: Oh god. Don't remind me.

JOYCE: It really bothered you. 'George, I think we're Jewish. I've done the research!' You never knew where he was going next.

HANNAH *(Defending Thomas)*: He was searching—

JOYCE: For what?? 'Thomas, what the hell are you talking about?'

MARY *(To George)*: You got really upset. Why did that upset you?

GEORGE *('I'm not the only one')*: Joyce got upset.

JOYCE: He's telling us what we are . . . He'd just go off half-cocked.

GEORGE: He could just dream things up.

HANNAH: He was a writer.

GEORGE: We're not Jewish.

JOYCE *(Over this)*: No.

MARY: He was only trying to figure something out—

GEORGE: What? Figure out what? He was just being— *(To Hannah)* you know what I mean?

HANNAH: I don't. What?

GEORGE: Romantic.

JOYCE: He's right. You're right.

HANNAH *(Over this)*: Being Jewish is romantic??

GEORGE: That's not what I'm saying.

HANNAH *(Over this)*: Try telling that to someone whose family—

GEORGE: He needed to feel *different*. That's what I'm saying. There's nothing wrong with being Jewish. Come on. *(Mocking, as Thomas)* 'What am I?' 'Who am I?' I really disliked that side of Thomas . . .

JOYCE: Me too. To be honest.

MARY *(Trying to explain)*: The way he explained it to me . . .

(Off, Patricia has stopped playing; no one notices.)

GEORGE: Do we have to talk about this?

HANNAH: Let Mary talk—

GEORGE: Joyce?

MARY: He said—he just couldn't understand where all this—the importance that your father and your mother placed on—on being cultured. Where had *that* come from? That's what he was asking.

GEORGE: 'Jewish people' want to give their kids culture and education. I know, Mary. But that's such a cliché. It's a cliché!

KARIN: I don't know about this.

MARY: Your relatives were farmers.

GEORGE: Why can't farmers—?

HANNAH: Isn't there some truth—?

GEORGE: I have friends who are farmers. They read!

MARY: Thomas wasn't putting down farmers.

GEORGE: I think he was. I live in the country.

HANNAH: So do I.

GEORGE: Well, that's how I took it.

MARY: George, I'm just saying I think Thomas was trying to figure out why he felt so different. Is there something wrong with that?

GEORGE: With feeling that? No. But what about telling us all what *we* should feel or think? Who *we* are? He wasn't just talking about himself.

MARY: Your grandpa was a mechanic for rich people's cars. *(To Karin)* Did Thomas ever tell you that?

KARIN: No.

MARY: I guess he only talked about that later . . .

GEORGE: He was ashamed.

MARY: I don't think so. Maybe. Maybe he was. But then he wasn't. And your grandmother—she was a maid.

HANNAH: For the Astors . . . Just down the road here.

MARY *(Over this)*: And your father was given piano lessons—at something like—

JOYCE: No more than five years old.

MARY: Your grandparents didn't play. *And* the fiddle. Your father played the fiddle. Thomas only wanted to know where that came from. Where the hell he came from.

GEORGE: Mary—

HANNAH: Let her talk.

MARY *(Another point)*: At the Jewish Museum in Manhattan—Hannah, I don't think we ever told you this. Thomas and

I were there once: and came across a plaque, I think it comes from Austria—

JOYCE *(To Karin)*: Our relatives came from there.

MARY: —listing Jewish soldiers from one village who had died in World War One. One name: Gabrielski.

GEORGE: What does that—?

MARY: I know that proves nothing. Thomas knew that.

KARIN *(Trying to keep up, over this)*: This is all new to me. Where in Austria?

JOYCE: Thomas dragged Mary to the 'ancestral' village.

MARY *(Over the end of this)*: That was wife number two, Joyce. This was before me. I didn't go. *(To Karin)* They made her wear a dirndl, Karin. I saw a picture . . . *(Smiles; then to George)* 'Where do I come from?' 'Where do I fit in?' 'Each day, why do I feel more and more different?'

(Then:)

I don't think that deserves to be mocked . . .

JOYCE: I don't think George is mocking the questioning, Mary. *(To George)* Are you?

GEORGE: No.

JOYCE: It's the being told what the answers are, Mary. Our big brother was always telling us what to do. What everyone had to read. What we had to read. What TV show— 'Quick, turn on channel . . .'

MARY: Thomas got excited about things. He wanted to share. For me that was a good thing.

JOYCE *(Over this)*: What hot actor to watch out for.

GEORGE: Who we 'had' to vote for—

MARY: What?

JOYCE: George and I were just talking about this on the phone last week. You probably don't even know this.

GEORGE: 'Obama, George . . .'

MARY: What are you talking about?

JOYCE: Just one example, Mary.

GEORGE: One day Thomas comes 'home'—

JOYCE: Like eight years ago. So he's not sick yet. I don't think you were here with him.

GEORGE: And, we're here in this kitchen. Joyce is visiting too. And Thomas tells us 'we gotta vote for Hillary.' The first woman blah blah blah.

JOYCE: 'It's so exciting.'

MARY: I remember him saying that.

GEORGE *(Over this)*: 'I've heard her speak in person.' He gets us excited.

JOYCE: Mom starts shouting: 'Where's the bell? Get out the bell.'

KARIN *(Over this)*: What? I don't understand.

JOYCE: Where is the bell?

HANNAH *(Over this)*: When the Gabriels start talking politics, Karin—

JOYCE: Mom has this little bell, you can ring the bell for—

HANNAH: For 'time out.'

JOYCE: Mary, where is it? It used to be in the kitchen.

MARY: It broke. The little clang-er broke.

HANNAH: During the conventions.

MARY: We had to throw it out, Joyce.

GEORGE: Anyway, two months later—Thomas is on the phone: *(Excited voice)* 'Forget Hillary, it's Obama! Oh my god have you been watching this guy? His speeches . . .' 'What about Hillary—?' I ask. 'No, don't be stupid, George. Obama: the first black blah blah blah. I thought I'd never live to see the day.'

MARY: I don't see why it's wrong, George, to keep asking: Who you are. Can't he ask that?

GEORGE: Well, he's not here to ask anymore, Mary.

(Then:)

MARY: No. No. He isn't.

(Doorbell off.)

And thank you for reminding us, George.
(Standing) That's the singer . . .

JOYCE: That was quick.

HANNAH *(To George)*: Shouldn't you be the one—?

MARY *(Wiping her hands)*: I'll go. I'll get it before Patricia scares her off . . .

(She starts to go.)

JOYCE: Don't let her do that. Please . . .

HANNAH *(Same time)*: George, go . . . Go . . . Let George, Mary. Please.

(This stops Mary. George gets up.)

Remember you like people to like you. That's not good . . .

(As he goes.)

Don't give it away . . . He's getting tougher. *(To Mary)* He'll do fine . . .

(Short pause.)

JOYCE: She came right away. She must be interested.

MARY: Must be.

HANNAH: Probably coming into the village anyway. Sounded like that. She's just checking it out . . .

MARY: Patricia going to stay in there? . . .

(Hannah shrugs.)

'Where do we fit in?' 'Where do we belong?' Thomas was just asking that. 'Why do I feel like a stranger in my own country?'

JOYCE: I remember Thomas saying that right here at this kitchen table. I think I know what he meant.

MARY *(To Hannah)*: You sure you don't want to be in there with him?

HANNAH: He's fine. I think he's going to be fine.

JOYCE: Think what Thomas would be feeling now, Mary . . .

MARY: Oh god. I don't even want to think about that. So maybe it's for the best, Joyce . . .

HANNAH: Mary, this morning—I think Thomas would have liked this. His warped sense of humor.

MARY: What? It wasn't that 'warped'—

HANNAH: George was talking to one of the weekenders that he does work for. A Democrat. When did the rich people become Democrats?

KARIN: I don't know.

HANNAH: How did that happen?

MARY: It just did.

HANNAH: For some reason George tells the guy about his mom and his problems. The mortgage. I don't know what he was expecting. But this guy just looks at George, looks him up and down, at his jeans that are stained, his dirty hands, and says, 'I hope, George, you're now not going to vote for—*him*.'

JOYCE: You're kidding.

KARIN *(Same)*: Trump?

HANNAH: That's what he said. George was just looking for a little sympathy. That's what he got instead . . .

JOYCE: People are scared. Everyone I know is scared.

MARY: So what did George say back?

HANNAH: The guy hadn't paid him yet. So nothing . . .

(Off, someone is playing various riffs or scales on the piano.)

JOYCE: She's trying it out.

(As they listen:)

It sounds good.

MARY: George got it tuned today.

JOYCE: Hannah said.

(Then:)

HANNAH: I wish I could just talk with him right now, Mary.

MARY: Thomas? Me too. He'd just let me rant. He always just let me rant . . . Now you just find yourself ranting along with everybody else and no one's listening. Thomas listened.

HANNAH: There's no news anymore, what happened to news? It's all screaming. It has just fucked up everything. Everybody I know seems fucked up by it. I'd like to talk about that with Thomas.

KARIN: The election?

HANNAH *(Over this)*: And it just makes me feel dirty, Mary.

MARY: I understand that.

HANNAH: Filthy. Like you just want to shower it off. That's what I feel.

MARY: 'Who are we?' I think we all should be asking that. 'Is this really our country?' Thomas was always asking that.

(Then:)

JOYCE: When I was serving the billionaires last night—you know, that's why my boss wanted us there, just to serve. I'd stand right next to some rich person, holding my tray. They don't look at you.

HANNAH: That's the job, Joyce. Welcome to my life.

JOYCE: And I overhear a woman say and this is a quote: "These days, Tony, I'm only reading things that I agree with."

MARY: Oh listen, I hear Thomas laughing . . .

(Scales have stopped.)

JOYCE: Maybe they're talking business.

(Scales start again.)

No . . .

KARIN: There's a teacher at my school who says she's pulled out the cable from her TV. Just yanked it out and used pliers to snap off that little metal pin inside. She did that, she said, in case she ever got tempted again.

JOYCE: Soon they debate. We should watch that. Shouldn't we? The debate?

(They think about this, then:)

HANNAH: 'Hillary, please be human.' Please.

JOYCE: *He* won't be human.

MARY: She's not—? *('human')*

HANNAH: Paulie doesn't think so.

KARIN: Getting sick is human . . .

HANNAH: And Paulie isn't alone.

(Then:)

JOYCE: Everyone last night at the party was talking about her 'coming back on the campaign trail.' How 'she's looking great.' She's going to be on Jimmy Fallon too. On Monday.

MARY: Too?

JOYCE: He was on last night . . .

HANNAH: You think she'll be human on Jimmy Fallon?

JOYCE: He wasn't.

HANNAH: He let Fallon rub his hair.

JOYCE: That's now the criteria for being human?

MARY *(Over the end of this; to Hannah)*: You watched Jimmy Fallon?

HANNAH *(Over this)*: I woke up. I couldn't sleep . . .

(Then:)

A friend of mine in the village. She owns a little dress shop.

MARY: I know who you mean.

HANNAH *(To Joyce)*: You don't know her. I don't know how she makes a living. *(To Mary)* Do you?

MARY: No.

JOYCE *(About the piano)*: When are they going to talk business? . . .

MARY: She hasn't left.

HANNAH *(Continues)*: There's nothing fancy in her store. Very basic stuff. Nothing special for the rich weekender—no exotic olive oils—

MARY: No five-dollar pieces of chocolate that are this big. *(Very small)* Five dollars.

HANNAH: No funny kids' T-shirts: 'London. Paris. Rhinebeck.' Just normal, real, human stuff. Anyway, whenever we run into each other now, and I just thought of this—she always says the same thing, and always with a smile: 'Hannah,' she says, 'what about us?' Thomas used to say that. 'What about us?'

KARIN: Did he?

JOYCE: I can hear his voice. 'What about us?'

MARY: What I hear is him always being hopeful.

JOYCE: What do you mean?

MARY: Thomas was always looking for something hopeful . . .

JOYCE: Hence—Obama . . .

MARY: For about five minutes, Joyce. *(To Hannah)* Anyway that's one thing I remember about my husband.

HANNAH: That's a gift. I wish I had it.

KARIN: Me too.

JOYCE: Me too.

MARY: 'Things will get better, Mary. You'll see things get better.'

(Then:)

Some days when I was tired, after a long day, I'd come home and he'd take one look at me and say: 'Mary, things get better.' I never said back what I was thinking: 'But, Thomas, can't things sometimes get worse?'

(The lights fade.)

What Did You Expect?

The same, a short time later.

The women wait.

Short pause. Joyce washes her hands. Mary works on her marinade. Then: off, someone has begun to play Bach's "Aria" on the piano.

HANNAH: I think that's George, he's showing off to the opera singer. That's not a good sign. You think I should—?

MARY: I do. I really do.

JOYCE: Me too. Go, Hannah. Go. Go . . . Hurry . . .

HANNAH: He'll want her to know he's a musician too . . .

(Hannah hurries off.)

JOYCE: What are we asking? Did George have it appraised?

MARY: We looked online. *(Shrugs)* It's an upright. Five thousand? It'll help. Fingers crossed.

JOYCE: Think of all the cans of Coke we spilled on that piano . . . I nearly broke my ankle on its leg . . . Thomas was chasing me. *(Another)* Once, Mary, Thomas climbed up and on it and sang "Kookie, Kookie, Lend Me Your Comb." Then he fell off. Mom and Dad were out somewhere . . . They never knew . . . Dad did the pedals for me, when I started, I sat on his lap. I did the keys, the ones I could reach . . .

(Off, the music has stopped. They all notice this.)

MARY: One of the notebooks Karin and I were looking through last night—about a show Thomas was writing . . . It's about a piano. A player piano. Set in Russia. He loved everything Russian.

JOYCE: Oh he did.

KARIN: I know.

MARY: There's a party, and the piano, all on its own, starts playing tunes everyone knows. How does it do it? How does it know? *(Shrugs)* But there's such a wave of 'comfort'—everyone at the party feels it; being accompanied, I think . . .

JOYCE: I was driving back from Tanglewood with Thomas. I was really young. He'd taken me to some piano concert. We'd just gotten off the Taconic. And we see, on a parallel road, a house on fire. We see the frame of the house through the flames. Everything else is quiet, but the house is totally engulfed. We stopped and watched for a while. Driving here from Hudson I suddenly remembered that . . .

(Hannah and Patricia enter.)

MARY: Dinner should be ready.

HANNAH: She's gone. George went down a thousand. Karin, will you please find something else to sell? Now!

MARY: Karin, Hannah was joking. We're doing our best.

(Karin starts to go back to the boxes.)

HANNAH: She told him there's a Bechstein upright for sale in Hudson.

JOYCE: She was negotiating . . .

HANNAH: So he went down a thousand. And she wrote a check . . .

(This sinks in. Then:)

I wonder how much it's really worth . . . *(To Joyce)* You okay?

(Timer goes off.)

MARY: Dinner's ready . . .
JOYCE: We heard you playing, Mom. I can't remember the last time I heard you play.
MARY: You all right, Patricia?
JOYCE *(Smiling)*: I was going to come in and say, 'Is that how you're going to play it? Is that how you're going to play it?'
PATRICIA: I don't understand, Joyce.
MARY: It's a joke, Patricia.
PATRICIA: I see . . .

(Off, George is playing Bach's Goldberg Variation Number 1. *They notice this.)*

JOYCE: I'll put away the rest of this picnic stuff, Hannah. Put some of it in the fridge?
PATRICIA *(To Joyce)*: She kept pointing out: 'Look at that chip on that leg. Look at that scratch.'
HANNAH *(Again)*: She was negotiating.
JOYCE: We've played on it . . . We were kids. What do you expect?
MARY *(To Hannah)*: He did okay . . . Dinner's ready, Patricia.
PATRICIA: What can I do?
MARY: We'll eat in the dining room?
PATRICIA: I hope so.
JOYCE: Where else? *(Handing her the guacamole in the Tupperware)* Here, you can put a top on this, Mom . . . Be careful. Don't spill it. George worked very hard on that . . .

MARY: Sometimes when Patricia visits we eat in the living room. The TV's there . . .

JOYCE: And watch the news? Not while I'm eating. Not now.

MARY: I can't get the story of the house on fire out of my head.

KARIN: I think George did a really nice job with the guacamole. Very nice . . .

MARY: Doesn't surprise me.

HANNAH: Me neither.

JOYCE *(Getting the silverware out of the table drawer)*: Excuse me, Mom.

(Off, in mid-phrase, the music has suddenly stopped; they all notice this.)

HANNAH *(Answering Mary's look)*: He's fine . . .

KARIN: What's George going to give his lessons on, now that the piano's sold?

MARY: He can go to his students' homes. Most of them have keyboards . . . *(To Hannah)* Right?

HANNAH: We still have 'our crap' piano. That's what he calls it. He can use that with the youngest kids. They don't know the difference.

(Patricia is having trouble with the Tupperware top.)

Let me help you with that, Patricia . . .

(Off, from the piano, Bach's Minuet in G Major. *This stops the others.)*

KARIN: What?

JOYCE *(Listening intently)*: That's pretty much the first thing any of us ever learned to play on the piano, Karin. On that piano. Right, Mom? Dad taught Thomas. Thomas taught George. George taught me . . .

HANNAH *(To Mary)*: Bread and butter?

MARY: There's a new loaf in the pantry . . . *(About the music)* Thomas once tried to teach me this . . . He said he can teach anyone to play this . . . Well he met his match . . . *(Smiles)*

(Hannah goes off and gets the bread.)

(To Patricia) You're wearing the scarf Joyce bought you in Paris. I recognize it.

PATRICIA: I am.

MARY: That's very thoughtful. I'm sure Joyce appreciates that.

JOYCE: I put it on you. I found it in the bottom of your drawer.

MARY: A scarf from Paris, Patricia. It's nice that you're wearing that. To have that.

HANNAH *(Returning with the bread, having heard the end of this)*: "Paris." I'm lucky if I get to Kingston. Bread Alone?

MARY: Tops Friendly.

JOYCE: What's that?

MARY: They ate up the Rhinebeck Stop&Shop.

JOYCE *(As she picks up)*: Oh, Hannah, I just remembered, I meant to tell George . . .

HANNAH: What?

JOYCE: In Paris—

MARY *(To Hannah)*: "Paris."

JOYCE: —near the Place de la Concorde. There's the 'Avenue—Gabriel.' It goes right past our ambassador's residence . . . I liked that it does. I don't know why.

HANNAH: Maybe we'd belong there.

(No one knows what to say. Then:)

JOYCE: And another thing I saw in Paris. An advertisement in the Metro: 'Learn Wall Street English.'

HANNAH: What the hell is that?

JOYCE: "Wall Street English." And there was a picture of this guy—screaming. Just screaming. Like this: *(She demonstrates)* It was really scary . . .

MARY *(To Joyce)*: At my birthday dinner, Patricia told us about this TV commercial she saw . . .

JOYCE: What commercial?

MARY: This politician, who was an actor.

KARIN: You said last night he actually was a senator.

JOYCE: You were at the birthday party?

MARY: It wasn't a party.

KARIN: I was. And he even ran for president.

MARY: You said he had such an honest face, Patricia.

PATRICIA: He had an honest face.

MARY: He was advertising mortgages on TV. "Spend down your home . . ." That's where she said she got the idea . . . He had a sexy voice . . . And an honest face . . .

KARIN: I can set the table, Mary. Pat, would you like to help me?

PATRICIA: He did have an honest face.

KARIN: I'm sure.

HANNAH: Why don't you take the bread and butter, Patricia? You're not going to get away with doing nothing . . .

(She hands Patricia the bread and butter.)

PATRICIA: I want to help.

MARY: She's teasing you. She's trying to be a Gabriel.

KARIN: You can help me, Pat. Mary, tablecloth or placemats?

MARY: Placemats. Tonight's nothing special.

PATRICIA: And you can't stay the night, Joyce?

JOYCE: I can't, Mom . . . I'm sorry. I can't.

PATRICIA *(As they go, to Karin)*: You're staying . . .

KARIN: I am. Pat, I live here now . . .

(Patricia and Karin go off to the dining room. Off, the music stops. They notice.)

HANNAH *(To Joyce)*: I can take some picnic stuff to our house.

MARY: There's also a cold cucumber soup. We just had it on Wednesday. Let's bring that out too. George liked it. *(Then)* He stopped.

HANNAH: Then we'll need soup bowls. And soup spoons . . .

(Then:)

I'll go get George . . . *(As she heads off)* I don't think he thought it would sell so fast . . .

(She is gone.)

JOYCE: I'll take in the wine, Mary . . .
MARY: What about your nice wine?
JOYCE: I think we drank that up.

(She takes a bottle of wine out of the refrigerator.)

I haven't told you this, Mary—what Mom said right in front of her roommate . . . Mom said she'd never imagined she'd end up like this. In a room that wasn't her own. And now they even want to kick her out of that. The roommate's right there. I bit my tongue— You're eighty-two years old, Mom, you spent all your money without telling us—

(Patricia comes from the dining room, unseen by Joyce.)

—what the hell did you expect?

(Joyce sees her mother.)

KARIN *(Entering from the dining room)*: Pat would rather we put on a tablecloth. Okay?
MARY: Whatever she wants. It's her house . . .

(Karin heads off.)

PATRICIA: What else can I do?

MARY: I think we have it all under control, Patricia.

(As Hannah enters.)

JOYCE: Where's George?

(George is behind Hannah.)

GEORGE: I'm here.
MARY *(To Patricia)*: I'll bet Karin needs help with the tablecloth.

(Patricia heads off to the dining room.)

JOYCE: I've got the vegetables, Mary . . . *(To Mary, as she goes)* Did she hear me? . . .
HANNAH *(Calls)*: Get out the soup bowls, Joyce . . .
GEORGE: What can I do?
HANNAH: He can take the soup. We had it on Wednesday. *(To George)* Mary says you liked it . . .

(As Mary takes the soup out of the refrigerator.)

MARY: You okay, George?
GEORGE *(Nods, then)*: And you?

(She nods as she hands him the soup.)

HANNAH: Mary said she used to make this same casserole for Thomas every Sunday night too. A Gabriel tradition . . .
GEORGE: But it's Friday . . .

(George goes off with the soup. Hannah hesitates.)

MARY: He did good. He did . . .

(Then:)

(At "Thomas"): "Things get better."

(Mary smiles. Hannah starts to go.)

I'll be right there . . .

(Hannah is gone.

Mary looks around the room. She looks at the boxes of Thomas's stuff. She fusses with the casserole.

Then:)

(To "Thomas," what she has said a thousand times before): 'Thomas, dinner's ready . . .'

(She hesitates. Then as she goes to put away some Tupperware in the refrigerator, we hear Lucius's "Don't Just Sit There" from the theater speakers.

Mary washes her hands, dries them, takes a quick taste of the casserole, and after one more look around the kitchen, she heads off to the dining room to join the others.

Blackout.)

END OF PLAY

WOMEN OF A CERTAIN AGE

For Oskar

PRODUCTION HISTORY

Women of a Certain Age was commissioned by and first produced at The Public Theater (Oskar Eustis, Artistic Director; Patrick Willingham, Executive Director) in New York City on November 4, 2016. The director was Richard Nelson; the set design was by Susan Hilferty and Jason Ardizzone-West, the costume design was by Susan Hilferty, the lighting design was by Jennifer Tipton, the sound design was by Scott Lehrer and Will Pickens; the production stage manager was Theresa Flanagan, the stage manager was Jared Oberholtzer. The cast was:

MARY GABRIEL	Maryann Plunkett
PATRICIA GABRIEL	Roberta Maxwell
GEORGE GABRIEL	Jay O. Sanders
HANNAH GABRIEL	Lynn Hawley
JOYCE GABRIEL	Amy Warren
KARIN GABRIEL	Meg Gibson

In December 2016, the complete series of *The Gabriels* was presented at The Public Theater with rotating repertory.

CHARACTERS

THOMAS GABRIEL, a playwright and novelist, died one year ago, at the age of sixty-four.

MARY GABRIEL, Thomas's third wife, and widow, a retired doctor, sixty-one.

PATRICIA GABRIEL, Thomas's mother, eighty-two.

GEORGE GABRIEL, Thomas's brother, a piano teacher and cabinet-maker, sixty-two.

HANNAH GABRIEL, George's wife, and Thomas's sister-in-law, works odd jobs, fifties.

JOYCE GABRIEL, Thomas's sister, an associate costume designer, fifties.

KARIN GABRIEL, Thomas's first wife, an actress and now teacher, fifties.

TIME

Election Day. Tuesday, November 8, 2016. 5:00 P.M.–7:00 P.M.

SETTING

The kitchen of the Gabriels' house, South Street, Rhinebeck, New York.

PUNCTUATION

Double quotation marks are used when someone is reading from something or directly quoting. Single quotation marks are used when someone is paraphrasing or generalizing.

. . . and something went—wiggle-wiggle.

—Anton Chekhov, The Cherry Orchard
(1903 version)

An empty room: the kitchen of the Gabriels' house. South Street, Rhinebeck, New York.

Refrigerator, stove/oven (electric), sink; large wooden and rustic table used as a kitchen counter (with a drawer for silverware) is set beside another smaller table making an L-shape; a bench with a back is to one side, facing the tables (on the bench, a small basketful of correspondence, bills, and small notebooks); a beaten-up armchair; upstage a small cupboard. Chairs and a bench are set upside down on the tables.

Exits: upstage to the unseen dining room; down left to the mudroom, back porch and backyard; down right leads to the rest of the house—living room, the stairs to the bedrooms on the second floor, and to the front porch.

In the dark, Lucius's "Until We Get There" plays through the theater's main speakers.

Mary, Hannah, Joyce, Karin and George enter with trays full of kitchen objects. They will create the 'life of the kitchen,' which includes a box of old children's books and magazines.

Patricia carries in a folded wheelchair, which she sets upstage by the sink. Though the character Patricia is partially paralyzed by a recent stroke, during the setup she walks in and takes her seat.

George leaves.

The lights change, the music fades.

Five Women

The women sit around the table; Karin peels potatoes. Hannah has just finished mixing cookie dough. She and Mary look through the box of old children's books, magazines, etc. Joyce sits looking through a children's cookbook: Betty Crocker's Cook Book for Boys and Girls. *Patricia is the center of the other women's attention.*

These five women have been talking here for a while:

PATRICIA: Who's there?

(All listen toward the mudroom.)

JOYCE: I don't hear anything, Mom. *(Looks to Mary, who shakes her head)*

HANNAH: What do you hear?

PATRICIA: I thought I heard a door close, Hannah.

JOYCE *(To the others)*: I didn't hear anything.

(Neither did the others.)

MARY *(To Joyce)*: I didn't . . .

HANNAH *(Shrugs)*: The wind?

KARIN: I'm sure I closed the door . . .

MARY: Sometimes if it doesn't click . . .

JOYCE *(To Patricia)*: We didn't hear anything, Mom. You want us to check?

MARY: Why don't I go and see . . .

(Mary heads off to the mudroom.)

JOYCE *(Back to the book in hand, to Patricia)*: So how about—a 'Bunny Salad'? Remember us making that?

HANNAH *(Mixing the dough)*: What's a 'Bunny Salad,' Patricia? *(To Joyce)* Show me.

JOYCE *(As she shows Hannah)*: I do remember us making this . . .

HANNAH: Cute.

KARIN: Why is it called a bunny salad?

MARY *(Returning)*: No one's out there, Patricia.

JOYCE: You okay, Mom? No one's out there . . . *(To Karin)* That's half of a sliced pear. See, sort of looks like a bunny lying down . . . *(Shows Karin)*

KARIN: Whose cookbook was this? . . .

JOYCE *(Pointing out where someone has written on the page)*: "George."

PATRICIA: George wrote his name in everything, Joyce. I don't remember a bunny salad.

JOYCE: I do . . . *(Turns the page)* "Candle Salad." I don't think we ever made that, Mom . . .

PATRICIA: I think we did, Joyce.

JOYCE: I don't think so. *(Reading)* "Muffins."

(Off, the phone rings.)

"Applesauce."

HANNAH *(To Mary)*: Phone . . .

(Mary wipes her hands and goes to get it.)

JOYCE: "Cinderella Cake." Too much work, and I don't think we ever made that either. *(Another)* "Choo-Choo Salad . . ."

KARIN: What's that?

JOYCE *(To Patricia)*: So, Mom—who is it?

PATRICIA: What? Who's what, Joyce?

JOYCE: On the phone. Who's calling? You're almost always right.

PATRICIA: What?

HANNAH: You are. *(To Karin)* She is. It's—

PATRICIA: What?

JOYCE *(Over this)*: Your—'amazing gift' . . .

HANNAH: Joyce.

JOYCE: I'm not making fun. Mom, you almost always know just as the phone rings—

PATRICIA: Know what?

JOYCE: Who's calling. You know you can do that, don't you? You know that?

PATRICIA: I know.

JOYCE: Still I've never really tested you. I've wanted to.

PATRICIA: Why do you want to—?

JOYCE: I'm going to test you. Come on, Mom. Tell us. It's all right, Hannah.

HANNAH: I didn't say anything.

JOYCE: So—Mom, who just called?

PATRICIA: It's probably, I think . . .

JOYCE: Who?

PATRICIA: George, isn't it?

JOYCE *(To the others, as fact)*: It's George. I'll bet she's right.

KARIN *(Peeling, over this)*: It could be for me.

PATRICIA: I don't know, Joyce.

JOYCE: Oh you know. I just don't know how you know, but you know. And it's spooky . . .

MARY *(Returning)*: It was George.

JOYCE: Yes! What did I tell you? Mom, you're amazing. You are just amazing.

KARIN *(Same time, to Hannah)*: She was right.

MARY: What—??

HANNAH: Patricia knew who was on the phone.

(Hannah will cover the cookie dough with Saran Wrap and put it in the refrigerator.)

MARY: George got stuck in traffic in Westchester; he just got off the Taconic. He didn't want us to worry. And he says cook whatever we want, he doesn't care.

KARIN: Pat, you really know who's calling—?

JOYCE *(Over this)*: You've always done it. You haven't lost your touch, Mom.

PATRICIA *(To Karin)*: I don't know.

HANNAH *(To Mary)*: And Paulie?

JOYCE *(To Mary)*: Did he say anything about Paulie?

MARY: No . . .

HANNAH *(Looking in Patricia's mug, to Patricia)*: Would you like more coffee? . . .

(Patricia doesn't.)

I sometimes know that it's Paulie calling. I just sense it sometimes.

MARY: You're his mother. Makes sense. That's not uncommon with mothers . . .

HANNAH: I'm not always right. *(About the coffee)* There's still some left. Anyone . . . ?

(No one wants coffee. Hannah will pour herself some.)

JOYCE *(The book)*: Mom, "Raggedy Ann Salad . . ." Can we do this? We have to do this . . .

PATRICIA: What do we need for that?

MARY: Joyce your mother had a very interesting—fascinating—dream just last night . . . *(To Patricia)* It was last night, right? It was last night. *(To Hannah)* We should tell her . . .

HANNAH: We should. *(To Joyce)* It's fascinating.

JOYCE: What dream, Mom?

MARY *(To Patricia)*: You told us about it just this morning. *(To Joyce)* Before you got here. We think she dreamed it last night.

JOYCE: What??

MARY *(To Patricia)*: Remember telling me and Hannah? We came to pick you up to vote. But you were too tired. You remembered so many details. I never remember the details of my dreams . . .

HANNAH: Me neither.

KARIN *(To Hannah, about the peeled potatoes)*: In quarters? . . .

(Hannah nods.)

MARY: All about your new roommate . . .

JOYCE: You have a new roommate, Mom?

PATRICIA: I do.

MARY: You'll meet her.

HANNAH *(Over this)*: Just this week. We've met her. The roommate kept saying, 'I don't belong in assisted living . . .' She wasn't saying this to us. She was just saying it . . .

MARY: In your mom's dream . . . *(To Patricia)* Remember? You described being in your bed—

HANNAH: Your mother's bed is now the one by the window.

JOYCE: Is it?

MARY: And the roommate, she is taking care of you. She's told Patricia that that was now her—the roommate's—job.

JOYCE: To take care of Mom?

HANNAH: Yeah.

MARY: Like she's now Patricia's nurse. When suddenly—in the dream—Patricia has her back to the roommate, and she hears this woman—

HANNAH: Gail.

MARY: 'Gail' say: 'Patty, I'm so sick and tired of taking care of you . . . So why don't you just get it over with, and jump out that window.'

JOYCE *(Quietly)*: What??

MARY: And Patricia turns to her and says . . . ? Remember . . . ?

PATRICIA: I remember.

MARY: You say: "Why are you saying this to me?" The roommate says back, "But I didn't say anything to you, Patty."

PATRICIA: "But I heard you say that to me, Gail."

MARY: "Did you see me say that?" Gail asks. In the dream. 'No. I didn't.' Am I telling it right?

(Patricia nods.)

Your mother hadn't seen her, because of course Gail was behind her. "Then next time, Patty, when you think I'm saying something, turn around and look for me." Patricia rolls over with her back to Gail again, maybe falls asleep?

HANNAH: And then it happens again . . .

(Patricia nods.)

MARY: She hears Gail say: "Patty, just kill yourself." Your mom wants to explain that because of the stroke she can't get herself out of bed, and so starts to turn around to tell her this, but Gail shouts at her: "Don't look at me. Just jump."

PATRICIA: "I can't. I can't get out of bed . . ."

HANNAH: 'I've had a stroke,' she explains.

MARY: Patricia just lies there. Then after a little while . . . She turns and looks at Gail. And asks, 'Why do you keep telling me that? Aren't you taking care of me?'

HANNAH: And Gail just says, 'Did you see me say that, Patty?' She'd been told not to turn around. 'Then how do you know, Patty, it was me?'

(No one knows what to say.)

JOYCE: Does anyone in assisted living know about this?

MARY: Not yet . . . When we take her back tonight . . .

HANNAH: Your mom's taking all these drugs now. She thinks they're what give her such dreams . . .

MARY: I'm sure Gail's taking all sorts of drugs too . . .

JOYCE: Gail wasn't there when she told you her dream.

MARY: She was there. Listening . . .

(At the sink, Mary will fill a large pot for the potatoes.)

JOYCE *(With the cookbook, back to)*: So, Mom—let's do a "Raggedy Ann Salad"?

HANNAH: What do we need for that?

JOYCE *(Reads)*: "Canned peaches . . . A cherry."

HANNAH: We don't have any of that, *(To Mary)* do we?

JOYCE *(Over this)*: "Raisins." For the buttons and the eyes and the shoes.

MARY *(To Hannah)*: I think we have raisins . . .

JOYCE: "Yellow cheese" for the hair.

HANNAH *(Over this)*: Joyce, you're going to have to go back to Tops Friendly—

JOYCE: I don't want to go back there . . . *(To Patricia)* You all right? Mom . . . Mom . . . *(Sings)* "My Raggedy Ann is a very old doll / She lay in the attic for years."

KARIN *(Over this to Hannah)*: What's this?

HANNAH: I don't know.

JOYCE *(Over this)*: "Hm, hum-hum, hum-hum-hum, my Raggedy Ann / With her legs doubled over her ears . . ."
Mom knows where that's from . . .

PATRICIA: Do I?

JOYCE: Come on. You remember. My little record player with the carousel that turned as it played . . . My carousel record player. *(To Karin)* She sold it at some garage sale. The second I left for college. *(Laughs)*

PATRICIA: Why would I do that, Joyce?

JOYCE: I don't know. I'd love to know.

PATRICIA: I don't remember any such record player.

JOYCE: I think you do . . .

(Mary will put the potatoes on the stove.)

HANNAH: Shepherd's pie and 'Paintbrush Cookies' that should be plenty . . .

MARY: That's enough. Agreed? Have we worked this out? We'll just do that.

(They agree.)

(To Patricia) I had a Raggedy Ann doll. I sewed it back together so many times—it looked like Frankenstein's monster. I used to operate on her . . .

KARIN: Pat. I have a question for you.

JOYCE: What?

KARIN: Today when I came back from teaching, and Joyce was here, she told me something—but I think she's just teasing me.

JOYCE: Oh that.

HANNAH: They don't tease. Do Gabriels tease?

MARY *(To Hannah)*: Thomas . . .

HANNAH *(The obvious)*: George . . .

KARIN *(Over this)*: About some sort of 'family ghost'—over in the guest room, above the office, where I'm sleeping? The room I'm renting? Joyce said as a kid—

JOYCE: And teenager.

KARIN: —she'd seen it a number of times. *(Smiles)* I don't believe her. But I thought I'd just ask. There isn't any ghost, is there? I think she's just pulling my leg. *(Looks to Joyce)*

PATRICIA: In the guest room? A ghost?

KARIN: Yes.

PATRICIA: There's never been a ghost in that guest room, Joyce. You know better.

KARIN *(Looks at Joyce)*: Thank you. *(Smiles)* I can't believe I even asked . . . I'm embarrassed to have brought it up. A ghost . . . *(Smiles)*

PATRICIA: It's in the basement, Karin.

KARIN: What??

PATRICIA: In the unfinished basement of the office; below where you're staying. Haven't you been down there?

KARIN: I looked— I opened the door, I didn't know where that door goes, so I looked . . .

PATRICIA: And you haven't heard anything?

KARIN *(Hesitates)*: Not really. No. *(Tries to laugh)*

PATRICIA: You haven't heard any scratching? Or some 'rapping'? 'Digging' noise . . . ?

KARIN: And if I had . . . ?

PATRICIA: So you have?

KARIN: I know that we have moles— *(To Hannah)* Didn't you tell me George set a mousetrap and caught a mole? And it's just dirt down there. So I figure moles could—

PATRICIA *(Over the end of this)*: I remember being over there once—when that was your father's office, Joyce. And cleaning up his stuff. He always left his coffee mugs . . . Just sitting in the sink. And I went down into the basement—we kept a few trunks down there. I can't remember what I was looking for. I'm down there. And the light goes out.

(Then:)

Must have burnt out, I thought. So it's pitch dark. When suddenly my hand—felt wet. I couldn't see anything. It was completely dark. I hurried back to the top of the stairs, I thought maybe I'd cut myself; was this blood? And I turned on the switch and the light came on. It wasn't burnt out. It had just gone out . . . And my hand, I could see—it was completely wet . . . But just water. Nothing else was wet. Nothing dripping. Except on one step—a puddle . . . I closed the door to the basement. And then I heard . . . this, *(Knock, knock, knock)* Karin, and—I told you there were only a couple of trunks there, but I heard—it sounded like chairs being thrown against the walls and smashed. A whole room full of furniture being broken up . . . And a voice . . .

(Then:)

A voice . . . My god, what a sound . . .
HANNAH *(To Karin)*: You know she's joking don't you?

(She didn't; all except Karin start to laugh.)

They tease . . .
PATRICIA *(To Joyce, over this)*: Thank you for letting me get that far.
HANNAH *(Over the end of this)*: The Gabriels, they tease.

(The lights fade.)

A Garage Sale

The same. A short time later.

Joyce looks through the children's book as Mary and Karin cut onion and garlic for the shepherd's pie.

HANNAH *(To Patricia, answering a question)*: We've found a lot of things—stuffed in the back of closets, in the attic . . .
JOYCE: George said he found Dad's fiddle . . .
HANNAH: He's been playing it all week.
KARIN: Joyce, I hadn't realized George played the violin as well as the piano.
PATRICIA *(Explains everything)*: Oh—he's a Gabriel.
MARY *(To no one)*: Thomas played the fiddle.
KARIN: I didn't know that . . . *(Having finished the onions, to Mary)* What else can I do?
MARY: Let me think . . .

(She goes and looks in the refrigerator.)

JOYCE *(Looking at the cookbook)*: What about Jell-O? With cut-up fruit. Look.

(Shows a picture in the book.)

When's the last time we had Jell-O? Mom, I'll bet you still have a box of Jell-O somewhere. From like a hundred years ago. It never goes bad, like the Twinkies you'd feed us . . .

MARY *(Over the end of this)*: There's no Jell-O. We don't eat Jell-O anymore. No one does . . .

JOYCE *(Putting down the book)*: I really wanted to make a 'Raggedy Ann Salad.' Shit. What are we going to do for a vegetable?

MARY: We have canned peas. Patricia likes them.

JOYCE: How can you eat those, Mom? You know they have like zero vitamins left . . .

HANNAH *(Over this)*: She likes them.

JOYCE: It's amazing we all survived our childhood . . .

PATRICIA: What? I couldn't hear . . .

JOYCE: You heard me, Mom.

HANNAH *(Over the end of this)*: Oh and we did a little scouting expedition this morning, Patricia. We all went to—here, you might be interested in this—

(Goes to pick up a big magazine from the bench.)

—a garage sale on Livingston.

MARY *(Explains to Joyce)*: Mrs. Voorhees.

JOYCE *(To Patricia)*: Not me.

MARY: You weren't here yet. We went right after we voted.

(Mary gets parsley, already washed, out of the refrigerator and will bring it over to Karin to chop.)

KARIN: You bought stuff? I thought you were trying to sell stuff.

HANNAH: For like twenty-five cents . . . Look at this. September—1910. *Ladies' Home Journal.*

PATRICIA *(Making a joke)*: I'm not that old.

JOYCE: You're not? Neither is Pam Voorhees.

HANNAH: Maybe it had been her mother's . . . ?

JOYCE: A garage sale on a Tuesday??

HANNAH *(After a look at Mary, corrects)*: An estate sale . . .

PATRICIA: Was Pam there?

HANNAH: No, she wasn't there.

JOYCE *(Over this)*: On a Tuesday. A garage sale . . .

HANNAH: It was a preview.

JOYCE: What did Paulie buy?

MARY: He stayed outside. He said everything smelled moldy . . .

KARIN *(To Mary about the parsley)*: Chop?

(Mary shows how small to chop it.)

HANNAH: A few others brought stuff to sell too. Barbara Apple had a whole clothes rack of her uncle's suits, jackets . . . shirts.

JOYCE: The actor.

KARIN: A good actor.

JOYCE *(About the magazine)*: Look at this . . . They made it so big . . .

HANNAH: Almost giving stuff away. George was like . . . *(Dumb voice)* "Oh my god, Hannah, look at all these neat clothes." I had to say to him: You wear the same thing every day. You're never going to wear this actor's things . . . Sometimes he doesn't see himself . . .

JOYCE *(Looking at the magazine)*: I thought you wanted to get George to dress better. Make him 'feel better about himself.' You're always saying that.

MARY: She was saying that just last night.

HANNAH: Not with those clothes. That's not him. In one of the upstairs bedrooms—there's still wallpaper with pictures of cowboys.

MARY: Her son must be fifty years old now.

JOYCE: Joey was our age, Hannah . . . And still is . . . *(To Mary)* Was Joey there?

(Mary nods.)

HANNAH: I wonder if he still sleeps there when he visits. I almost asked him. Little cowboys with lassos . . . *(Then explaining about Tuesday)* He told me today's a preview just for the village . . . Before the weekenders get their hands on anything . . . He put a yard sale sign by the Town Hall. So we'd all see it when we went to vote.

MARY: The villagers . . .

JOYCE: You think they chose election day on purpose?

HANNAH: Only people from the town vote there. Only we would see it . . .

JOYCE: Good for him.

HANNAH *(To Patricia)*: We went to get some tips for our own sale . . .

PATRICIA: Did you get any?

HANNAH: Not much.

JOYCE: Here . . . *(Reads)* "The Girls Club. With One Idea: To Make Money." Maybe we should all read this . . .

HANNAH: I haven't had a chance to even look at that—

JOYCE *(Reads)*: "An open letter to the American Girl." That's us. You too, Mom . . . *(Reads)* "I want to talk straight and without mincing words. Has your mother ever said to you: If I could have had as much when I was your age as you have now I should have been the happiest girl in the world"?

MARY: You didn't say things like that to your children, Patricia, did you?

PATRICIA: Joyce?

JOYCE *(Mimes locking her mouth with a key)*: Tick a lock . . . *(Continues to read)* "The chances are that when your mother was a girl she did have an overdose of self-denial and unsatisfied longing . . ."

KARIN: Pat, is that how you felt growing up?

PATRICIA: My mother did. That's my mother to a T.

JOYCE: Want to say anything more, Mom?

(They wait for more. Then:)

I guess that's all we're going to get . . . *(Reads)* "Your mother had precious good times. She dressed simply . . . And when you came along—" Her children . . . ". . . the memory of her own girlhood heartaches stirred all her tender love of you and so she gave you whatever you wanted. She gave you clothes which her own judgment told her were not suited to you." We just had fights over my clothes, didn't we, Mom?

PATRICIA: I don't remember any fights, Joyce.

MARY: Who didn't fight with their mom about clothes?

KARIN: I wore a lot of my mother's clothes.

JOYCE *(Continues to read)*: "Your mother gave you money, of whose value you had not the faintest conception." I'll skip this part . . .

PATRICIA: I'm interested in that, Joyce.

JOYCE *(Continues to read)*: "She gave you praise you hadn't earned."

HANNAH: Is that true, Patricia?

JOYCE *(Before Patricia can answer)*: Maybe. That's maybe true, Mom. I give you that. *(Reads)* "She gave you privileges which you just abused—"

PATRICIA: Oh that's true.

JOYCE *(Reads)*: "She gave you devotion that you accepted as a matter of course . . ."

HANNAH: Patricia?

KARIN: Pat? True?

PATRICIA *(Mimes locking her mouth with a key)*: Tick a lock.

JOYCE: Maybe I didn't appreciate everything you did . . .

PATRICIA *(Mimes again)*: Tick a lock . . .

MARY: One of Thomas's students—when Thomas was teaching . . . He came home one day, *(As Thomas)* "Mary, this student said the most amazing thing today." This relates to that. The student said that her parents keep telling her they just want her to be *happy*. But she told Thomas, "Don't my parents realize the pressure that puts on me?"

(At some point Mary gets a frying pan and begins to brown the onions.)

PATRICIA: I don't understand . . . What did her parents do wrong?

MARY: Pressuring her to be 'happy,' Patricia.

PATRICIA: Why is that . . . ?

JOYCE: Sometimes, Mom— I know just what Thomas's student meant. Sometimes, it's— *(Searches for the word)* 'helpful' to think of 'being happy' as something that's not in our own control. There are *other* factors. So, if/when we aren't happy, maybe then we won't feel so damn guilty about that. Like we've fucked up. Or have let others—our parents—down . . .

(Then:)

(Back to the magazine) Here's an article for you, Karin—

KARIN: What's that?

JOYCE *(Reads)*: "How to Furnish My Entire Flat from Boxes."

KARIN: Save that! I'm going to need that! Can I see? Let me see . . .

(Laughter; Joyce hands her the magazine.)

PATRICIA *(Confused)*: Why does Karin need—??

HANNAH: For her new apartment. *(To Karin)* I still don't know how you're going to make that commute every day from Kingston . . .

KARIN: We'll see . . .

PATRICIA: I thought you were living in the guest room?

HANNAH *(Continues)*: To Hotchkiss.

MARY *(Over this)*: She is, Patricia . . . But she's moving on . . .

(Mary will brown ground beef with the onions.)

KARIN *(To Joyce)*: Look: an ad for Jell-O.

JOYCE *(Joking)*: We should have had Jell-O . . .

KARIN: It looks good.

HANNAH: It always 'looks' good.

PATRICIA: My mother was like those mothers in that magazine . . .

(They wait for more.)

JOYCE: Is that it? Why was she like them, Mom? Tell us.

PATRICIA: She never wore makeup in her whole life. I can still hear her voice . . . You are very lucky, Joyce. I could have been my mother.

(No one knows what to say. Then:)

JOYCE *(With the cookbook)*: A picture of "Raggedy Ann Salad." In color . . .

HANNAH: Patricia, do you remember where we keep all those cookie cutters? You had whole boxes of all kinds of cookie cutters.

JOYCE *(Turns page)*: Hannah: They have a picture. "Paintbrush Cookies . . ." Do you need a picture?

KARIN *(Starting to stand)*: I know where they are. I saw them the other day . . . Two boxes of cookie cutters, way in the back of the pantry . . . I was cleaning out stuff . . . I can get them. Should I get them?

HANNAH: Sure. Great.
KARIN: I'll get them then . . .

(She goes.)

HANNAH: Thanks, Karin . . . *(To Mary)* Karin knows where the cookie cutters are?
JOYCE: Is Karin wearing one of Thomas's shirts, Mary? I've been waiting to ask.
HANNAH *(To Joyce)*: Mary gave it to her.
MARY: She's been helping to clean out Thomas's clothes closet. We've been going through stuff. It's dirty work. She only has nice clothes.

(She covers the frying pan.)

PATRICIA: Why was Pam having a garage sale? Has she died, Hannah?

(Then:)

HANNAH: Last month . . . While you were in the hospital, Patricia . . .

(Then:)

We'll need paintbrushes. The littlest ones. Patricia, do you still—?
MARY: Where they've always been, the 'junk' cabinet in the living room. We haven't started on the living room yet.
PATRICIA: Pam's son was there?
HANNAH *(Nodding)*: Joey even asked after you, Patricia. He'd heard you'd been ill.
PATRICIA: Pam probably told him.
HANNAH: Probably. And he'd heard about your selling the house. *(To Joyce)* He hasn't changed as much as a lot of men do . . .

JOYCE: That's good to hear.

MARY: You all right, Patricia?

JOYCE: When Joey Voorhees was something like eight . . . *(To Patricia)* See if you remember this, Mom. Joey was playing ball just across the street in the schoolyard. I think I was jumping rope. And two kids grabbed him, and started hitting him. And all of a sudden, Mom, you run out of our house, and across the street and you push those boys away. You take Joey inside, into the kitchen. *(Gestures: 'here')* I found you both in the kitchen . . . You'd given him a piece of cake. Do you remember that?

(Then:)

PATRICIA: No.

JOYCE: You don't? Come on, Mom, you need to remember the good things you do too.

(Karin interrupts with two plastic boxes—the cookie cutters.)

HANNAH: I'll take those, Karin . . . *("the plastic boxes")*

MARY: What else do we need for the cookies?

HANNAH *(Again)*: Paintbrushes . . .

KARIN: There are paintbrushes in that cabinet in the living room . . . *(Points)*

HANNAH: Are there?

KARIN: The junk cabinet, I call it. Want me to get them? I can get them.

HANNAH: Sure. That would be a big help, Karin . . . Thank you.

MARY: Thank you, Karin.

(As Karin goes off to the living room:)

HANNAH *(Calls)*: They might need to be washed.

MARY *(Calls)*: You can use the downstairs bathroom sink . . .

(Karin is gone.)

JOYCE *(Continuing the conversation)*: You've done a lot of good things. Nice things . . . You need to remember them too.

PATRICIA: I don't remember those things, Joyce.

JOYCE: Yes, you do. You're just being stubborn. *(After a look at Mary)* Mom, Mary's been finding all sorts of things. Cleaning out stuff.

PATRICIA: I know.

JOYCE: Mary told me on the phone about a box of letters . . . I don't think she's said anything . . .

MARY: To Patricia. No. Not yet.

(Then:)

PATRICIA: Can I see some of those, Hannah? *('the cookie cutters')* I want to pick mine before Joyce takes all the good ones . . .

(Hannah sets a box in front of Patricia.)

JOYCE: A box, she found way in the back of your and Dad's bureau. And . . . And on the top of the box—she just showed it to me when I got here—you'd written: "Burn after I die." Well Mary decided not burn them, Mom, because you're not dead.

('Smiles' at her 'joke.' Then:)

HANNAH: Not just Mary. I agreed too. So did George.

JOYCE: Mary, Hannah, George have read them, Mom. I read them while Mary was picking you up . . . ?

(Patricia looks one-by-one through the cookie cutters.)

They're all about your sister . . .

MARY: I was just cleaning out the bureau, Patricia . . .

PATRICIA *(Looking at the cookie cutters)*: I know the box, Mary.

JOYCE: All the letters are to you when you were a girl . . . How sorry everyone was when Ellie died. Nothing we read seemed like it needed to be burned . . . *(To Mary)* Did anything to you?

HANNAH *(Answering)*: No.

MARY: I'm sorry if I should have destroyed them, Patricia . . .

HANNAH *(To Mary)*: You need help?

MARY: Sure.

(Hannah and Mary find work to do: getting cans of tomato paste and broth for the shepherd's pie, etc.)

JOYCE: I want to talk with you about this . . .

PATRICIA: What's 'this,' Joyce?

JOYCE: Reading the letters, and seeing you as a girl of thirteen, and how people wrote to you . . . How your dad wrote you. The fact that he wrote you; you were in the same house, weren't you? Or had you gone away? One of the addresses was away . . .

PATRICIA: I went to stay with my aunt for a while.

JOYCE: I hadn't known that. How could I know that? Thirteen. Ellie was my aunt.

(Patricia looks at her.)

Of course I never met her. The photo you keep at the home; was when she got married, right? She's so beautiful in the photo. You once told me, I'll bet you've forgotten this, that she'd been your best friend.

PATRICIA: She was older.

JOYCE *(To Mary)*: What was her husband's—? George knew the name. *(To Patricia)* George told me something really interesting on the phone. I don't think he's told you yet.

HANNAH: He hasn't.

JOYCE: He did some 'exploring' on the internet, right? Ellie's husband . . . He was a model for advertisements? Wasn't he?

PATRICIA: Yes, Joyce, he was.

JOYCE: A very handsome man. Very attractive. George even came across one of the advertisements he was in . . .

(Patricia looks at her.)

For hats . . . And he found out other very interesting things too. I think they're interesting. I think we all do . . . The best man at Ellie's wedding . . . ?

(Then:)

You want to know?

PATRICIA: What?

JOYCE: There had been this big scandal—someone even recently wrote about, made a play out of it. Some Harvard students way back were thrown out of school for being homosexuals. Being gay. George discovered that one of these students was Ellie's husband's best man, Mom. At their wedding. Do you know what I'm suggesting?

(They hear Karin returning with the paintbrushes.)

PATRICIA *(About a cookie cutter)*: Hannah, shooting star. I forgot we had one of them . . .

HANNAH *(Stopping Karin)*: Karin . . .

(She gestures and Karin goes back out again into the living room.)

JOYCE: Mom? I'll stop. Never mind . . . Want me to stop?

(Patricia looks at her.)

(And she continues) George speculates—and this does make a whole lot of sense to me, Mom. What if your sister—What if she hadn't known that her husband was a gay

man. He might have thought he needed—'a cover.' That's what gay people had to do then. There's actually a name for this. The world made us do that then. So maybe— Ellie at the Christmas party she went to on that night? She was at a Christmas party, right?

PATRICIA: Yes.

JOYCE: And she sees something at this party that makes her realize her situation. She leaves her husband at the party—we know she did this. And goes back to their apartment . . . We know she did. But she leaves no note . . . What could she write? Mom?

PATRICIA: My sister was high-strung.

JOYCE: What does that mean, Mom? Anyway, just suppose what I'm suggesting is what happened—just think what your big sister would have been going through. She was trapped.

(Patricia looks at Joyce.)

She was nineteen. Nineteen. She couldn't tell her parents. Couldn't tell your mother. Grandma would have told her to— *(In a voice)* 'make the best of it, dear.' Right?

(Patricia 'laughs' to herself.)

PATRICIA: I don't know.

JOYCE: Or 'you must be doing something wrong.' That's what she would have said. Right? Right?

PATRICIA: He—played sports.

JOYCE: Mom.

PATRICIA: He was a good swimmer . . .

JOYCE: You know better. It wasn't her fault. And—it wasn't your fault.

(Patricia looks up.)

PATRICIA: I never said . . . *(Stops herself)*

JOYCE: What? You never said what? You didn't have to say . . .

(Then:)

But I think that is what you thought. That it was your fault? I read these letters to this thirteen-year-old child, and everyone is saying, in their own way, the exact same thing—Patty, it's not your fault. Cousins, an uncle, Grandma's friends, one of your teachers . . . It's not your fault, Patty. Or your mother's fault. Or Ellie's . . . Or her husband's . . .

(Then:)

What can we say to make you believe that?

(Short pause.)

PATRICIA: I don't know, Joyce.

(Then:)

Who's making the paint for the cookies?

HANNAH: I will, Patricia. How many colors?

JOYCE *(To Mary)*: Karin can come back in . . . *(To Patricia)* Can't she?

(Patricia nods.)

MARY *(Calls)*: Karin!

(Mary gets up.)

She can't hear me . . .

(She heads off.)

HANNAH: I think you have four colors of food coloring. And we can make more from that . . .

JOYCE *(To Patricia)*: You all right?

(Then:)

(With the cookbook) Look, Mom, there's a 'letter' in the front from *Betty Crocker* herself. "Dear Boys and Girls: Cooking is an adventure. It's really easy to cook, once you know how. You'll be trying all sorts of things—even a supper for the family some night to give mother a holiday . . ."

PATRICIA: You know, there was no 'Betty Crocker,' Joyce. They made her up.

JOYCE: I know, Mom . . .

(Karin and Mary return.)

HANNAH: Sorry, Karin . . .

(The lights fade.)

Paulie

A short time later; the same.

Mary, an old book in hand, and Joyce, leaning over her. Patricia, having just heard a noise in the living room:

MARY: That's just the front door, Patricia. It's just George . . . He's back from taking Paulie to his college . . .

HANNAH *(To Patricia)*: When he's ready, he'll come and join us.

JOYCE: Mary, she said, found this old songbook in the attic, Mom . . .

PATRICIA: Paulie was upset?

HANNAH: He was.

JOYCE: We told you.

HANNAH: It had to have been a shock. He grew up playing in this house. His grandma's house. I'm sure he's calmed down by now. He'll get over it.

JOYCE *(Showing her the book)*: *Sing for America. (Shows her the 'signature')* "George."

MARY: I used to sing this to my dog Cleo.

JOYCE: You used to sing that to me, Mom . . . Remember singing this? *My Old Dog Tray.*

PATRICIA: I do.

HANNAH: I never sang that to Paulie. I don't know it.

JOYCE *(To Patricia)*: You want to sing it with us?

HANNAH: You okay, Patricia?

MARY *(To Joyce)*: Just the chorus?

MARY AND JOYCE *(The chorus)*:

Old dog Tray's ever faithful,
Grief cannot drive him away;
He's gentle, he is kind,
I'll never, never find,
A better friend than old dog Tray . . .

(Off, from the living room, George has begun to play an old fiddle tune. They listen. Then:)

HANNAH: We found your father's old fiddle-tune book. It was in the attic too . . . George was thrilled. He said he'd forgotten half the tunes. So he's just been practicing. He broke a string yesterday. We found a whole package of strings in the case. *(Amazed)* Still good.

KARIN: May I see . . . ? *(Takes the songbook)*

MARY *(To Joyce)*: You know, there's research out now about how a child's brain isn't completely formed until his mid-twenties . . .

JOYCE: I didn't know that. *(To Hannah)* Did you?

HANNAH: She's told me. It's good to know.

MARY: And yet we expect them to . . .

JOYCE: To what?

HANNAH: To understand, Joyce—complex, confusing things . . . *(Shrugs)* Loss . . . Life . . .

(When the potatoes are done, Mary will take the pot to the sink and strain them.)

JOYCE *(To Hannah)*: Kids, Hannah. I don't know how you do it.

KARIN: Me neither.

HANNAH: You do what you do. Paulie's a good guy.

MARY: He really is. Smart. I love having him around. I miss that.

HANNAH: Though sometimes . . . As you've seen today, Joyce.

JOYCE *(Shrugs)*: You should see some of the actors I deal with. That was nothing.

HANNAH: We knew he'd be upset.

MARY: You know kids when they go away to school they like everything to be exactly the same when they come home.

HANNAH: This is a bit more than that.

MARY: I know.

JOYCE: I'll bet there were times when I was a lot worse than Paulie was. Right, Mom?

PATRICIA: When, Joyce?

JOYCE: As a kid, Mom. I'm sure I said things to you and Dad too . . . I know I gave you some pretty rough times . . .

PATRICIA: Oh god, yes. Joyce, you really did . . . And you said things . . .

JOYCE: You don't have to say it like that. And I don't think I caused you any more trouble than Thomas or George . . . The things they did and said, and got away with.

PATRICIA: Joyce, you were so much worse than your brothers. Much much worse . . .

JOYCE: Are you joking? Is she joking?

(Joyce looks to Mary.)

Mom, what are you talking about?

PATRICIA: I'm not saying you're like that anymore . . . Not that you're now perfect . . .

MARY: You all right there, Patricia, you need anything?

PATRICIA: I'm fine, thank you, dear.

MARY: Joyce you want to do the potatoes? You always do great mashed potatoes. Never a single lump.

JOYCE: I get out my aggressions . . . My frustrations.

HANNAH *(Holds up a tiny cookie cutter, to distract her)*: Look at this one, Patricia. What do you think that is?

JOYCE: That's a Christmas stocking, Mom.

MARY: A Christmas stocking . . . I love the little ones. I'm so glad you didn't throw those out.

JOYCE: Unlike my little record player carousel . . .

(Fiddle music continues off.

Mary will check on the frying pan and get out a large casserole dish.)

MARY: When Paulie got here this morning he really seemed excited. About voting.

HANNAH: His first time.

JOYCE: He's going to be scarred.

HANNAH: He *was* like a little kid, Joyce.

MARY: Nice to see that again.

HANNAH: He probably wouldn't have wanted you to see him like that, Joyce. Being an excited kid. 'How do I do it? I want to do it right, Mom.' 'Fill in the circles. Put it into the machine . . .' He couldn't stop smiling. You're his 'cool aunt from New York City.' He wouldn't have wanted you to see that.

JOYCE: I was looking forward to calling him tonight, once the election results— Knowing it was his first time. And we'd talk about how his vote counted. If it mattered in any race . . .

HANNAH *(A race where his vote would count)*: Teachout/Faso . . .

MARY: A nice aunt thing to do . . .

JOYCE: They need to hear that. The kids. That it matters.

MARY: I think so too.

JOYCE: I won't bother him tonight. Maybe later in the week.

KARIN *(Having turned a page in the songbook)*: Mary, you can't sell this in your garage sale . . . That's the idea, isn't it?

JOYCE *(Over this)*: Why not?

MARY *(Over this)*: What? Why?

(Fiddle music has stopped.)

KARIN: Look at this picture. Look. A little white boy in black face . . . Jesus. It's racist. *(Reads the book's title)* "*Sing for America*" . . . Incredible . . . *(Setting the book down)* This was in your attic? . . .

JOYCE: Throw it out.

MARY: Recycle it.

JOYCE: Mom, *that* you keep?

MARY: I'll put it out later with the newspapers. I'll rip out that page . . .

(As George enters:)

HANNAH: Hi.

GEORGE: Mom, you're looking good. How do you feel?

PATRICIA: How's Paulie?

HANNAH *(Points to a sweater on the bench)*: He left his favorite sweater.

GEORGE: He was in a hurry to get out of here . . .

HANNAH: We told your mother.

PATRICIA: Why did you have to tell Paulie, George?

GEORGE: He needs to start taking out loans, Mom.

HANNAH *(To Patricia)*: We told you this.

GEORGE: He needs to sign things. He needed to know why.

HANNAH: We didn't want him to come home for Thanksgiving and just see a sign on the lawn.

GEORGE: We only waited till today so we could tell him in person.

MARY *(To George)*: You want anything? There's beer.

JOYCE: I'll get you a beer.

(He doesn't want one.)

PATRICIA: He was upset?
JOYCE: He's still a kid, Mom.
HANNAH: He's not a kid, Joyce.
GEORGE: Good to see you in your kitchen, Mom. We don't see that very often anymore . . .
PATRICIA: Tell me what he said, George?
GEORGE: In the car, Mom?

(George sits.)

In the car . . . Let's see. His exact words, Mom? *(Laughs)*
JOYCE: What's funny?
GEORGE: What were our son's exact words to his father? Mom, I think they were something like: 'Dad, so you're just going to let them fuck Grandma over?'
HANNAH: What?
GEORGE: Sorry, Mom.
MARY: What does that mean?
JOYCE *(Over this)*: He said that to you?
HANNAH: What does he think we can do? Who's them?
MARY: He's upset.
GEORGE: After saying like nothing for a half an hour. Just staring out the window. Then: 'Dad, you're just going to let them fuck Grandma over?' That's what I said too, Hannah: 'Who's them? Paulie? Who is them?'
JOYCE: Where to begin?
GEORGE *(Smiles)*: Right. Right. Where to begin . . .

(Then:)

I tried to explain that it's not going to help anything by getting angry. Getting angry will not help you, Mom.

'The best we can do, to hope for—is to make all this as painless as possible for Grandma.'

HANNAH: He must have understood that. He had to hear that.

GEORGE: He asked why we hadn't told him, Hannah. 'I'm a grown-up now, Dad.'

HANNAH: Come on. We waited so we could tell him in person.

GEORGE: That's what I said to him.

HANNAH *(To Joyce)*: He's been loving his school . . . He hasn't wanted to come home.

GEORGE *(Over this)*: I know. I know.

HANNAH: Today we got him home. To vote . . .

(Then:)

JOYCE *(To George)*: He's a kid.

GEORGE *(Goes to get himself a beer)*: He's not a kid, Joyce.

(Then:)

MARY *(To Joyce)*: You said you'd mash the potatoes . . .

KARIN: For what it's worth, the things some of my students say—and with so much confidence. So damn confident? Then the next day . . . something else.

GEORGE: So what's all this? What are you doing? I haven't seen these cookie cutters for years . . .

JOYCE: We're making dinner—and, George, everything, we all agreed, has to come out of that book . . .

HANNAH: *Betty Crocker's Cookbook for Boys and Girls.*

GEORGE: I remember that.

HANNAH *(Lists)*: Shepherd's pie. Paintbrush cookies.

JOYCE: Mary and Hannah found that book in the attic . . .

MARY: And all that stuff . . . *('the piles of books on the table')*

JOYCE: We even thought of making Jell-O . . .

MARY: Remember Jell-O?

JOYCE *(Over this)*: You used to love your Jell-O . . . Or was that Thomas? . . .

GEORGE: I don't remember.

JOYCE: Raggedy Ann Salad.

GEORGE *(Over this)*: I don't understand. Why?

HANNAH: It was sort of Paulie's idea.

GEORGE: Paulie's . . . ?

HANNAH: When he'd just got here this morning. Before we told him anything. You saw how happy he was.

MARY: He told us about a game his friends sometimes play at—

HANNAH: This is where we got the idea. From Paulie.

MARY: At dinner in the cafeteria: *(In a voice)* "If you knew it was your last meal, and you could have anything, what would you have?"

GEORGE *(To Hannah)*: Why would they play that?

HANNAH: I don't know, George. Kids . . . It's an icebreaker, he said.

MARY: He said the responses always fell into two categories—those who want something 'extravagant,' to indulge themselves, a fancy bottle of wine—

JOYCE: Wine? He's eighteen.

HANNAH: Come on, Joyce.

MARY: —that costs god knows what—some meal from some expensive restaurant . . .

GEORGE: Is that what Paulie would want?

HANNAH: No.

MARY *(Over this)*: And the other category: those who want something that they remember having already had. So with a nice memory attached . . . A nostalgic thing I guess.

HANNAH: He wanted that, George.

KARIN: What are kids doing thinking about 'last meals'? I don't think I'd even be hungry . . . If I knew it was my last meal. I wouldn't be thinking about what to eat . . .

MARY: It's just a game, Karin. And Hannah and I had just found in the attic—*Betty Crocker's Cookbook for Boys and Girls.* So we all got the idea to make everything out—

HANNAH: —of that. Paulie loved that. He had even agreed to stay for dinner, George. I hadn't told you. I was going to surprise you. And not only going to stay, but he was going to help us cook.

(Then:)

GEORGE: Where was I?

HANNAH: We were in line to vote. Paulie, Mary and I. I think you were talking to someone.

(Then:)

This could be maybe the last chance to have a dinner together here. All make a dinner together. In your house. This house.

GEORGE: You said that to Paulie?

HANNAH: No. No.

GEORGE: We had to tell him, Hannah. He's not a kid.

HANNAH: I know.

(Then:)

GEORGE: So when will this fantastic dinner be ready?

JOYCE: Don't make fun, George.

MARY: Give us about an hour.

GEORGE: Then, Mom, I'm going to go play Dad's fiddle for a bit. I'm getting better. It's all coming back . . .

(He starts to leave.)

JOYCE: You sounded good.

HANNAH: George, while you were gone, the real-estate agent for the house came by.

(This stops George.)

He just walked into the kitchen. Didn't even knock.

GEORGE: What did he want?

HANNAH: He took pictures. Can he do that? Just walk in?
GEORGE: He has keys.
MARY: He scared your mother.
GEORGE: I'm sorry, Mom.

(He goes. Short pause.)

KARIN *(With the songbook)*: "*Sing for America*"? Recycle . . . ?
MARY: Thanks, Karin.

(Karin goes to put the book on a pile of newspapers by the sink.)

PATRICIA: Paulie's angry?
HANNAH: I think, more like disappointed, Patricia. In us. *(Sees Patricia's face)* Not you. Not you. Just—in us.

(The lights fade.)

Cutting an Apple

A short time later.

Off, George plays through the basic fiddle tunes book.

Joyce mashes the potatoes. Hannah will get the dough from the refrigerator and roll it out. All listen to Karin, who is in the middle of quoting from a 'monologue'; she directs this to Patricia and Joyce (the others having heard it last night):

KARIN: Pat, then she says *(Quoting)* "Part of the problem with empathy, is that empathy doesn't do us anything. We've had lots of empathy, but we feel that for too long our leaders have used politics as the art of the possible . . . But the challenge, now, is to practice politics as the art of making the impossible, possible . . ."

MARY: She was like twenty years old, Patricia. We don't see this side of Hillary now.

JOYCE: It must be there. Somewhere. Don't you think?

MARY: I don't see it.

HANNAH *(Over this)*: Wellesley . . .

MARY: She's twenty. Twenty-one. Karin did a lot of it for us last night.

KARIN *(Quotes)*: She said, "We are all of us, exploring a world that none of us understands, and attempting to create *within* that uncertainty."

JOYCE *(To Mary)*: That's true . . .

KARIN: "But there is the feeling that our prevailing culture, and its corporate life . . ."

HANNAH: "Corporate life . . ." Hillary. Where is this Hillary? Come on . . .

KARIN *(Continues)*: "Corporate life which tragically includes, universities—"

MARY: Thomas would have really agreed with that . . .

JOYCE *(Over this)*: "—is not a way of life for us."

MARY: Hillary Clinton, Patricia, at twenty-one.

JOYCE *(Correcting her)*: Rodham. Hillary Rodham.

KARIN: Here's something the kids at Vassar couldn't believe.

HANNAH *(To Patricia)*: She did her show last week at Vassar—

KARIN: "Trust . . ." she said—

HANNAH: Listen to this.

KARIN *(Quotes)*: "Trust is the one word that when I asked my graduation class what it was they wanted me to say for *them* in my speech, everyone came up to me and said, 'Talk about trust.'"

(Then:)

JOYCE: I wonder if she remembers that . . .

HANNAH: I wonder if when she looks back . . . Does she look back? Can she look back? What she thinks . . .

KARIN: Pat, I end my play with a poem that she also recited at her graduation.

> My entrance into the world of so-called social problems
> Must be with quiet laughter, or not at all.
> The Hollow Men of anger—and bitterness
> Must be left to a bygone age.

MARY: "Quiet laughter, or not at all . . ." Karin said she wanted to end her show hopeful.

KARIN: I think that's important. Especially this year. Especially when there are kids . . .

JOYCE: "Hollow Men—"?

KARIN: "—of anger and bitterness."

JOYCE: They've been left behind?

(Hannah looks through the cookie cutters.)

HANNAH *(To Patricia)*: So you going to come with us? *(To Karin)* What time's your show?

PATRICIA: Where?

JOYCE: Who wants to be alone tonight?

HANNAH: At the theater society. The barn . . . We've been there. We saw *Godspell* there. Are you going to come with us? We're all going.

PATRICIA: I don't think—

MARY: Come on, Patricia. It's a special night.

HANNAH: If you get tired, we'll bring you back to the 'inn.'

KARIN *(Answering Hannah)*: Nine? Around nine? I don't think things are that tightly scheduled. I suppose it depends on . . . How things go tonight.

HANNAH: Sure. We'll see.

KARIN: Sometime after the polls close. It's just excerpts . . . They want like twenty minutes . . .

JOYCE: I voted today for that Hillary. She must be in there. Somewhere in there . . . You think she's still in there?

MARY: Long lines in Brooklyn?

JOYCE: Very long. I got talking to the young woman in front of me. I said, 'Pretty exciting, right.' She said, 'I just hope Hillary knows that my vote is not him.'

HANNAH *(To Karin)*: You want to do any cookies? You want to choose a cookie cutter? . . .

KARIN: I should get ready soon.

MARY: And she's wearing your glasses, Patricia.

PATRICIA *(Confused, touching her own glasses)*: What? Why?

MARY: Not those. We're not taking away those.

HANNAH: We'll have fun . . . With us girls . . . Joyce is right—it's good to be together tonight. *(To Joyce)* Karin's found some other neat stuff for her show . . . *(To Karin)* What's that weird bit—?

JOYCE: What bit?

HANNAH *(To Karin)*: About the collars . . .

MARY: Why is that weird?

HANNAH: She'll like that. It's about clothes.

KARIN: She says, "Instead of the closed collars I usually wear, I've been told to change my wardrobe to a more open-necked look. To convey, I'm told, more openness."

JOYCE: One of Bill's pollsters told her that. Do what the pollsters tell you—that'll make you seem human.

KARIN: Then she says, "But I just tell them, I get colds frequently, and I need to keep my neck warm to avoid them."

(Laughter.)

JOYCE: Good for her.

MARY: Makes sense to me. Doesn't that make sense?

HANNAH: Hillary's just saying 'fuck you.' Sorry, Patricia.

MARY *(Over this)*: You think so?

JOYCE: She is definitely saying 'fuck you.' "Convey more openness . . ." A man definitely told her to do that . . .

KARIN: Maybe Bill . . .

MARY: 'Fuck you.' Where is that Hillary?

(They notice Patricia starting to nod off.)

JOYCE: Mary . . .

HANNAH: Patricia? You want to cut out some cookies? We've got plenty of dough . . . The Famous Paintbrush Cookies. Why don't we set up Patricia so she can . . . We're choosing cookie cutters . . . *(Continues, about Hillary)* And I give her this: she never quits. I do like that . . .

MARY: I do too.

HANNAH *(Putting an apron on Patricia)*: Patricia, Karin bought a pantsuit.

PATRICIA *(Confused)*: Why?

JOYCE *(Obviously)*: For the show. To be Hillary.

PATRICIA: A pantsuit . . . ?

JOYCE *(A joke)*: I guess she couldn't fit into any of yours, Mom.

PATRICIA: I have a pantsuit??

MARY: Joyce . . .

HANNAH *(To Patricia)*: We can hang around here until almost nine, and then all go together to see Karin's show. And if you get tired, or whatever, we'll take you right back to the 'inn.' It'll be fun. I don't want to think of you alone in your room on this election night.

JOYCE: She has her roommate.

PATRICIA *(Reaching)*: I'd like an apple, please.

JOYCE: You want an apple??

MARY *(Same time)*: You hungry, Patricia?

PATRICIA: I would like an apple.

HANNAH *(Takes an apple)*: Here. You want me to cut it into slices?

PATRICIA *(Taking the apple)*: I'll cut it.

MARY: Help her cut it.

HANNAH: Let me—

PATRICIA: I can cut it, Hannah.

(Hannah hesitates, then hands Patricia a knife. During the following, Patricia—with only one hand, because of the stroke—tries to cut the apple into two. This is very difficult to do, and

even painful to watch. Once or twice it nearly gets away from her. This takes a lot of struggle.

All watch this, though try not to show that they are watching.)

MARY *(A joke, to Karin)*: You going to wear the pantsuit on your date?

PATRICIA *(Totally focused on cutting the apple)*: What? What date?

HANNAH: Karin has a date, Patricia . . .

JOYCE: Be careful, Mom . . .

MARY: She's not eating with us. She's just been helping us out.

JOYCE: Hannah told me.

KARIN *(To Patricia)*: Just your family tonight . . .

(They try and not watch.)

PATRICIA *(Cutting)*: A date?

KARIN: It's not a real—

MARY: He's taking you to Gigi's.

JOYCE: You sure you don't want some help, Mom??

MARY *(Over this)*: Sounds like a date to me.

KARIN: He's part of the Rhinebeck Theatre Society. I think he just wants to thank me for the show. I'm not being paid. There might even be other people with us at the restaurant.

JOYCE *(To Patricia)*: Don't hurt yourself . . .

(She looks to Mary—no one knows what to do.)

HANNAH: It's a date. If she bought a dress.

KARIN *(It was cheap, 'the dress')*: At Marshalls . . .

MARY *(Over the end of this)*: She bought a new dress.

JOYCE: I got new jeans . . . *(To Patricia)* You want me to hold it? It keeps slipping . . .

(Patricia ignores her.)

MARY *(To Joyce)*: What do you mean?

JOYCE: For voting. She gave everyone who promised to vote a new pair of jeans. My boss.

HANNAH: Isn't that patronizing?

JOYCE: She's rich. Welcome to my life, Hannah. If you went to Ohio to canvass? You got new boots . . . I came here instead.

HANNAH: How much did the jeans cost?

JOYCE: I don't know.

(They try not to watch.)

(Nods to Karin) She's here like two months and she's got a date . . .

MARY: He's in real estate. The date . . .

PATRICIA *(Trying to cut)*: Is he selling my house?

JOYCE: No. They've gone with someone else for that.

PATRICIA: My children grew up in this house.

JOYCE: I'm one of your children. I know.

(She can't take it anymore:)

Let me cut that for you . . . Okay? It's hard with just one . . . hand. Give that to me.

(She slowly takes the knife out of Patricia's hand.)

MARY *(To distract her)*: Patricia, you want more coffee? You need anything?

(Joyce begins to slice the apple.)

JOYCE: There . . . That's better, isn't it?

(Patricia tries to take off the apron with one hand.)

What, Mom? What are you doing?

HANNAH *(Over this)*: What do you need, Patricia?
MARY: Tell us what you need.

(Patricia starts to stand.)

JOYCE: Where are you going?
PATRICIA: I want to go home.
JOYCE: What do you mean?
HANNAH *(Over this)*: You are home, Patricia. This is your home. *(Looks to Mary)*
MARY: Patricia, what's wrong?
PATRICIA *(Quietly)*: I'm sad . . .
MARY: You can't stand on that leg.
PATRICIA *(Over this)*: Please, take me home, Mary. I don't want to come here anymore.
JOYCE *(Over the end of this)*: We're going to have dinner, Mom. We're making dinner—
HANNAH: Joyce is here. She came for dinner.
MARY *(Comforting her)*: It's all right, Patricia. It's all right. Come on . . .

(Off, the fiddle music has stopped.)

JOYCE *(Over this)*: Get George. Karin, could you get George?

(Karin hurries off.)

Tell him we need him . . .
PATRICIA *(Over this)*: Where's my wheelchair?
HANNAH: It's over by the sink.
PATRICIA: Where is it, Mary?
MARY: It's right over there . . . *('by the sink')* It's just folded up.
JOYCE: It's— *(Shouts)* George!!
HANNAH: Joyce.
JOYCE *(Points it out)*: Your wheelchair's right there, Mom . . . It's just right there. Mary's got it.

(Mary has gotten the wheelchair and is unfolding it as George hurries in.)

HANNAH *(To George)*: Your mother wants to go home—

GEORGE: Mom . . . ? *(To Joyce)* What's going on?

JOYCE: Nothing.

HANNAH: She said she's sad.

PATRICIA *(Same time)*: Please. Please, George . . . Take me home.

GEORGE: I thought you were going to have dinner with all of us. They're making a real nice dinner. Joyce is here.

HANNAH *(Over the end of this)*: You've been helping us, Patricia.

JOYCE *(Over this, to George)*: She doesn't want to be here.

PATRICIA: George . . .

GEORGE: I'm right here, Mom.

MARY *(Bringing over the wheelchair, over this)*: Maybe you need to go to the bathroom first, Patricia? You want to go to the bathroom before we go home?

JOYCE: George . . .

PATRICIA: I do.

(Patricia nods.)

MARY: She needs to go to the bathroom. *(To Patricia)* Not by yourself.

JOYCE: Mom. Help her, George.

MARY *(To Patricia)*: You can't move that leg . . . Remember? Let George help you. You don't want to fall down. You don't want that. Do you?

(George has gotten her up.)

HANNAH: Hold on to—

JOYCE: What can I—? Let George . . .

GEORGE: Onto my neck, Mom. Hold on tight.

JOYCE *(Without moving)*: I want to help.

(As he lifts her into the wheelchair:)

GEORGE *(Over this)*: And I'm going to swing your . . . We've done this many many times. There. Good. Good work. Really good work . . .

(She is in the wheelchair.)

You just got a little tired . . . *(To Mary)* I think it's what she wants—the bathroom. Joyce, will you take her?

MARY: I'll do that, Joyce. I can do that . . .

(Mary and Patricia head off.)

JOYCE: I can do it . . .

HANNAH *(Suddenly)*: George, has she been in her living room since they picked up the piano?

GEORGE: We always come in through the back . . . Up the ramp . . .

JOYCE *(About all that has just happened)*: Fuck . . .

HANNAH: I think she's been in there . . . She's seen. I'm sure. Never mind . . .

(No one knows what to do or say. Then:)

KARIN: I should get changed . . . *('Smiles')* For my date . . . ? You don't need me for . . . ?

HANNAH: No. No, nothing. Thanks, Karin.

KARIN: You all okay?

(Karin heads off to the office.)

HANNAH *(To Karin as she goes)*: I thought it wasn't a date. *(To George)* Mary gave her one of Thomas's shirts . . .

(George shrugs.)

Maybe Mary is going to need some help . . . getting her off the toilet . . . ?

JOYCE *(Innocently)*: She's a doctor . . .

GEORGE: I'll go see if she . . . needs help . . . And I can drive Mom back to her 'inn' . . . Sorry, Joyce.

(He is gone.)

JOYCE *(Calls after)*: And I'll go with you. *(To Hannah)* I have to leave early tomorrow . . . I want to make sure to say goodbye . . .

(Then:)

I really thought she was going to hurt herself with that apple . . . I couldn't watch . . . She seems better though. When I was up last month . . .

HANNAH: She'd just begun P.T. then. She's better.

JOYCE: I'm glad we're taking her back. She's tired. Oh Mom . . . *(Laughs to herself)*

HANNAH: What?

JOYCE: This afternoon, when I was reading the letters? I was sitting in Mom and Dad's room. And while I was lost, reading . . . I hear *(In a voice)* 'Hi.' A high voice. *(Then)* 'Hi.' I look around—nobody there. 'Hi.' It sounds like it's coming from Mom's closet. 'Mom? Mom? Hi.' And I'm about to go and look in the closet, when I realize—it's just my stomach. *(Makes a noise)* Sort of sounds like 'hi' doesn't it? *(Then)* Doesn't it? You know how when your stomach is grumbling and it sounds like it's—out there somewhere? Like a thrown voice? 'Hi.' It was like that . . . It was my stomach . . .

(She sees Mary entering with Patricia in her wheelchair.)

Everything all right?

HANNAH *(Same time)*: That was fast.

JOYCE: You okay, Mom? I mean—

MARY *(Over the end of this)*: False alarm. We're fine. Aren't we, Patricia? We're just fine.

JOYCE: I'm going with George, Mom, and take you home . . .

MARY: That's no longer necessary . . . Your mother wants to stay. Don't you? How often do we have dinner with Joyce. Right? You want to stay with your family. You want to sit at the table? Stay in your chair—? *(Then, as an explanation)* She's wearing . . . *('Depends')* She forgot she was. She just got worried. It happens. No one likes to embarrass herself. *(To Patricia)* What about the chair there? . . . You sometimes like to sit in this beautiful chair.

PATRICIA: The chair . . .

MARY: Okay. It's more comfortable.

JOYCE: You're going to stay for dinner, Mom? That's great.

(George has returned.)

(To George) Mom's staying for dinner . . .

GEORGE: I know.

MARY *(A joke, to Patricia about her new position on the armchair)*: A change of scenery.

HANNAH: Let me help, Mary . . .

(As Hannah and Mary help Patricia into the armchair:)

GEORGE *(To Joyce)*: Dad's old chair . . .

JOYCE: I know. Good idea to move it into here. How much did you get for the desk?

GEORGE: Eighty-five on eBay.

MARY *(Helping Patricia)*: I reminded Patricia what day today is. You'd forgotten.

PATRICIA: I did, Mary. I forgot . . .

MARY: Thomas would have wanted all of us to be here . . . He'd have been very upset . . . One year. One very long year.

HANNAH: How about a chair? . . . For your legs, Patricia.

(Patricia doesn't want one.)

JOYCE: What can I do?

MARY: Let me put a towel down . . . Under . . . Just a second . . . Could you get me a towel, Hannah? In the sink drawer . . . We'll use one of those.

(As Hannah gets a dish towel:)

You just forgot, what today is . . . *(Explaining again)* Actually it was on the ninth, tomorrow; but Joyce has to get back . . . *(To Hannah)* I'll hold her up . . . Put it under.

(As Hannah puts the towel under Patricia:)

Now you can sit here in comfort and watch over us. You do like doing that don't you?

JOYCE *(A joke)*: And give advice, Mom . . . You love giving advice . . .

PATRICIA: Do I?

(As soon as Patricia is comfortable:)

MARY: What were we talking about?

(The lights fade.)

The Buzzards

A short time later.

George sits on the bench. Patricia sits in the armchair, watching the others.

Hannah makes the base for the cookie paints; Joyce chooses cookie cutters.

MARY: I was in the Kingston Mall—
JOYCE: I always hated—
MARY *(Over this)*: —the other day. What a depressing place that's become . . .
HANNAH *(To Joyce)*: You used to like it. We used to go together.
JOYCE: As kids.
MARY: Half the stores are closed.

(Patricia shifts in her seat.)

GEORGE: You all right, Mom?
PATRICIA: I'm enjoying watching these girls work.
HANNAH *(To Joyce)*: I think she means us.
MARY *(Continues)*: And—I was in that big shoe store, what's it called? I was the only person in there. And I am sitting and then I look up and there's this mirror on a pillar . . . *(She hesitates)*
HANNAH: What?
MARY: For some reason I wasn't—prepared . . . *(Shrugs)* I had my makeup on. Maybe I put it on a little too quickly . . . The light in our upstairs bathroom—you need natural light . . . And I'd certainly looked hard at myself before. To see what more will need to be done? Do I start coloring my hair? I think now it's a bit late for that.
JOYCE: Hillary still colors her hair.
MARY: But to *start* now? . . . Who wants those questions? Still I'd never been *surprised* like I now was. Startled. I look up and it isn't just—oh there's something new, another—whatever to be covered. But what I see is a stranger . . . Do I want to know that person? *(As if looking at herself in a mirror)* Who is there? *(Remembers something and smiles)*
HANNAH: What?
MARY: Thomas used to say that one day he wanted to write a play with that opening line. The greatest opening line of all time of any play, he said.
GEORGE: What line?

JOYCE *(Obviously)*: *Hamlet.* "Who's there?"

MARY: That's how every play should begin, he said. "Who's there?" *(Shrugs)* I didn't understand.

(Mary will go and look in the refrigerator for tomatoes for a salad.)

JOYCE: Mom, you are going to live to be a hundred and five. And I think that's really good. Means I've got those genes.

HANNAH *(To Mary)*: Could you get me another egg, Mary? For the paint.

JOYCE *(Over this, to George)*: You too . . .

(Mary will prepare a simple salad.)

MARY: I read somewhere—some book about dealing with a loved one's death.

(They are all interested.)

(Checking the tomatoes) I already washed these . . . *(Continues)* How it was the custom, years and years ago, in a lot of places in America—in the home where there'd been a death, to drape black curtains over all the mirrors . . .

HANNAH: Why?

(Hannah mixes the egg yolks for the paint. Joyce will then make the colors from this food coloring.)

MARY: I just remembered this. *And* over any paintings or photographs of landscapes . . . Landscapes. *(Answering Hannah)* So that the soul, as it left the body, would not be distracted by a reflection of itself. Or by a last look at the world now being lost. I think it was out West . . . In log cabins . . .

GEORGE *(As a joke)*: You probably saw all that as a kid, Mom . . .

PATRICIA: I don't think so.

JOYCE: My boss? In her office in the shop, she keeps a print of Titian's *Venus*. You know, the one where she's a plump girl, lying on the bed, naked, proud of herself and her sexiness . . . She says it's her inspiration—and her solace, and joy . . .

GEORGE: Is your boss—chubby?

(He joins the women at the table.)

JOYCE: No, she's very thin . . . But maybe that's how she sees herself . . .

GEORGE: I don't understand . . .

(None of the women want to explain this to him.)

HANNAH *(To George)*: You going to paint some cookies?

JOYCE: You and Thomas always liked to paint the cookies.

MARY: Did they, Patricia?

PATRICIA: I don't remember. Maybe.

JOYCE *(To George, with the cookie cutters)*: What do you want to do? A—duck? Here's a duck. Or a fish? . . .

HANNAH: Let him pick his own cookie cutters—

JOYCE *(Over this, with a cookie cutter)*: What's this supposed to be? You know what this is, Mom? *(Shows her)* I think it's supposed to be a squirrel.

PATRICIA: That's Santa Claus with his sack.

JOYCE: I think it's a squirrel, Mom.

(As they work: Mary on the salad; Joyce on the paint; Hannah begins cutting out the cookie shapes:)

MARY *(To Hannah)*: Paulie didn't seem bothered about having to take out loans . . . That didn't seem to be what really upset him.

HANNAH: No. I don't think it was. *(To George)* Did he say anything about the loans on your car ride? Did you bring it up?

GEORGE: I did. He said, "What the fuck, Dad, I'll just default. Fuck 'em."

HANNAH: Fuck who? Who does he think is out there to fuck for having to take out loans?

JOYCE *('A joke')*: You mean, where do you start?

GEORGE *(Smiling)*: Maybe that's what he means. Maybe, Hannah.

HANNAH *(Smiling)*: 'Fuck them.' Maybe . . . Sorry, Patricia. Good luck, Paulie. Go ahead and try . . . See how far *you* get.

(Then:)

George, tell your sister what you wrote under that guy's desk . . .

JOYCE: What desk—?

HANNAH: He built a small desk for a client—what does he do?

GEORGE *(Shrugs)*: A financial guy.

HANNAH: For his home.

GEORGE: He has a 'home office.' In his 'weekend' house. Some scam to get a tax deduction, I'm sure. I used to think there were *rules*. To them it's just a game . . .

JOYCE: What about this desk?

HANNAH: George wrote underneath . . . You know so, say this guy drops his 'Montblanc pen,' and has to crawl under to get it, and then he happens to look up . . . What will he see? What did you write? It's a quote. He knows it by heart. Tell her . . .

GEORGE *(Quotes)*: "I speak not the triumph of the sword, nor the wonders of science, nor of grandiose economic achievement, but only of the brotherhood of man."

JOYCE *(Confused)*: That's what you wrote? All that? That's a lot to write underneath a desk.

HANNAH: It's from the grave of a famous poet—

JOYCE: And what does it mean?

HANNAH: It's obvious what it means.

GEORGE: I'm not saying it's going to change anything, Joyce.

JOYCE: What could it change? You scribbled that underneath—?
GEORGE: It's not scribbled.
HANNAH: I thought it was a pretty cool thing to do.
GEORGE: It made me feel good.
HANNAH: He wrote it in pen, Joyce.

(Karin enters in a dress; carrying the manuscript for her show.)

JOYCE: All dressed up.
MARY: Look at you.
KARIN *(Over this)*: Don't tease—
JOYCE: I'm not teasing.
KARIN: It's not a date.
PATRICIA: She's teasing.
JOYCE: You look—great. Doesn't she look great?
KARIN: Is it too—?
MARY: Karin, you really look good.
HANNAH: You do.
MARY *(Over this)*: It really fits great. And I for one can't believe she got that at Marshalls . . . *(To the others)* I can never find anything there . . . Did you want to wear my—? *('earrings')*
KARIN: These are fine. What's wrong with them? And it's not really a date.
GEORGE *(To Joyce)*: Mary was asked out on a date . . .
HANNAH: She doesn't want you to—
JOYCE *(To Mary)*: What are you talking about?
MARY *(Same time)*: Come on. Stop it. I didn't go.
HANNAH *(Over this, to George)*: She doesn't want to talk about that.
JOYCE: Who was he?
MARY: Please don't talk about me.
JOYCE *(Over this)*: That's a good thing, isn't it?
MARY: Shut up.
JOYCE: A year's a long time. And taking care of him for years—
GEORGE: I agree.
MARY: Shut up.

PATRICIA *(To Karin)*: Put an apron on over that . . .
KARIN: I'm just— *('waiting')*
JOYCE *(Pointing out an apron)*: There's one on the . . .

(Karin looks at her watch.)

What time is he . . . ?
KARIN: Any time. It's not a date.
GEORGE: Hannah, Paulie also said in the car . . .

(All are interested.)

"Uncle Thomas would have fought all this . . ."
JOYCE: What's 'all this'? The mortgage?—
GEORGE *(Over the end of this)*: I guess, everything.
HANNAH *(Over this)*: How? How would he? Mary?
MARY: I don't know.
GEORGE: I think Paulie said it to hurt me. He misses his uncle too. We've watched this, haven't we, Hannah?
HANNAH: We have.
GEORGE: We've tried to talk to him about it. And we all know Thomas would not have known how to fight any more than we do. Or who . . .
MARY: No. I don't think he would.
JOYCE: No.
GEORGE: I started thinking, driving back—remembering, it just popped back into my head. When Thomas had just gone off to college. And how that was really hard on me. I felt such an incredible loss. My big brother gone. I didn't tell anyone I felt that. *(To Joyce)* You were too young. *(Continues)* And finally he came home at Thanksgiving, and he didn't seem all that different. And he still seemed interested in me, spent time with me. He told me about school. And, Mom, do you remember how he and Dad fought at dinner? They really fought: "We're going to make things better, Dad!"

MARY: Thomas said that?

GEORGE: 'More just.' "Well you just do your homework, Tommy." Dad. "And never sign your name on any kind of petition, Tommy. Never." He was always afraid of that. Really worried about us doing that. "You're there to get an education. Period. That's why you're in college." Remember?

PATRICIA: I do . . .

GEORGE: Thomas looked at me across the table, winked at me, and I knew what he was thinking: 'Little brother, look at how scared our father is.'

(Then:)

Thomas was exactly Paulie's age . . . And Dad was mine . . .

(Then:)

HANNAH: George and Paulie had a big fight over Bernie this summer.

GEORGE: Bernie's looking better every day, Hannah. Maybe the only one who is . . .

HANNAH: You need to say that to Paulie.

(Then:)

Mary, you want to know what Paulie shouted at George when they were fighting about Bernie?

GEORGE: What?

HANNAH: "Dad, what about us?"

GEORGE: He did.

JOYCE *(To Mary)*: Thomas would always—

MARY: We know. We all know that.

HANNAH: "What about us?" Just like Thomas.

PATRICIA: Your father only wanted you to not make a mistake that you'd later regret. He always said he only wanted you children to be happy . . .

JOYCE: Happy, Mom? Do you remember what Mary was telling us about Thomas's student?

PATRICIA: I heard.

GEORGE: What? That's all we want too for Paulie, isn't it, Hannah? That's what we say. 'Just be happy.'

PATRICIA: I always wanted more than that for you.

(Then:)

MARY: Hannah's now working as a maid, Joyce.

JOYCE: What?? What are you talking about?

MARY *(Over this)*: They haven't told Paulie. You didn't know that. I thought you didn't know.

HANNAH: Just part time—

MARY: At the Rhinecliff Hotel.

HANNAH: We're not 'hiding' it, Mary.

GEORGE: We just haven't told him yet.

JOYCE: When did this start?

HANNAH: We need the money. The catering has slowed, who gets married in November?

MARY: She makes the beds. Cleans the rooms. Cleans the bathrooms. You told me you're the only maid there who speaks English. So she's started helping the other maids. On your breaks, right? With their English. Good for you. That's a good thing to do.

HANNAH: Thank you.

JOYCE: I didn't know.

GEORGE: Just until Mom can come and live with us. 'Assisted living' is even more expensive . . .

HANNAH *(To Patricia)*: You are getting so much better, Patricia . . . *(To Joyce)* Every day. We're taking things one month at a time. We're 'working' through our savings . . .

MARY: Paulie's 'fund' . . .

(Then:)

GEORGE: You know what's funny, Joyce?

JOYCE: What? What is funny?

GEORGE: Less than two miles from the Rhinecliff Hotel is the Astor estate. And Joyce, our grandmother—Dad's mother—she was a maid there, for the Astors . . .

JOYCE: I know that.

GEORGE *(Over this)*: So I've been kidding Hannah that it's like we've gone back in time . . . Gone backwards . . .

JOYCE: I don't think you should tease her about that.

HANNAH *(Trying to make a joke)*: I've got like the same damn job now as your grandmother . . .

(George will hand out the parchment paper sheets for the cookies.)

JOYCE: So, Mom, you are going to move in with Hannah and George. I didn't know that was completely decided.

HANNAH: When she's ready.

GEORGE *(Same time)*: When she can.

HANNAH: Her bedroom will be the living room. Because of the stairs . . .

JOYCE *(To Hannah)*: Don't you need a living room?

HANNAH: I have a kitchen . . .

(Off, the doorbell rings.)

JOYCE: Karin, there's your date.

KARIN *(Getting up)*: It's not a date.

(Joyce is getting up.)

What are you doing?

JOYCE: I'm going to answer the door.

KARIN: No.

MARY *(Over this)*: I'll go with you.

KARIN *(Over this)*: I can answer the door myself.

JOYCE: I don't think that's right . . . Is that right? Should she answer the door? *(Chorus of: "No!")* Wait . . . *(Fixes Karin's collar)*

KARIN *(Over this)*: Come on.

JOYCE: That's better.

(Another doorbell ring.)

(Teasing) Oh he's eager . . . Come on.

(The three are on their way out.)

PATRICIA: Order something really expensive.

KARIN: I will.

JOYCE *(Suddenly worried)*: Karin . . . *(Stops her)* You have 'protection'? *(Her joke)*

KARIN: Oh fuck off . . .

(Joyce, Mary and Karin are gone.)

PATRICIA: Joyce teases too much . . .

HANNAH *(To George)*: I am going to call Paulie tonight.

GEORGE: He's not going to answer, Hannah. He doesn't want to talk to us.

HANNAH: Then I'll call his roommate. I have that number.

GEORGE: How did you get that?

HANNAH: When we moved him in. The mothers exchanged phone numbers. Mothers do that. Just in case, we said. Please, don't try and talk me out of it. Please . . .

PATRICIA: George, do you remember your grandmother and the mashed potatoes?

GEORGE: No, Mom. No. I don't.

PATRICIA: She'd have to clean out the cracks in their dining room table—

HANNAH: Who?

PATRICIA: The Astors. Clean out mashed potatoes with a knife. They'd let their kids shove them in the cracks. She said she overheard once someone saying, pointing to her, 'That maid will clean it up . . .'

(As Mary and Joyce return:)

JOYCE *(Entering)*: He had his nose pressed against the window . . .
HANNAH: Did you meet him?

(Hannah moves the cookies onto plates.)

MARY: She wouldn't let us.
JOYCE *(Over this, to Mary)*: I think she bruised my arm. *(To the others)* Like in one second, she was right out the door—
MARY *(To Joyce)*: He looks like a real-estate agent.
JOYCE: That's what I thought. *(To Hannah)* Let me do that.
GEORGE: Isn't that what he is?
MARY: Yeah. But he also looks like one. I think I've seen him around.

(As George, Hannah and Joyce set themselves to paint, cut-out cookies passed around, etc.)

HANNAH: And, Joyce, you probably don't know this either. About Mary . . . *(Looks at Mary)*
JOYCE: What?
HANNAH: Mary can't renew her doctor's license. And it's not just a few tests. She'd have to take everything all over again.
MARY: I can't do that, I'm too old. I was stupid.
HANNAH: So Mary's thinking of being a substitute science teacher over in Ulster.
MARY: They need them. And if you don't have a teacher's license you can still substitute up to sixteen weeks in the district. So I figure, I'll sign up in three or four districts. I should be able to get enough work.

JOYCE *(To George)*: Did you know that?

(He nods.)

In Ulster? Kingston?

MARY: And my daughter's very clear now she doesn't want me in Pittsburgh.

HANNAH: She hasn't actually said, Mary . . .

MARY: She's 'said,' Hannah. I think it's her father she doesn't want to upset . . . They are close.

JOYCE *(To Hannah)*: When did this happen?

HANNAH: Her daughter called last night . . .

(Mary smiles.)

JOYCE: What?

MARY: It's like *she* discovered Hillary! Like until about two months ago she'd have nothing to do with her. *(As her daughter)* 'I'll never trust her . . .' Now she's calling 'making sure' I vote today. 'It really matters, Mom. She came to Pittsburgh today, Mom! I saw her in person. We can't let him win. And remember she's a woman.'

HANNAH: I think we already knew that.

GEORGE: She's in Pennsylvania. So that's good . . .

JOYCE: Kingston? You're moving there?

(Mary shrugs.)

HANNAH: Mary, tell Joyce about the lawyers' office in Kingston—

MARY: You tell her.

JOYCE *(Over this)*: What?

HANNAH: There's a law office—

GEORGE: Two houses down from where Karin's new apartment is—

MARY: We all went to look at Karin's new apartment. You went with us too, Patricia, remember?

HANNAH: It's called "Rounds and Rounds: Attorneys at Law." Rounds and Rounds—we go . . .
GEORGE: 'We've got you coming and going.'
MARY: 'And we'll take forever doing it!'

(Laughter.)

GEORGE: Out of Dickens . . . Like us. *(Laughs)*
HANNAH *(Over this)*: It is. You're right . . . We are. He's right . . .

(Mary works on the salad.)

JOYCE: We could all start a NORC . . .
PATRICIA: What's that?
JOYCE: We could take care of each other. Grown-ups. Who needs kids?
MARY: A NORC, Patricia, a community of people of a certain age *(Like us)* who take care of each other. Live together . . .
JOYCE *(Painting)*: When I was in Paris—
HANNAH: Oh, 'Paris, I go to Paris.'
JOYCE: Shut up. This is an entirely different subject. I visited this famous cemetery there.
GEORGE: A NORC, a cemetery. Is this really a new subject?
JOYCE *(Continues over this)*: A huge place. Like a city itself. Lots of famous people—Oscar Wilde. Lots. A crematory where the ashes are put into a wall in like little slots. Isadora Duncan is there. *(Smiles)* She's just called 'Dora Duncan.' I guess her whole name didn't fit. There was a workman there, cleaning out a slot. I learned later that these 'slots' are just rented and so when . . . Then—you're forgotten . . . Thrown away? I don't know. He's cleaning out the 'slot' and there's another empty slot just above, and he puts his plastic bottle of apple juice in there. I'm looking and there are all these names and then this plastic bottle of apple juice . . . Taking up its own slot . . . Why do I keep remembering that?

HANNAH *(Painting)*: NORCs. Cemeteries. When do we start talking about our illnesses? Come on, we're fucking Gabriels.

PATRICIA: What does that mean?

GEORGE: I don't know, Mom . . . Anyone know?

(Karin returns, still with her script.)

MARY: Karin? Why are you back?

HANNAH *(Over this)*: You okay?

KARIN: He uh . . .

GEORGE: What? He what?

JOYCE: Where is he?

KARIN: He's—gone to dinner. I want a beer.

(George starts to get up.)

I can get it . . .

(He goes to get a beer from the refrigerator.)

We got as far as the traffic light. We're waiting for the Walk Sign . . . Sometimes that seems to take forever.

HANNAH: It can . . .

KARIN *(Taking the beer)*: Thank you.

MARY: You want a glass?

(She wants a glass.)

KARIN: I do. I like a glass.

(Mary goes to the sink, gets Karin a glass.)

He asked if later he could see upstairs. Your second floor. For a minute, a very stupid minute, I thought he—you know—thought that I was sleeping up there. So I said—

I'm staying in the office, in back, upstairs *there*. He said, he'd probably like to look at that too.

JOYCE: I don't understand.

KARIN: But the upstairs here really interested him. How big are the bedrooms? . . . The square footage. He had a tape measure with him.

HANNAH: What??

KARIN *(Taking the glass)*: Thank you. The second we left *(Snaps her fingers)* he started asking about the house. Leaks? The basement? We're walking down the street, and it's all he will talk about. How—when it's listed this week, it could still be listed with him too. They do that. 'We can do that.' He has someone interested. I ask him, are we only going to talk about the house? And he said—is that all right? *(Sips her beer)*

HANNAH: You never got to the restaurant.

KARIN: No. "I have a headache."

(Then:)

GEORGE: The buzzards are circling . . .

PATRICIA: What do you mean?

GEORGE: Where's my gun? *(To the buzzards)* 'We are not dead yet . . .'

PATRICIA: I don't understand.

JOYCE *(Over this)*: It's all right, Mom . . .

MARY: You'll have to eat with us, Karin . . .

KARIN *(Getting up)*: I can't do that. This is your— It's a family thing. I know that . . . *(Then)* One year after Thomas's death . . .

HANNAH: Almost . . . It's tomorrow.

KARIN *(To Mary)*: You're the widow . . . I'll get something in town . . .

MARY: You're welcome to join us. Isn't she?

HANNAH: Stay.

JOYCE *(Over this)*: Of course.

MARY: Stay. Stay with us. And paint a cookie . . . We're all Gabriels.

KARIN *(As she sits)*: I just kept the name— My agent said I shouldn't change it . . .

JOYCE: We just chose the shapes.

MARY: Get her some paper, George . . .

(George cuts another sheet of parchment paper.)

You want to change your dress?

KARIN: I'm fine. I'll take off these . . . *(Takes off her heels)*

MARY: Where's Patricia's apron?

HANNAH: I put it back.

(Hannah will get the apron and Karin will put it on.)

JOYCE *(Looking at George's work)*: George has chosen Christmas trees.

GEORGE: They're autumn trees, Joyce. I'll paint them with fall foliage.

JOYCE *(To George)*: They'll look like lights. I think that cookie cutter is meant to be a Christmas tree—

HANNAH: Leave him alone. They'll end up looking beautiful. Everything George touches ends up looking beautiful. He's an artist.

GEORGE: A craftsman.

HANNAH: That's an artist too.

MARY *(To Karin)*: Here . . . *('the parchment paper sheet')*

JOYCE: Give her a couple of cookies.

HANNAH: Pick what you want.

(Karin will put a couple of cut-out cookies onto her parchment paper sheet.)

JOYCE *(Half to herself)*: Why didn't we make the Raggedy Ann Salad? That would have made my day . . . Aren't I easy to please, Mom? . . .

(Joyce looks at Patricia, who is asleep.)

Mom's asleep.

(They all look at Patricia.)

HANNAH *(To Karin)*: Let's not get your play script dirty . . .

(Hannah moves it out of the way.)

KARIN: Oh I meant to show your mother these . . . *(Takes out glasses from her purse)*

JOYCE: What?

KARIN: Your mother's glasses . . .

HANNAH *(Same time)*: Those were your mother's . . .

(As Karin puts them on:)

(Explains to Joyce) For Karin's show . . .

JOYCE: I know . . .

KARIN: She had glasses just like these. Young Hillary . . . *(Puts them away)*

MARY: My daughter was fifteen when the whole Monica mess . . . I was visiting her and her dad. *(To Karin)* They're in Pittsburgh. *(To all of them)* And she said about 'Monica and Bill': 'Oh, I'd never stay married to someone who cheated on me.' I know she meant to hurt me . . . I tried to explain—things are complicated. *(To Joyce)* She's started calling more.

JOYCE: Good.

MARY: She's just feeling guilty . . .

(No one knows what to say.)

JOYCE: I can't believe that real-estate guy, Karin. Your 'date' . . . Unbelievable.

KARIN *(As a joke)*: Well now everyone knows it wasn't a date.

GEORGE *(Getting ready to paint)*: The real-estate agent handling Mom's house called me last Friday, Joyce. And says, he has potential clients who are visiting from the city, could he bring them around? I tell him, it's not even listed yet. And I hang up. Could you pass the red?

(Joyce hands him the red paint.)

KARIN: I'll use this brush.

JOYCE: Don't ask. Just take it.

(Karin takes the brush.)

GEORGE: He then calls right back and says he wishes to remind me of the fact that we don't actually own this house anymore. So he was just being polite and neighborly. And they'll be here in an hour. I explain we were busy. He says, he doesn't give a fuck. And 'please don't ever hang up on him again . . .' Could you hand me the green?

(The lights fade.)

Done

The same, a short time later.

George, Hannah, Joyce and Karin paint cookies. Mary cuts vegetables for the salad. Patricia is in a restless sleep.

In the middle of a conversation:

JOYCE *(Painting)*: Why Kinderhook? . . .

KARIN *(Half to herself, a joke)*: 'Old Kinderhook': Okay.

HANNAH *(To Joyce, over this)*: Some very rich gallery owner from Manhattan bought their high school.

JOYCE: What??

MARY: I don't know about this. Why don't I know about this?

HANNAH: Their high school. Right in the middle of Kinderhook. I guess they'd built a new one? I don't know. I hope so. And completely renovated it.

GEORGE *(Painting)*: Open one day a week.

JOYCE: How do they make any money?—

HANNAH *(Over the end of this)*: I don't think they have to, Joyce. *(Looks to George)* I don't understand either.

GEORGE *(Painting)*: I don't know how those games are played . . .

HANNAH *(To Mary)*: I forgot to tell you. We saw this show by an African artist—Anatsui. I think that's how you say it. Do you know his stuff?

(Neither Karin, Joyce nor Mary knows his work.)

(Explains) He makes these giant—very colorful—

GEORGE: Beautiful—

HANNAH: —objects, most of them hang on a wall.

GEORGE: Out of thousands of little tiny bottle caps. All sewed together with wire.

HANNAH: They end up looking like magnificent tapestries. *(To George)* Don't they?

GEORGE: Incredible.

HANNAH: They flow . . . Then you get close and you see—it's all these found things.

GEORGE: All real stuff.

HANNAH: Then you step back again and it's— *(Looks to George)* —magnificent. Spiritual.

GEORGE: That's how we felt.

HANNAH: It made me happy just to be there. Among his whatever they are—in their presence.

JOYCE *(To George)*: From bottle caps?

(He nods as he paints.)

HANNAH: They just seem to be—and George and I said almost the same thing—overflowing with life. We kept thinking: they are living and breathing. And human. And real. These wired-together tiny bottle caps. You read on the wall that they are from liquor bottles; the sort imported into Africa from Europe . . . So I guess there's some 'dark' thing too: Colonialism . . . *(Shrugs)* Yet out of that—from that—these things have been created, and they are beautiful. We were both just blown away.

(Then:)

Then on the way out, there's a little room with some books, catalogs about the work, Anatsui's life . . . George picked up one—

GEORGE: And I happen to turn to one page where there's this 'intriguing' photograph . . . Of one of Anatsui's big pieces hanging in the lobby of the Bill and—whatshername Foundation.

HANNAH: I forget.

GEORGE: The Bill and whatshername Gates Foundation.

KARIN: I think it's M-something.

GEORGE *(Over this)*: And alongside the work on their lobby wall is a handsomely printed description about the making of it. It explains how village children in the artist's African town—

HANNAH: And there's a little photograph of them—

GEORGE: —how they help hammer the bottle caps and tie them together with the wire. *And* for this the artist, El Anatsui, repays their labor by sending them to school.

JOYCE: Huh . . .

HANNAH: Obviously this is something this foundation wants to celebrate—trumpet—how through his artwork this great artist gives back to his community, by helping poor children go to school.

JOYCE: What's wrong with that? Sounds—

HANNAH: All this is explained in this catalog. *(Puts down her paintbrush)* And then it says that this isn't true . . .

MARY: What isn't?

HANNAH: Someone at the Gates Foundation seems to have just made this all up.

JOYCE: What?

GEORGE: There's a photo in the catalog of Anatsui looking incredulous, maybe thinking: 'Where the hell did they get this idea?' He doesn't pay for poor kids to go school. It probably never even occurred to him to do that. He pays them what he pays them, a going rate, for where he lives and works; a rate we'd probably cringe at, but that's what they get. They're paid to help him make art. Which doesn't have to justify itself by quote unquote doing something else.

(Then:)

Just Art 'that shows' or 'proves'—the capacity we, human beings, have to create, out of 'our mess.' I'm trying to quote him now. 'And while never denying that the mess is there, we—by using just stuff, even found stuff, bits of this and that, everyday normal stuff, even if it's bottle caps—we celebrate being human.'

MARY: I like that, Hannah.

GEORGE *(Over this)*: But billionaires, we guessed, didn't we, Hannah? Must need to feel that they are buying more than just that. Things they can turn into something else.

(Patricia coughs in her sleep.)

KARIN *(Noticing Patricia)*: You think your mother's comfortable there?

(Mary goes to Patricia, and moves a blanket or pillow to make her more comfortable.)

JOYCE: Don't wake her up . . . Please. I'm joking, Hannah . . . I'm so glad you finally got her wearing those things.

MARY *(Over the end of this)*: *Depends.*

JOYCE: Thank you for doing that.

GEORGE: Are you taking credit? It wasn't your idea.

HANNAH *(Back to artists)*: George told me a story about Alexander the Great and this great great artist.

GEORGE: You told me that it was sexist.

HANNAH: Not when I tell it. *(Continues)* What art can do as just art. What it shows. Allows us to see. Alexander commissions a portrait of his mistress. Then when he sees the painting finished, he realizes that this painter must appreciate her more and understand her better than he, Alexander, ever could. He sees that. He sees what he hasn't been seeing. So he just gives his mistress to the painter . . . *(To George)* That's the sexist part . . .

(Then:)

MARY: A friend of mine, from Yale— I don't know why that made me think of this. Ancient Greece I guess. She wrote Thomas maybe three, four days before he died.

JOYCE: So, like a year ago.

MARY: She's a Greek and biblical scholar and she wanted to tell him about some new research into the New Testament. There's all sorts of electronic research now going on, she said. And so it's now being thought, that the word for the profession of Saint Paul? I forget the Greek word. But forever it's been translated as 'tent maker.' But now they think that's not what it really means.

HANNAH: You never told me this.

MARY: So I still have some secrets.

KARIN: What does it mean?

MARY: 'Prop maker.'

KARIN: You're kidding.

HANNAH: What???

MARY: 'Prop maker.' In a theater. The person who does the—props for a play. *(Picks up something off the table)* So it seems—that Saint Paul, the Saint Paul, got his start in theater! *(Smiles, shakes her head)*

HANNAH: Thomas must have loved that . . . Was he even able to hear that?

MARY: He always said theater and religion, they were like this . . . *(Fingers together)* I'm not sure I completely understood what he meant . . .

(Joyce has paused from painting, and has picked up Karin's play manuscript.)

JOYCE *(To Karin)*: Mind if I . . . ?

KARIN: No . . . *(Explaining)* I jump from quote to quote. All her words. I've added nothing. *(Points)* Here . . . I like this . . . She's trying to find her feet again as First Lady. After that mess—

JOYCE: Which one?

KARIN: Health care . . . *(Explains)* At this point she's really lost.

GEORGE: Not for the first time and not the last.

JOYCE *(Reads)*: ". . . how best to make sure that children and families flourish . . ."

KARIN: I think she's trying to find her way back to that. The children. At this point.

JOYCE: In the early nineties.

KARIN: With health care.

GEORGE: I remember . . .

KARIN: To try and remember who the hell she really is . . .

HANNAH: So you think she keeps forgetting?

JOYCE *(Reads)*: "What we need is a new Politics of Meaning . . ." That just sounds ridiculous now. *(Reads)* ". . . a society that fills us up again and makes us feel that we are a part of something bigger than ourselves . . ." Good luck. *(Reads)* ". . . coming off the last year when selfishness and greed . . ." "What does it mean to be educated? What does it mean in today's world to be human?" Ask him that. Ask him. Where is this Hillary now?

KARIN: Mostly from letters. Speeches . . .

HANNAH: Emails . . . ?

KARIN: I love doing the moment when she's changing her name to Clinton . . . She both did and didn't want to do that. I understand that.

JOYCE *(Continues, as she looks through the script)*: "The séance" . . . ? What séance?

KARIN *(Explaining)*: Her dark days in the White House, debilitating self-doubt . . .

JOYCE: I didn't know about this. Why don't I know about this? I thought we knew everything—

MARY *(To Karin)*: You told me she was quite religious.

GEORGE: I didn't know that.

JOYCE *(Reading, the 'séance')*: Look who Hillary wanted to talk to: "Are you there, Eleanor Roosevelt?" "Eleanor, how did you, put up with all this?" She wanted to ask Eleanor that? *(Reads)* "Did you ever feel that you were carrying the history of womankind on your back?"

MARY: You think Eleanor answered her back?

JOYCE *(Looks at Patricia)*: Mom told me on the phone this week that she'd voted twice for Eleanor Roosevelt. 'No, you didn't, Mom. She didn't run for anything . . .'

HANNAH: May I see? *(To Karin)* Do you mind?

(Joyce hands Hannah the manuscript.)

JOYCE: I went back to Val-Kill recently.

HANNAH: When did you—?

JOYCE: Six, seven weeks ago? After coming here. When I came up to see Mom, after the stroke. A friend met me there.

GEORGE: What friend?

JOYCE: She'd never been. She lives over in New Paltz, but she'd never been to Val-Kill. Anyway, you know Hillary's photograph is all over . . .

KARIN *(Over the end of this)*: She loves Val-Kill. I was just going to say that.

JOYCE *(Over this)*: My friend and I—

HANNAH: Who is she?

JOYCE: We were in the little gift shop. We were the only two in there except for the lady behind the counter. My friend asks if the planks out there on the lawn were where the swimming pool used to be. The woman explains that the first pool was on the other side of the house. 'Why are you ladies interested in the pool?' she asks. My friend says she's just curious about Eleanor's friends, the women who lived here with her. The couples. This woman, she looks at the two of us, obviously she sees there is no one else in the shop; she then lifts out from under the counter a kind of scrapbook of photos: 'Here,' she says. 'Look here . . .' And she opens it up.

(Then:)

There are all these black-and-white photographs of Eleanor—in her bathing suit. By the pool laughing. Her arm around one woman. Both of them are laughing. Just being . . . I suppose—herself. Allowing herself to be herself . . .

HANNAH: Did you tell your mom that?

JOYCE: About Eleanor?

HANNAH: Everything, Joyce. Visiting there with a friend . . .

JOYCE: Why would I?

HANNAH: You should.

JOYCE: I don't think she'd be interested . . .

HANNAH: Don't just assume.

(They paint.)

MARY: Your mom and I went to a séance.

JOYCE: Why would you—?

KARIN *(Same time)*: I don't know about— *('this')*

MARY *(Over this)*: I think she remembers going . . . It was her idea. Some place on Long Island. You pay six hundred dollars—

JOYCE: When was—?

HANNAH: Last winter.

MARY: We didn't know we were broke then. We'd read about it in the *Times*. How—even being around other people 'pretending.' How that could be helpful. And so we went to try and talk with Thomas.

(George looks at Hannah.)

HANNAH: I didn't tell you, George.

MARY: A Mr. Edward was the medium; he called himself something else. There were seven of us. Each one of us, I guess, just wasn't ready to let go of someone . . .

JOYCE: Did you talk to Thomas?

MARY *(Smiles)*: No. Of course not. *(Looks at Patricia)* It was in his basement rec room. Golf trophies in the bookcase. A folded-up ping-pong table. But there was something in it though, that we all needed . . .

JOYCE: What?

MARY: I suppose: to accept that it was okay to not want to just cut it off. Accept that it can and maybe even should be a long journey. Not to try too hard to 'move on'—rather, when things are really hard, you can tell yourself, it was okay just to 'move.'

(Then:)

(Changing the subject) It's election day. We should be talking about that, shouldn't we?

HANNAH: Paulie's first time.

JOYCE *(To George)*: So Paulie was excited voting. Hannah said he was like a kid.

GEORGE *(Smiling)*: But holding his nose. Just before he went behind the voting desk, he turned to me and held his nose. Like a kid.

HANNAH: It was a joke.

GEORGE: When we were walking out of the Town Hall, Hannah, he said to me, 'Dad, it could have been about so much more . . .'

HANNAH: Sorry, son. They're usually not like this.

MARY: We're better than this, Paulie.

JOYCE: We sure about that?

GEORGE: "I thought I'd be inspired, Dad. Not just scared."

KARIN: He said that?

JOYCE *(Same time)*: Wrong election.

(Then:)

GEORGE: My first time voting. Like Paulie, I'd come back from college just for the day. My dad wanted me to go with him, and for some reason we'd waited until around about this time at night, so it was dark out . . . And a beautiful fall night. Like tonight. The crunch of leaves under our feet; the Dutch Reform's church bells. The Town Hall lit up. Dad said to me, 'Everyone should have his first experience voting for Jimmy Carter—in Rhinebeck.' Dad . . .

HANNAH: The first time I voted . . .

GEORGE: Where were you—? *('living')*

HANNAH: Pine Plains then.

GEORGE: Right. With that guy with really long— *(Gestures 'sideburns')*

HANNAH *(Ignoring him)*: I got Mondale . . . I finished, pulled that lever to open the curtain, and suddenly thought—did I do it right?

GEORGE: What do you mean?

HANNAH *(Over this)*: Did I make a mistake?

GEORGE: What choice did you have?

JOYCE *(Over this)*: I often think that, Hannah.

HANNAH: I mean, George, did I miss voting for some question? I remembered there were going to be questions, but I didn't see them. Later, my mom asked me if I'd voted yes on some—very very important question. I felt like I'd fucked up . . .

GEORGE: Because you fucked up.

MARY: I was visiting my daughter; they'd just moved away to Pittsburgh, to my ex's family. This isn't about a first time, but about an election day. And I'm staying in a motel. She was allowed to come over and stay one night with me. I'd completely forgotten it was election day. That happens. I'm sure that happens to a lot of people when you're overwhelmed . . . I turned the TV on; there were the results. We're lying each in our twin bed . . . Natalie Merchant starts to sing . . . And we then see the two of them walk out holding hands. This is of course in Little Rock.

(Then:)

My daughter says all excited: 'Oh she looks so beautiful . . .' I look at my daughter in her bed, and I say, 'She's the wife . . .' I reminded her of that last night when she called, Hannah.

HANNAH: Did she remember?

MARY: She did. I was surprised. *(Then)* I said—'Well, now she's not just the wife . . .'

(Then:)

GEORGE *(To Karin)*: Natalie Merchant lives in Rhinebeck.

KARIN: Does she?

HANNAH: We've seen her two, three times in the health food store. I think she moved.

MARY: Can I paint a cookie? . . . I want to paint one cookie . . .

HANNAH *(Over the end of this)*: Of course . . . Why are you asking? . . .

JOYCE *(Same time)*: Mary. Give her a brush.
HANNAH: Get her a cookie . . .
GEORGE: One left.
KARIN: Take a paintbrush . . .

(Mary sits and joins them.)

HANNAH: By now Faso and Teachout together have spent thirteen, fourteen million dollars to win our little rural district.
MARY: I read that too in the *Freeman*.
HANNAH: And nearly all of that—both sides—they say, has come from people who don't live here. This morning, I left that circle empty . . .

(Then:)

KARIN: In my show I want people to see Hillary, the person . . . One of the women who invited me . . . She kept saying: 'Tonight, just do the nice parts. Only the nice parts . . .'
MARY: Just her better angels . . .
KARIN: Right.
MARY: A friend wrote me the other day; she lives in Chicago. She said there's a billboard in one of those really tough neighborhoods on the South Side—
GEORGE: Where all those kids are being killed—
MARY: Yeah. And it says: 'Your ticket out of here.' It's for the state lottery. The Illinois State Lottery. My friend wrote: 'See, Mr. Trump, he's not alone. What have we become?' Who are we? 'Who's there?' *(Smiles)*
JOYCE *(To Hannah)*: Careful . . . You're dripping . . . *('on Karin's manuscript')*

(Picking up the script, to Karin) I'll put this over on the bench, Karin . . . Get it out of the way . . .

(She will set the script on the bench and sit there, watching her mother.)

KARIN: Good idea. Thanks.

(Patricia mumbles in her sleep.)

JOYCE: Mom's dreaming . . . *(Looking at her mother)* George, did you hear what she said? 'I wanted more than that for you.' More than what?

GEORGE: I don't know . . .

MARY *(As she paints)*: Ever feel like this? I take a shower, and all I'm thinking—is I'll be over with that soon. Then I have breakfast, while I'm thinking: What's next? I'm putting on my face—getting that over with. Check. Check mark. Over with that. Done with that.

(The timer goes off.)

What now? Now what?

(Then:)

HANNAH: Your timer . . .

MARY: I know. Dinner. Someone should set the table.

GEORGE: I can do that . . .

JOYCE *(Having noticed a notebook on the bench)*: Listen to this. I just saw this . . . This is one of Thomas's notebooks?

MARY: Shit, leave that in the basket.

GEORGE *(Surprised)*: Mary?

HANNAH *(Over this)*: What is it?

JOYCE *(Ignoring her)*: He's written here: "A play where everyone is always cooking."

KARIN: We read that.

MARY: Joyce, just give that to me . . . *(Reaches out for it)*

KARIN: Hold on, Joyce . . . There's something else in that notebook.

MARY: Karin. Give it to me . . .

JOYCE: What?

KARIN: Mary, show them what we did in that notebook yesterday.

JOYCE: What? Why is it in here?

KARIN: I'll show you. Let me have it.

MARY *(As Joyce starts to give it to Karin)*: Don't give it to her.

HANNAH: What's this about?

MARY *(Over this)*: Karin, they don't need to see—

HANNAH: See what?

MARY: Joyce!

HANNAH *(Over this)*: Mary, I've never seen you like this.

KARIN *(Same time, to Joyce)*: Give it here. *(Taking the notebook and going through it)* I think they do, Mary. I think they'd be really interested in this . . .

JOYCE: Mary's blushing . . . I'm interested. Why are you blushing?

HANNAH *(Smiling)*: I don't know anything about this.

MARY: It's not funny. Fuck you . . . *(To George who has stopped to watch)* I thought you were going to set the table.

GEORGE: I'm interested.

MARY: Damn it, give that to me, Karin!—

KARIN: No! We wrote something— *(Corrects herself)* *rewrote* something—

GEORGE: In Thomas's notebook?

KARIN: In this one. *(To Mary)* Didn't we? What did we write—?

MARY *(Over this)*: George, tell her to give me back the notebook.

(He ignores her.)

Dinner's ready.

(She will take the shepherd's pie out of the oven as:)

KARIN *(Finding the page in the notebook)*: Here it is. It's a monologue. We just came across this, didn't we? *(Holds it up)* He'd written the whole thing out. *(To Mary)* Right? Come on, it's funny. *(To the others)* Mary said he used to do that, as notes for a play. To use later . . . We've come across a bunch of them. Different people. This one . . . *(Looks at Mary)*

JOYCE: What?

KARIN: This one . . .

(Holds the notebook out to Mary, she doesn't try to grab it.)

You want to explain?

(Mary busies herself with the peas.)

We just happened across it. It's about a . . .

JOYCE: What?

KARIN: A female doctor . . .

EVERYONE *(Interested)*: Oh! Mary . . .

JOYCE *(Over this)*: About Mary. Something Thomas wrote.

GEORGE: What about Mary?

KARIN *(Over this)*: Her same age. The doctor here. Exactly Mary's age when he wrote it. We figured that out, didn't we? He wrote in the dates . . . Anyway, so 'Vi'—he calls her 'Vi,' the doctor. She—*you* want to tell them? *(Continues)* She comes home from work one day, from her practice, wearing a—what? A brown pantsuit. And a pretty much nondescript—his words—gray sweater.

MARY: It's not really gray. And I don't know why it's 'nondescript.'

KARIN: She knew the sweater . . .

MARY: It's very comfortable.

KARIN: And 'Vi' throws herself into a chair—*that* seems to be the set—one chair—and begins to—what? Complain? Worry? She's been shaken up by something at work.

MARY: She's not complaining.

KARIN *(Over this)*: You told me you'd said some of these exact things. About—feeling hopeless.

MARY: Not always. Sometimes.

KARIN *(Over this)*: Impotent. Being—a doctor. In this—that very day, she'd seen one of her patients die.

MARY: I think he was trying to turn her into one of those Russian doctors—in the plays he loves so much. Full of frustrations—

KARIN: Mary— I read it to Mary. And she says, 'Let me see that . . .' And she takes a pencil and begins crossing things out—

GEORGE: In his notebook?

KARIN: And adding things. What did you add? Tell them . . .

MARY: We cut the pantsuit. That was the first thing we cut.

KARIN *(Reads)*: 'Vi' now "enters, having changed from her drab doctor's work clothes into . . . a powder blue silk dressing gown with a sweet butterfly pattern." Where online did we see that? We researched . . .

GEORGE: I can't believe this—

HANNAH: When did you do this?

KARIN *(Holding up the notebook)*: She *(Mary)* wrote all over it . . . *(Reads)* "That catches all the lovely curves of her exquisite body . . ."

HANNAH: What website?

MARY *(To Karin)*: You added that. We crossed out stuff too. *(Answering Hannah)* Way beyond J. Crew, Hannah. Way beyond your imagination.

HANNAH: What the fuck does that mean?

MARY *(To Hannah)*: You should shop online with Karin sometime.

KARIN: And we put her into some very nice pajamas. I'd like to have those pajamas. And then here as she's beginning to talk—she makes herself a cocktail.

MARY *(To Karin)*: Karin knows the names of all these fancy cocktails . . . What did we decide?

KARIN *(Over the end of this)*: We hadn't made a final choice. We were testing . . .

MARY *(To Hannah)*: I don't know how she knows them.

HANNAH: Were you both drunk? Was this at night?

KARIN *(Paraphrasing)*: 'Mary has a cocktail—' *(Corrects herself)* '*Vi* has a cocktail in hand . . .' *(To Hannah)* '. . . *middle* of the day.' *(Continues)* She is *not—no longer*—sitting on a chair, but now she sits on a *divan.*

MARY: I always wanted a divan. Thomas said they're 'too pretentious . . .'

KARIN *(Continues)*: And she leans back on the divan . . . And this was a nice touch. Whose idea was this? *(Shrugs)* "As she begins to calmly talk to us—"

MARY: I added 'calmly.' What did he write?

KARIN: We crossed it out. I can't read it. *(Continues)* "One hears the soft sensual rustle of her nylons as she crosses her legs . . ."

(Off, the phone rings.)

JOYCE AND HANNAH: Phone . . .

GEORGE: I got it.

HANNAH *(To George)*: Maybe it's Paulie.

GEORGE *(To Mary and Karin)*: I can't believe you two did that . . .

(He heads off.)

JOYCE: I thought she had pajamas on.

MARY: What do you mean?

JOYCE *(Over the end of this)*: Then why is she wearing nylons?

MARY *(To Karin)*: We need to change that.

HANNAH *(To Mary)*: That is so unlike you. It's childish . . .

KARIN: We know.

MARY: I know. But he's not here, Hannah. So fuck him. He shouldn't have died.

(At first no one knows how to respond, then she smiles.)

HANNAH: Then I guess it serves him right? . . . Can I see? Fuck him . . .

(Then:)

KARIN: There's almost nothing left of the thing Thomas wrote . . . We spent like what? Like five hours on it.

MARY: Give me that.

(She takes the notebook:)

(Speaks to the notebook) She doesn't just complain. She isn't always unhappy. She's fucking sexy. And she's hopeful. And she's getting on with her goddamn life!

(She puts the notebook back on the bench, then to the notebook:)

Or she will.

(Then:)

Let's have dinner. George was supposed to set the table . . .

KARIN: I can do that, Mary. I'll do that . . .

(Karin heads off to the dining room.)

JOYCE: Does she know which plates to use?

MARY: She knows . . .

JOYCE *(Calls)*: The white plates . . .

MARY *(Over this)*: She knows. I just want to finish painting my damn cookie . . . Joyce, you better wake up your mother.

(Mary sits and paints her cookie.
Joyce sits on the bench and looks at her mother.)

JOYCE: You know I almost forgot Mom was here. No, I didn't. Mom . . . today I kept hearing your voice . . .

HANNAH: I thought that was just your stomach . . .

JOYCE: You do sound like my stomach . . . Hearing you say: 'We're putting on a show.' *(To Mary)* I think because of the stuff you've been digging through. I remembered this . . . She used to do for my birthdays—wonderful puppet shows. Did you know that?

(Mary shakes her head.)

HANNAH: I remember those.

JOYCE: Down in the rec room. She'd ring a bell: 'We're putting on a show.' Someone could be crying, or fighting. And that was her answer to everything: 'We're putting on a show.' All my friends thought you were so amazing . . .

HANNAH: I know I did . . .

JOYCE *(Gently waking up Patricia)*: Mom? Hi . . . Mom? Hello? Hi . . . We're having dinner . . . Wake up . . .

PATRICIA *(Waking up)*: What . . . ??

JOYCE *(At the same time)*: You were asleep.

PATRICIA: What?

JOYCE: I think you were voting for Eleanor Roosevelt. Mom, someone's just phoned. *(After a look at the others)* Can you tell us—who's on the phone? Use your magical powers.

HANNAH: Joyce . . .

PATRICIA: What . . . ? I wasn't asleep.

JOYCE: Who's on the phone, Mom? Come on, you always know . . . And I've always found that really creepy. Is it Paulie? We think it's Paulie.

HANNAH *(To Joyce)*: Your mom's wheelchair, it's . . . *(Points by the sink)*

(Joyce looks at Hannah.)

Will you do it?

(Joyce looks at Mary.)

MARY *(Painting)*: I'm busy, Joyce.
JOYCE *(Getting the wheelchair)*: Who is it, Mom? Is it Paulie?
PATRICIA *(Half asleep)*: It's Paulie.
JOYCE *(To Hannah as 'fact')*: It's your son. He's on the phone.
PATRICIA *(To Joyce)*: It's Paulie . . .
JOYCE: We know, Mom. We know. You always know . . . *(About the wheelchair)* Mary, how do you open this up?
MARY: Figure it out.
HANNAH: You need to learn . . .

(Joyce looks to Hannah.)

The handles . . .
JOYCE: Why are you doing this?
MARY *(Painting)*: Doing what?
HANNAH: I'll take the salad, Mary. And see how Karin's doing . . .

(They see George returning. Hannah stops.)

Was it Paulie?
GEORGE: No, Karin's date.

(Joyce looks at her mother.)

JOYCE: Mom . . .
PATRICIA: What, Joyce?
HANNAH *(Over this)*: Calling to apologize? . . .
MARY: Fuck him. *(To Hannah)* I'm on a roll.
GEORGE: He wanted to know how far back the property goes . . .

(Hannah heads off with the salad bowl.)

How can I help?
MARY: Karin is setting the table.
JOYCE *(Still with the folded-up wheelchair)*: George, how do you do this?

MARY: Let her do it, George. She'll work it out.
GEORGE: Are we drinking wine?
MARY: We don't want wine, do we?
GEORGE: We might need it . . .

(Joyce opens the wheelchair.)

MARY: See. She did it. Good for you, Joyce.
JOYCE: Here we go, Mom . . .
GEORGE: Put the brakes on . . .
JOYCE: Where are the brakes?
GEORGE: Those things right there.
JOYCE: This?

(She puts the brakes on. Karin returns.)

KARIN *(To Mary)*: We're doing a tablecloth or placemats? I set out placemats. Hannah thinks we should have a tablecloth. Mary, if you want a tablecloth . . .
MARY: Placemats are fine. It doesn't matter . . .
JOYCE *(To Patricia)*: Okay, Mom?

(All watch Joyce.)

Put your arm . . . Mom . . .
GEORGE: She can't move that arm, Joyce.

(He will get a pitcher of water out of the refrigerator and refill it.)

JOYCE: I know!
MARY *(Still painting, before George can help)*: They're doing fine. Let them . . .
JOYCE *(To Patricia)*: Put your arm, that arm, Mom. Here.

(They all watch.)

(As she gets ready to help up her mother) I've been wanting to ask you, George, what did the guy from New York think

about the house? Who came to see it last week. He did come, right? I'm just curious. *(To Patricia)* Ready?

GEORGE: He said it was too small.

(Patricia loses her grip on Joyce.)

JOYCE: It's okay. *(To the others)* We're fine.

(Hannah has returned. She will strain the peas in the sink and put them in a bowl.)

GEORGE *(Back to the house)*: I heard him ask if the house could be knocked down . . .

PATRICIA: Knocked down?

(She looks up at Joyce.)

JOYCE: We don't own it, Mom.

GEORGE *(Continuing)*: I guess so he could build something bigger . . .

JOYCE *(To Patricia)*: One more time. Ready? . . . Good. Good. There. Good. You're in . . . Are you in?

(Patricia is in the wheelchair.)

There you go . . . *(To the others)* I did it. I'll take you into the dining room . . . *(A bad joke)* Fasten your seatbelt . . . I know—you're not a child. It's a joke, Mom. *(To the others)* I'll sit with Mom, keep her company. Please don't be too long.

(As they go:)

You want to sit at the table in your wheelchair or in a grown-up chair? I'm teasing you, Mom . . . *(To the others)* Don't be long.

(They are gone.)

GEORGE *(About Joyce and Patricia)*: Let's give them about—a half an hour alone together . . .

KARIN *(Getting out silverware)*: I thought the village was an historic district, so you can't just knock things down . . .

GEORGE: They get around that. Just let a property go to hell . . . They let you knock it down then.

MARY: It's not right . . .

GEORGE: What does 'right' have to do with anything? *(With the water pitcher)* I'll set out water glasses . . . *(Goes off)*

HANNAH *(To Karin)*: The church across the street did that with a house . . . Just let it go . . . The church. Karin, can you also take the peas?

KARIN: My mother used to always say: "Pray for peace and spiritual food and for wisdom and guidance, for all these are good. But don't forget the potatoes . . ." *(Looking at the shepherd's pie)* Smells good, Mary.

(Karin goes off with the silverware and the peas.)

HANNAH *(To Mary)*: I put on a tablecloth . . . Are we still taking Patricia to vote? . . .

MARY: If there's time . . . Is there time?

HANNAH: I think she's forgotten about it . . .

MARY *(Shrugs)*: She's going to win. The other is unthinkable.

HANNAH: And if she doesn't?

MARY: Maybe we just follow the crowds to the cliff, Hannah, hold hands, and jump. Shouting: 'What about us??' We should probably ask Patricia, let her decide. There's still time . . .

(Hannah has gone to get napkins out of the table drawer.)

HANNAH: Karin was just telling me that she's now thinking of moving on Friday. I guess she's in a hurry . . .

MARY: Just one day sooner. She doesn't teach on Fridays . . . Kingston's nice . . .

HANNAH: I'll get George to help Karin.

MARY: She doesn't have much stuff . . .

HANNAH: What cookie did you choose?

MARY: I didn't choose anything. The only one left. A person. But I'm giving her a nice big smile, Hannah . . .

HANNAH: I think Uptown Kingston does kind of feel how Rhinebeck used to. You know what I mean? It's only the people who live there. That's nice.

MARY: It is.

HANNAH: George was telling me that just a few doors down from Karin's new apartment—not the lawyers out of Dickens, in the other direction, is the house where John Wilkes Booth's brother, the famous actor, where he hid out, after his brother had shot Lincoln. He came and stayed, and I guess felt safe there. *(The joke)* George said—see, even then no one went to Kingston . . . *(Smiles)*

MARY: That's funny . . . Hannah. "Things do work out . . . That's what we have to keep telling ourselves, damn it."

HANNAH: Thomas?

MARY: Yeah.

(Hannah goes off to the dining room with the napkins.

Mary has finished her cookie and begins to collect the others onto a cookie sheet. Piano music from the living room: Schumann's Album Pour La Jeunesse, No. 6, *"Armes Waisenkind."*

She sits and listens to the music.

Hannah returns.)

What do you need?

(Hannah goes to the refrigerator.)

HANNAH: George wants wine. I saw an open bottle of white . . . I'll smell it . . . Joyce doesn't like my salad dressing. She wants the Paul Newman. I'll call Paulie after we eat. *(The wine)* Smells fine. Patricia wants a pillow for her back . . .

(She goes to pick up a pillow from a chair.)

MARY: Hannah, we did sell the piano, didn't we? And they took it away? . . .

(Hannah just looks at her.)

I still hear him . . . Even after a year . . . He used to play this to me . . . *(Obviously)* You can't hear it.

(Hannah shakes her head.)

HANNAH: No. What are you going to do?

(Then:)

MARY: I've finished my cookie. I'm gathering the others. I'll put them in the oven. Then set the timer. Remind me, we might not hear it in the dining room. Then I'll bring in the shepherd's pie. We'll have dinner . . . I've got it all planned out, Hannah. *(Smiles)* I'll be right there.

(Hannah goes.

Mary continues to collect the cookies and listen to the short piano piece. It finishes. After a moment:)

You done?

(Silence.

As Mary puts the cookies in the oven and sets the timer:

Music: Lucius's "Until We Get There" plays from the theater speakers. She looks over the table and the room, puts on oven mitts, picks up the shepherd's pie; after one more look across the kitchen table, she goes to join the others in the dining room.

Blackout.)

END OF PLAY

AUTHOR'S NOTES

The Presidential Election and the Theater

From The Public Theater's Programs

Shakespeare understood us. His (and Fletcher's) *Henry the Eight* is a play about political power and backroom politics, interrupted by occasional political pageantry to appease the common citizen. It carries this extraordinary subtitle *All Is True*. Of course, if all is true, then also nothing is.

In troubled and troubling times, theater has not only an opportunity, but the responsibility, to portray this confusion, and articulate the ambiguities, doubts, and fears of its time. The goal then being not to argue a side or a point, but to attempt to portray people and worlds as they are, not as we wish them to be. Theater, to my mind, is not an argument, but an effort to create and portray human complexity, which we then share with a living audience, at the same time, in the same space: human being to human being.

In this way, as a playwright, I try not to be co-opted by arguments and agendas, especially those I may agree with as a citizen. Of course, it is a great temptation, in troubled times, to try and use the theater as a weapon. My theater, however, is more temple than weapon; a place to come together, where we perhaps will see ourselves and others, see our world and other worlds, while all the time relishing that we are not alone in our fears and confusions, as we sit together struggling to understand and work things out.

In other words, my theater is not a place to shout in, or be lectured at, nor where we go to be incited; rather a place to come together, sit among strangers in the dark, and recognize the complexity of the world before us. As the great English playwright, Harley Granville Barker, wrote over a hundred years ago: "Dramatic art is the working out—in terms of make-believe, of society itself."

The Plays: A Rhinebeck Panorama

Each of these plays is set at a distinct moment over nine months of the nation's 2016 presidential election: the Friday after Super Tuesday when primary season was in full swing; the middle of September when the general election was in full swing; and election day itself. When first performed, neither the characters nor I (nor the audience) knew what was going to happen during this memorable election, nor what would happen on election day itself. So in part, they constitute three real-time snapshots of one family's life during this past election year.

The subtitle for these plays is *Election Year in the Life of One Family*. Given the anxieties we all faced as we approached a resolution to this election and now given its unsettling conclusion, it is completely understandable that the subtitle for these would be misread as simply: *The Election in the Life of One Family*. But these plays follow not just an election, but one year in the lives of these characters; a year that reveals their hopes and losses, their fears and resiliency, and how these entwine with a political season few of us ever imagined. My goal then, in part, has been to weave together an unruly and contentious national event with the small (and large) events of private life; and in doing so, perhaps portray a world where the personal, the cultural, the societal, the familial, the artistic, and the political are viewed not as separate categories, but as dependent aspects of each of our lives. At least that has been one ambition.

These plays are set in Rhinebeck, New York; a village, one hundred miles north of New York City; a place the *New York Times* once called "the town that time forgot." It's a very small place, yet the more I write about it, and populate it with my characters, the larger it has come to loom in my imagination. Years ago I came across a very large (8' by 3') watercolor panoramic panel hanging in the Museum of London, in England, with the fascinating title: "The Rhinebeck Panorama." Unfortunately, from the perspective of someone who lives in Rhinebeck, this massive watercolor does not depict a panoramic view of my tiny Hudson Valley village, but rather is a bird's-eye view of London, England, in the 1830s. My village, I have learned, *did* however give this picture its name; in 1941, this work was discovered in the attic of a Rhinebeck house, lining the inside of a barrel of pistols. (How it got there, and why pistols were kept in a barrel, remain mysteries.) Still the phrase "*Rhinebeck Panorama*" has stuck with me and, I think, inspired me, suggesting, as it does, *a grand view of wide expanse, but of a very small place.*

Another ambition for these plays, I think, lies somewhere within this phrase.

Richard Nelson
Rhinebeck, New York

ACKNOWLEDGMENTS

For *Hungry*:

I consulted and read numerous books while writing *Hungry*; the most useful are the following: Jean Anthelme Brillat-Savarin's extraordinary *The Physiology of Taste or Meditations on Transcendental Gastronomy*; M. F. K. Fisher's *The Art of Eating*; Priscilla Parkhurst Ferguson's *Accounting for Taste*; Mrs. Child's *The American Frugal Housewife* (1833); Laurie Colwin's *Home Cooking* and *More Home Cooking*; Luke Barr's *Provence, 1970*; Anne Hollander's *Feeding the Eye*; Matt Taibbi's *The Divide*; Laurence Tribe and Joshua Matz's *Uncertain Justice*; Michael Lewis's *Flash Boys* (which both Hannah and Thomas/Mary must have been reading; the former tries to quote from this when he talks about the vultures on the savanna, and the latter when a blue sky is called green); Stacy C. Hollander and Valerie Rousseau's *Self-Taught Genius: Treasures from the American Folk Art Museum*; Elizabeth Warren's *A Fighting Chance*; Rand Paul's *Government Bullies*; Mark Leibovich's *This Town*; Edward M. Smith's *History of Rhinebeck*. Among the articles

I consulted was Jeff Gordinier's "A Confidante in the Kitchen: Laurie Colwin Used Simple . . ." *New York Times*, April 2, 2014.

The piece from the *New York Times Magazine*, which is quoted from in the "Brigadoon" scene, is "Getting Out" by Colette Dowling (March 28, 1976).

The gift Joyce has bought Mary at Val-Kill is *Cookies for Eleanor* by Chandler Roosevelt Lindsley.

In the "Common Sense in the Kitchen" scene, my characters read extensively from Marion Harland's nineteenth century *Common Sense in the Household: A Manual of Practical Housewifery*.

I also found the following interview very helpful: Priscilla Parkhurst Ferguson on the Criterion DVD of the film *Babette's Feast*.

Hungry is a play and a work of fiction, and is not based upon any living person or persons.

For *What Did You Expect?*:

I consulted and read the following books while writing *What Did You Expect?*: Anne Hollander's *Feeding the Eye*; Edward M. Smith's *History of Rhinebeck*; Oliver Sacks's *On the Move*; Joseph E. Stiglitz's *The Great Divide*; Matt Taibbi's *The Divide*; Peter Schweizer's *Clinton Cash*; Michael J. Sandel's *Public Philosophy*; Edwin Haviland Miller's *Salem Is My Dwelling Place* and *Melville*; James R. Mellow's *Nathaniel Hawthorne in His Times*; Peter Brook's introduction relating to Oliver Sacks in his play *The Man Who*; *Women in Clothes* (edited by Sheila Heti, Heidi Julavits, Leanne Sharpton).

The translations of the fragments of Euripides' *Melanippe the Captive* are adapted from C. Collard, M. J. Cropp and K. H. Lee's *Euripides: Selected Fragmentary Plays, Volume 1*.

The play Thomas has supposedly co-translated, and which Karin describes, is Maurice Maeterlinck's *Interior* (translated by William Archer); the musical Thomas has supposedly co-written is *Unfinished Piece for a Player Piano*, written by myself and Peter Golub, and based upon the film of the same name (which is based upon Chekhov's *Platonov*); the fragment from

Edith Wharton's unfinished novel, *Beatrice Palmato*, which Karin reads, was first published as an appendix to R. W. B. Lewis's *Edith Wharton: A Biography*.

I am grateful to Robert Marx, Joe Mitchell, Dr. Julio Urbina, Lauren Weisenfeld of The Fan Fox and Leslie R. Samuels Foundation for their thorough answers to my questions regarding elder care; and Jocelyn and Evan for their thoughts about this election.

What Did You Expect? is a play and a work of fiction, and is not based on any living person or persons.

For *Women of a Certain Age*:

I consulted and read the following books while writing *Women of a Certain Age*: Carl Bernstein's *A Woman in Charge*; Dick Morris's *Behind the Oval Office*; Peter Ackroyd's *The English Ghost*; Matt Taibbi's *The Divide*; *Women in Clothes* (edited by Sheila Heti, Heidi Julavits, Leanne Sharpton); M. F. K. Fisher's *The Art of Eating*; Jean Anthelme Brillat-Savarin's *The Physiology of Taste or Meditations on Transcendental Gastronomy*; Anne Hollander's *Feeding the Eye*; *Olivier Assayas* (edited by Kent Jones); Alice Munro's *Runaway*; Oliver Sacks's *On the Move* and *Hallucinations*; W. G. Sebald's *The Rings of Saturn*; Laurie Colwin's *Home Cooking*; Claire Bidwell Smith's article in the *New York Times* ("What the Psychic Showed Me," August 22, 2015), about visiting a psychic.

The Ladies' Home Journal, which Joyce reads, is issue September 1, 1910; the cookbook they use is *Betty Crocker's Cook Book for Boys and Girls* (1957); the songbook is Opal Wheeler's *Sing for America* (1944); the story about Edwin Booth comes from *Jervis McEntee* (published by the Friends of Historic Kingston); the discovery about Saint Paul's life in the theater comes from my friend Larissa; the "ice-breaker" comes from Jocelyn.

Women of a Certain Age is a play and a work of fiction, and it is not based upon any living person or persons.

R. N.

Richard Nelson's other plays include *Illyria*, the four-play series *The Apple Family: Scenes from Life in the Country* (*That Hopey Changey Thing*, *Sweet and Sad*, *Sorry* and *Regular Singing*), *Nikolai and the Others*, *Farewell to the Theatre*, *Conversations in Tusculum*, *How Shakespeare Won the West*, *Frank's Home*, *Rodney's Wife*, *Franny's Way*, *Madame Melville*, *Goodnight Children Everywhere*, *New England*, *The General from America*, *Misha's Party* (with Alexander Gelman), *Two Shakespearean Actors* and *Some Americans Abroad*. He has written the musicals *James Joyce's The Dead* (with Shaun Davey) and *My Life with Albertine* (with Ricky Ian Gordon), and the screenplays for the films *Hyde Park-on-Hudson* and *Ethan Frome*. He has received numerous awards, including a Tony (Best Book of a Musical for *James Joyce's The Dead*), an Olivier (Best Play for *Goodnight Children Everywhere*) and two New York Drama Critics' Circle Awards (*James Joyce's The Dead* and *The Apple Family*). He is the recipient of the PEN/Laura Pels Master Playwright Award, an Academy Award from the American Academy of Arts and Letters; he is an Honorary Associate Artist of the Royal Shakespeare Company. He lives in upstate New York.

On the cover: Archangel Gabriel Weathervane, c. 1840.
Paint on sheet metal. 35 x 32 1/2 x 1 1/4". Gift of Adele Earnest. 1963. 1.1.
Photo: John Parnell. Location: American Folk Art Museum, New York, NY, U.S.A. Credit: American Folk Art Museum / Art Resource, NY.